PEACE &
PARSNIPS

PEACE & PARSNIPS

ADVENTUROUS VEGAN COOKING FOR EVERYONE

LEE WATSON

Photography by Alistair Richardson

THE EXPERIMENT

NEW YORK

The Experiment, LLC
220 East 23rd Street, Suite 301
New York, NY 10010-4674
www.theexperimentpublishing.com

The Experiment's books are available at special discounts when purchased in bulk for premiums and sales promotions as well as for fund-raising or educational use. For details, contact us at info@ theexperimentpublishing.com.

Library of Congress Cataloging-in-Publication Data

Names: Watson, Lee, 1978- author. | Richardson, Alistair.
Title: Peace & parsnips : vegan cooking for everyone / Lee Watson ; photography by Alistair Richardson.
Other titles: Peace and parsnips
Description: New York, NY : Experiment, LLC, 2016. | Includes index.
Identifiers: LCCN 2015041608 (print) | LCCN 2015051408 (ebook) |
    ISBN 9781615193219 (cloth) | ISBN 9781615193226 (Ebook) | ISBN 9781615193226 (ebook)
Subjects: LCSH: Vegan cooking. | Vegetarian cooking. | LCGFT: Cookbooks.
Classification: LCC TX837 .W335 2016 (print) | LCC TX837 (ebook) | DDC 641.5/636—dc23
    LC record available at http://lccn.loc.gov/2015041608

ISBN 978-1-61519-321-9
Ebook ISBN 978-1-61519-322-6

Cover design by Penguin Random House UK

Manufactured in China
Distributed by Workman Publishing Company, Inc.

First printing May 2016
10 9 8 7 6 5 4 3 2 1

For Sweet Jane
and my little family
(Carol, John, Laura and Paul)
and my big family (all of you). xxx

CONTENTS

**Recipes with page numbers in blue in the table of contents are gluten-free,
or offer a gluten-free alternative.**

Introduction

Vegan cooking is all about creativity; it's full of surprises, new techniques and ways of using ingredients. Anybody can have a go at being vegan. I know that anybody can do it because I have – me, the mightiest nose-to-tail carnivore of them all, and look at me now. After leaving meat off my plate for the last five years, I've never felt more energetic, happy and healthy. Since then, I've made it my mission to travel the globe looking for new dishes, scouring food markets and hanging out with locals, and learning that vegan cooking is a global craze and always has been. Many of the recipes that I've collected here have been brought back to my home in Wales and served up at the Beach House Kitchen, where I do most of my cooking and write my blog (beachhousekitchen.com). The way we eat reflects so much about who we are, and vegan food puts a huge emphasis on amazing fresh produce, food bursting with vitality and a generally more peaceful approach to life.

There's so much more to vegan cooking than tofu and rubber-like nut cutlets. I'm going to show you, with minimal fuss and plenty of accessible ingredients, how to make food that would satisfy both a fully fledged vegan and someone new to the idea, who is dipping their toe in the water. I'll be bringing the wonders of veganism into your kitchen, showing you new ways of preparing some of your favorite dishes. It will teach you to be resourceful – stews can be stuffed into roasted vegetables, soups can be made into sauces, smoothies can be thickened up and eaten as desserts; this kind of flexibility is the hallmark of a happy cook. There are recipes here designed to be rustled up in a hurry and others for more fancy occasions. The truth is, making delicious, varied, nourishing vegan food is easier than you thought.

More and more people are realizing that the way we are producing food, especially meat, is unsustainable. Veganism is the best way to protect our environment and the welfare of animals; even by cutting back on meat and dairy just once a week (or once a year!) you are making a very positive statement.

A vegan diet can fulfill your nutritional requirements, pack your belly with goodness and consistently boggle your mind with new culinary angles and diversity. You'll end up saving money, you'll feel healthier, you'll have energy, you'll feel satisfied and you may just save the world, one meal at a time! Why not feel good all the time? A vegan diet is a big stepping-stone to a brighter, lighter way of being.

The recipes in this book are mere guidelines – I am terrible at following rules. No matter how closely you try to follow a recipe, the dish will often alter and you will produce something unique, to be proud of and savored.

Peace and parsnips,

Lee x

Eating from the soil, shoot or branch

"Nothing will benefit human health and increase the chances for survival of life on Earth as much as the evolution to a vegetarian diet."— Albert Einstein

For me, organic and seasonal eating are the most natural ways of acquiring the sustenance we need to live the lives we want to lead. All energy comes directly from the sun – without it, we'd struggle! Plants transform that energy into something we can live on, which is one of the coolest, if not *the* coolest, things about nature. I break it down like this: organic = perfectly natural, chemical-free; seasonal = perfectly natural, vastly superior nutritional content. Both make a lot of sense.

I believe that we feel instinctively and know what foods do us good. Some people can eat loads of meat, dairy, gluten, etc., without any obvious issues, but eating high levels of these foods will affect us at some point in the long run. Sometimes these negative effects are subtle and do not show immediately.

We are all unique, and therefore need to find a diet that suits us as individuals. Veganism takes experimentation, an open mind and a greater sensitivity towards sourcing and combining ingredients. I see choosing to eat plant-based food as the best experiment possible for your body! No dairy, low saturated fats, normally lower levels of gluten (which is almost indigestible); most food allergies are readily catered for, without a need to think twice about recipes. The majority of these recipes are gluten-free or offer gluten-free options (but always check ingredient labels to make sure they're GF).

Eating food that grows directly from the earth, fed by the sun, dangling from trees, does not seem like a bad way to approach food. Nature gives us ample plant-based foods to nibble on; in fact, nature has given us the perfect way to fuel ourselves with optimum, pure, high-grade wonder-fuel: this way is veganism. Our furry friends would agree.

Dynamic ways of consuming vegan produce to boost your system

Raw power!

Research has shown that living plants contain unique health-giving properties, special energy that is destroyed when foods are cooked or processed. Raw foods (meaning the food hasn't been heated above 115°F) are used by many doctors to restore the health of patients. Even eating a diet based on 50 percent raw foods will have a huge effect; 75 percent raw and you are flying! We still don't understand the exact relationship of the subtle energies contained in our bodies and those contained in "living" foods, but the positive effects they have are irrefutable. They encourage detoxification, improve cellular metabolism, heighten enzyme activity and generally restore and nurture the body.

Raw power = a more energetic, slimmer and healthier way of being.

Fermented food

Fermented foods are becoming ever more popular and their health benefits widely acclaimed. Fermentation is the process in which ingredients such as cabbage and cucumbers are left to sit and steep until their sugars and carbs become bacteria-boosting agents that lift the immune system. We already consume plenty of fermented food: leavened bread, beer, wine, cider, yogurt and, increasingly, sauerkraut and kimchi.

Seasonality

Spring

Fruit:

Apricots, avocado, lemons, limes, oranges, rhubarb, strawberries

Vegetables:

Artichokes, asparagus, bean sprouts, beets, broccoli, broccoli rabe, celery, fava beans, garlic, leeks, mushrooms, nettles, new potatoes, peas, purple sprouting broccoli, salad greens, scallions, wild garlic

Herbs:

Bay, chervil, chives, cilantro, dill, marjoram, oregano, parsley, rosemary, thyme

Foraging/Other:

Asparagus, chanterelles, chickweed, dandelion leaves, fiddlehead ferns, elderflowers (for cordials), nettles (for soups, teas, etc.), burdock, morels, oyster mushrooms, ramps, seaweeds (dulse, Irish moss, kelp, rockweed, sea lettuce), *Viola odorata* (sweet violet), wild garlic

Summer

Fruit:

Apricots, avocado,
blackberries, blueberries,
cherries, crab apples, currants,
figs, grapes, nectarines,
melons, peaches, pears,
plums, raspberries, rhubarb,
strawberries

Vegetables:

Beets, chard, chilies,
cucumbers, garlic,
eggplant, fennel,
mushrooms, peas, peppers,
potatoes, radishes,
runner beans,
salad greens, shallots,
scallions, string beans,
sweet corn, tomatillos,
tomatoes, zucchini

Herbs:

Basil, bay, cilantro,
dill, marjoram, mint,
oregano, parsley,
rosemary, sage,
summer savory,
tarragon, thyme

Foraging/Other:

Blackberries,
blueberries, borage,
calendula (pot marigold),
chamomile, chanterelles,
dandelion leaves,
lamb's quarters, lavender,
nasturtiums, purslane,
sea kale, sorrel, wild cherries, wild
marjoram (oregano),
wild strawberries,
zucchini flowers

Autumn

Fruit:

Apples, blackberries, blueberries, clementines, cranberries, figs, grapes, kumquats, nectarines, pears, persimmons, plums, quinces

Vegetables:

Beets, bok choy, broccoli, broccoli rabe, brussels sprouts, cabbage, carrots, cauliflower, celeriac, celery, eggplant, fennel, Jerusalem artichokes, kale, kohlrabi, leeks, lettuces/salad greens, mushrooms, onions, parsnips, peppers, potatoes, pumpkin, radicchio, radishes, rutabaga, string beans, sweet potatoes, tomatillos, tomatoes, turnips, winter squashes, zucchini

Herbs:

Basil, bay, chives, marjoram, mint, oregano, parsley, rosemary, sage, thyme

Foraging/Other:

Barberries, blackberries, blackthorn (sloe) berries (for flavoring – gin mainly!), chamomile, chanterelles, currants, dandelion roots (dried and roasted for a coffee substitute), elderberries, heather, hen-of-the-woods mushrooms, horseradish, huckleberries, juniper berries (for flavoring gin again, mainly), pecans, porcini, rowan berries (for jam), salsify, walnuts, wild cherries (great for flavoring brandy)

Winter

Fruit:

Blood oranges, clementines, cranberries, grapefruit, kumquats, oranges, pomegranates, quinces, tangerines

Vegetables:

Broccoli, brussels sprouts, cabbage, cauliflower, celeriac, celery, endive, Jerusalem artichokes, kale, kohlrabi, leeks, onions, parsnips, potatoes, rutabaga, salsify, spinach, turnips, watercress, winter squashes

Herbs:

Bay, rosemary, sage

Foraging/Other:

Hazelnuts, field mushrooms, oyster mushrooms, porcini, *Viola odorata* (sweet violet), walnuts, watercress

A very meaty problem

"If anyone wants to save the planet, all they have to do is just stop eating meat. That's the single most important thing you could do. It's staggering when you think about it. Vegetarianism takes care of so many things in one shot: ecology, famine, cruelty."— Paul McCartney

My "veganity" didn't just sprout from my love for nutritious and super-tasty food; it was also an ethical decision: I decided that the way the large-scale meat and dairy industries were treating the animals in their care was just not acceptable. Animals were suffering to put cheese in my sandwich, and that was enough to turn me off dairy for good.

The meat industry is now a larger contributor to climate change than the entire transport industry. Going vegetarian is one big step in the right direction, but going vegan is a giant leap of positive intent. Veganism moves us forward in the way that we coexist with our planet. The more people who choose to eat vegan meals regularly, the greater the opportunity we have to stem the tide of pollution and disruption to nature and the greater the hope we offer to future generations.

Another consideration is that eating meat is tough on the digestive system. It requires digestive juices high in hydrochloric acid to break it down. The stomachs of omnivores and herbivores produce a twentieth of the acid produced by carnivores. Our bodies are not naturally disposed to eating large quantities of meat.

This sounds quite gross, but meat decays and becomes toxic when dead, and after we consume it, it rots within our bodies, releasing putrefaction poisons. Our bodies go through this process every time we eat meat. Carnivores are designed with a much shorter digestive tract than humans – they basically expel their dinner more quickly than we do. Like humans, non-flesh-eating animals have a digestive tract twelve times the length of their bodies; carnivores have a digestive tract only three times the length of theirs. Carnivores also eat their meat raw, and humans prefer it cooked. Cooking meat (and vegetables for that matter) decreases the natural enzymes that help true carnivores digest their meat. This leads to the pancreas being put under pressure to produce more digestive enzymes, so that it eventually becomes overworked and weak.

Meat has a toxic effect when we digest it, which the liver must try to cope with. Generally the livers of meat-eaters are forced to work much harder to extract poisons from the blood than those of vegans. This is just one considerable example of the increased likelihood of disease and potential organ failure that big-time meat-eaters face.

Carnivores are also experts at digesting huge amounts of animal fat and cholesterol without a large number of adverse effects. We all know the dangers of clogged arteries, strokes and the like; these conditions are often a direct result of eating too much saturated animal fat. Cut that out and you'll have a healthy ticker. Putting it into numbers, vegetarians, on average, have 14 percent lower cholesterol than meat-eaters, which equates to half the risk of serious heart disease. For vegans, consuming zero saturated animal fats, it would be even lower.

This was morbid, but important for me to get off my chest. I care about the health of my family, my friends ... in fact, all of us. I hope this has put part of the ethical, non-meat-eating approach into some form of context. A no-meat or low-meat diet equals a better world for all of us. Choosing to leave meat off our plates has huge implications. Also, health-wise, vegan vs. meat can only have one undisputed champion.

Jane with our neighbour Dawn's chicken Pinky. Perky is just out of shot!

Food myths

1. **MYTH:** Vegans struggle nutritionally and are generally skinny weaklings.

FACTS: There are vegan bodybuilders, big beefy folk who pump iron (if you're into that). There are also millions of vegans around the world living very healthy lives. With a little nutritional information (all contained in this book, I may add), a vegan diet can provide the body with all it needs, and probably more! People who take the plunge and give a plant diet a go generally feel lighter, imbued with greater energy levels, with shinier hair and skin, sparkling eyes and . . . you get the picture. They feel pretty damn good.

2. **MYTH:** Fats make you fat.

FACTS: Almost complete nonsense. Fats (with the exception of some saturated fats and the alien hydrogenated fats) are essential for the maintenance of a healthy body, especially relating to the nervous system and brain, which are, of course, very sensitive and best looked after carefully.

Sugars are generally what pile the pounds on. You have to eat high levels of fats, many handfuls of cashews, before the body begins to think of storing these fats as bottom bulge.

3. **MYTH:** Meat is the best source of protein/vegans don't get enough protein.

FACTS: Plants are packed with protein, and a balanced plant-based diet provides all the proteins needed to conduct a healthy and happy lifestyle. They're guilt-free, ethically clear and easily digestible. The body thrives on plants; the body buckles and stutters on meat.

Here are the facts, produced by men and women in white coats:

Studies have shown that people who eat a plant-based diet have a lower BMI (Body →

Mass Index), lower cholesterol and lower blood pressure. Plant proteins are lean, so you will be ingesting considerably lower levels of saturated fats.

Quinoa and soy provide what is called "complete" protein, which means that all our amino acid needs are taken care of. Eating a balanced veggie diet will always fill in the protein blanks left by "incomplete" proteins.

Most of us actually eat too much protein, and this excess cannot be broken down properly by the body and is turned into toxins. It has been said recently that eating too much protein is as bad as smoking, especially if those proteins come from animal sources. In middle age especially, it is better for our health to eat a lower-protein diet.

So the question is not how do we get more protein into our diet, but how do we eat a reasonable amount that will not harm our health? We need much less protein than we have been led to believe.

4. **MYTH:** Milk is the best source of calcium.

FACTS: Milk is not the elixir of life we thought it was. We need milk for a while – for a baby it's essential. After that, we can drop the bottle and pick up the leaf or berry with no detriment to our health (see page 37 for more info on dairy nutrition).

There are plenty of very rich sources of calcium, even richer than the mighty milk! Kale, arugula . . . green leafy veggies in general, sesame and tahini, white beans, bok choy, molasses, oranges, okra, broccoli, sugar snap peas, almonds, whole wheat grains, legumes, dried figs and other dried fruits, seaweed, tofu.

5. **MYTH:** Orange juice is the best source of vitamin C. →

FACTS: *Here is a list of fruits and vegetables that contain higher levels of vitamin C than oranges: papaya, peppers, broccoli, brussels sprouts, pineapple, strawberries (most berries, in fact).*

Other great sources are kiwi, tomatoes, cauliflower, cabbage, grapefruit, parsley, spring greens, spinach, sweet potatoes.

6. MYTH: We have incisors and we know how to use them.

FACTS: *When was the last time you saw a human fell a wildebeest? Our incisors are tiny, and all physiological evidence would suggest we are omnivores at best. Our teeth are generally quite flat, better for grazing than for tearing at legs of meat.*

7. MYTH: Eggs are essential for vitamin B12, thiamine, niacin, riboflavin and the other B vitamins.

FACTS: *Egg yolks do contain some special things, but these can be found from other sources. The B vitamins are quite a complex bunch, generally helping our body's cell and nerve functions and metabolism. They include thiamine, riboflavin, niacin, folate (think foliage), B12, B6, biotin and pantothenic acid. Apart from vitamin B12, a well-balanced diet will cover all these more than adequately by including plenty of green leafy vegetables, nuts, whole grain cereals, fresh and dried fruit, rice, potatoes, capers, most spices, black pepper, bananas, asparagus and lentils.*

Vitamin B12 is a little tricky in a vegan diet, as it is normally contained only in animal products. Many tofus and whole grain cereals are fortified with B12 and nutritional yeast flakes contain B12. Some people even say that if you leave a little soil on your veggies, you obtain B12. (This approach probably isn't for everyone!) With a well-balanced plant-based diet, there is no evidence to suggest a greater risk of vitamin B12 deficiency for vegans. It is something we should all be aware of. →

The evidence relating to the B12s is still quite contentious due to the way they are measured, and the many different scientific bodies doing research all have their own opinions. We need only a very small amount of vitamin B12 to be very healthy, but if you are thinking about becoming a full-time vegan, it's worth reading up on and, to be cautious, taking regular supplements.

8. MYTH: Things just aren't creamy without cream.

FACTS: *Nonsense really. Tofu and soaked nuts/seeds, when blended, give a very acceptable "creaminess" to dishes that can even fool some non-vegans into thinking cows are involved. Nut milks are also a brilliant way of adding richness to a vegan dish.*

9. MYTH: Vegans don't get enough vitamin D and iron.

FACTS: *Vitamin D is mainly found in animal-based foods, but there are plenty of sources outside the animal world. The plant world is blessed with many excellent sources of iron. Iron is best absorbed when combined with vitamin D. Worth bearing in mind!*

Non-animal sources for Vitamin D: the sun! Mushrooms (especially those grown outdoors; shiitake are best), fortified foods (cereals, soy drinks), and you may even look at venturing into supplements (if you don't like the sun and mushrooms). Make sure that vitamin D supplements come from lichen and not from animal sources.

Mushrooms can even be charged with sunlight after they're picked. Put them on a sunny window ledge for a day and this will boost their vitamin D content. In wintertime, you may like to get your Speedos on and take a sun bath. Watch out for excess UV rays, but generally, blue and broad spectrum lights will give a real vitamin D boost.

Iron: legumes, whole grains, sprouted beans and legumes, date syrup, molasses, green leafy vegetables, nuts, dried fruits.

The Vegan Pantry

A vegan's pantry is not that different from a non-vegan's pantry, and most of these recipes are flexible and do-able, without difficult-to-find ingredients. You will almost certainly have the majority of them already knocking about in your kitchen.

I know that not all local shops stock all the ingredients in my recipes. "Do you carry seitan?" will normally raise a few eyebrows down at the corner shop (I live halfway up a mountain in North Wales). However, with the advent of online food shopping, combined with a visit to your local health food store and "Asian" market, none of these ingredients should be too tricky to unearth. Buying grains, seeds and legumes is always best done in bulk, if you have the space to store them. This method may seem like a lot at first, but when you break it down, it works out loads cheaper. You may be able to find a delivery service for bulk orders, and it works well when a group of friends get together to order once every so often. These services may also offer some of the more difficult to source vegan ingredients and you can kill two peanuts with a potato.

Some "speciality" ingredients are superfluous to a balanced vegan diet. If you have a decent selection of veggies, fruits, legumes and nuts, you are well on your way to vegan-hood.

I tend to gather odds and ends when I see them at local markets or in shops. My pantry grows organically from little gems picked up on travels, such as spices or herbs from a certain region, and most have sentimental value. Some people bring back silk scarves and jangling trinkets from vacation; I return laden with spice mixes and cocoa beans. This kind of providence can only add to the magic and enjoyment of cooking and eating, bringing together so many disparate and wonderful ingredients, transforming them into something completely new, harmonious and unique.

I am not going to go through the entire range of items for the "ideal pantry," as there is no such thing, but if you start with a core selection of spices and dried herbs you can branch out steadily. Each new recipe you try will normally add one or two new additions to your pantry gang.

Grains

Grains are a cheap and plentiful way of filling ourselves up, and have been ever since humans started wandering around the earth. However, grains can offer us so much more, particularly if their natural nutritional properties are maintained and not processed away.

Buying whole grains is essential – anything refined should be avoided like a nutritional plague, since when grains are processed they lose many of their good bits, from vitamins to fiber.

Grains should be kept in jars or containers away from sunlight, and never left in torn plastic bags exposed to harsh pantry elements (air and occasional damp spells are no good for grains). Grains will keep for ages if stored properly – we even have some leftover grains in clay pots from the Harappan civilization in northern India, circa 3500 BC! They knew how to look after their pantries.

Most grains need a good rinsing before using, and some will appreciate a little soak before cooking, but this does change the quantity of water needed and the cooking time, so soak with caution. All grains require slightly different cooking times and water quantities for best results, although covering them with roughly ¾ inch of water, bringing them to a boil and popping a lid on, then simmering for half an hour was a general rule of thumb that I used throughout my student years. It never let me down, apart from one memorable voyage into accidental black rice!

I like to use gluten- and wheat-free grains regularly, normally buckwheat and millet.

Barley: Whole barley is best. Pearl barley has been refined and has lost lots of its integrity and nutritional content. Barley is becoming increasingly popular as a substitute for, say, rice in a risotto (a farrotto!) – it's a full and very wholesome grain.

Buckwheat (gluten-free): Not actually a grain but a seed, buckwheat has a strong earthy flavor and is best paired with other hearty ingredients. Buckwheat flour adds something a little different when used in baked goods, and makes a mean pancake.

Bulgur wheat: This is like a rougher, more nutritious cousin of couscous. It has been parboiled, meaning it takes only a short time to cook. Bulgur is used extensively in the southern Mediterranean and Middle East. For me, it's best served as a warm salad, with luxury adornments like almonds, dried apricots, herbs and spices.

Couscous: Made by coating semolina grain with flour and parboiling. In some places in North Africa this is still done by hand. Couscous is a labor of love, a grain that is becoming a staple in the US and rightly so. Very easy to cook, with a lovely light texture. You should always fluff up couscous with a fork, and I also like to add a glug of olive oil just before serving. It doesn't need much more than that!

Millet (gluten-free): This is another very nutritious grain and has been eaten for millennia – it's cheap to buy and makes a hearty accompaniment. Like buckwheat, millet is best roasted slightly before cooking, to lessen the stickiness. Its stickiness makes it ideal for forming vegan burgers and sausages.

Corn (gluten-free): Boasts plenty of nutrition. Ground corn, or cornmeal, is where we get polenta. Like all grains, whole grain is best since it retains all the nutrition. Corn also has an awesome color that brightens up the plate or bowl.

Quinoa (gluten-free): A high-altitude, super-nutritious grain (well, it's actually a sprout) that the Incas couldn't get enough of. Quinoa is a delicious and highly nutritious option, but the price and distance it travels means that I only use it on occasion.

Oats: Very rich in nutrients and good fats, oats can actually lower cholesterol. We're all familiar with them as oatmeal, but they can be used as a coating before frying, in soups and stews, and as a great ingredient for baking (they add substance to all they touch). Oats are naturally gluten-free, but may be packaged in a non-gluten-free facility, so make sure to check the label if you're strictly gluten-free.

Rice (gluten-free): The Daddy grain. Most of the world lives on the stuff, and they all cook it in different ways. Many people struggle with cooking rice, but it doesn't need to be taxing. It is actually very simple, and there are a couple of foolproof techniques. Rice should always be washed before cooking – rinse with cold water until the water runs clear. Brown rice is more nutritious and flavorful than white, but will take a little longer to cook. I normally keep brown rice (without it vegans wilt), red, black (if I'm feeling flush), wild, Arborio, jasmine and basmati rices on hand. What can I say – I eat a lot of rice!

Semolina: A wheat-based grain. It is milled in a variety of grades – fine, medium or coarse. Fine and medium are good for pasta and for desserts like *halwa*, while coarse is normally made into couscous.

Tips for cooking grains:

- *Do not stir grains when they are cooking; it makes them mushy and sticky.*
- *Never remove the lid when grains are cooking; the trapped steam is what cooks the grains evenly.*
- *Add flavorings to your grains, i.e., stock, herbs, chopped onions, tamari, seaweed, etc., to give them an interesting edge.*
- *Always cook grains on a very low heat after initially bringing them to a boil. The slower they cook, the lighter the results.*
- *Leftover grains make perfect frying material. Once cooled, pop them into the fridge, and the next day they can be mixed with vegetables in a frying pan and transformed, with a little sauce, into a super-quick meal.*

Beans, peas or legumes

Beans are powerhouses for lean plant protein and nutrients. Wherever these legumes grow, they actually enrich the earth with nitrogen and are therefore a very beneficial crop. Dried beans do need soaking and proper cooking, since they contain proteins that are hard for the body to break down (leading to bouts of whistling windiness), especially red kidney beans. Lentils and split peas do not need soaking, but do need to be washed before cooking. Sometimes I will soak beans and lentils until just softened and then blend them into a purée. This is great for a twist on a pancake batter or for thickening soups and stews.

There is such a variety of beans on offer that I normally keep a few staples, like chickpeas, mung beans, red kidney beans and yellow split peas, and vary the rest as I need them for a recipe. Of course, it doesn't always work out like this, and you can end up with a kaleidoscope of beans in your pantry.

Most beans and legumes take different lengths of time to cook, depending on variety, size, age and how dry they are. Just test them: if they're remotely "chalky" between the teeth, let them simmer on.

Dried or canned?

Dried. For me, always dried. You need to be a little bit ahead of yourself, as most beans need at least 6 hours of soaking, and overnight is best. Dried beans are always cheaper and have a fuller texture.

Tips for cooking beans and legumes:

- *Soak all dried beans overnight, roughly 8 hours, in fresh, cold water. They will expand to at least their original size, so always cover the beans with three times their volume of water. Little pieces of grit, stones or weird-looking beans may float to the top – remove them.*
- *Always preserve the cooking liquid from beans; it contains vitamins and loads of flavor and is ideal for soups and stews. I normally try to incorporate it into the dish involving the beans.*
- *Cooking beans and legumes on a low simmer will preserve their shape and texture. Do not add salt to the cooking water for beans: this will make the skins tough. Chickpeas and kidney beans foam when being cooked – just remove the foam with a slotted spoon.*

Below are some guidelines to how long different beans, peas and lentils should take to cook:

- *45 minutes – 1 hour: adzuki, black-eyed peas, navy, red kidney beans, soy, mung beans (or less), all lentils and peas (red split lentils, think more like ½ an hour).*
- *1¼–1½ hours: black beans, chickpeas, flageolet, pinto, butter beans.*
- *Check the beans by pressing one against the side of the pan with a spoon. If it's soft all the way through, it's cooked. I always like to nibble one, just to double-check.*
- *Stir salt into the pot just before the cooking time ends.*
- *If you'd like to cook your beans more quickly, add ½ teaspoon of baking soda to the water. This will cut the cooking time by roughly a third.*

These are what I normally keep handy:

Beans: adzuki, butter beans, red kidney beans, black beans, pinto, rosecoco, flageolet, navy, mung (whole and split), black-eyed peas, soy

Peas: chickpeas, brown chickpeas, split green and yellow peas, dried whole green peas

Lentils: green, brown, Puy (petite French green) and red lentils (I'll normally have a variety of Indian lentils kicking around, but they are only recommended for the hopeless dal addict)

Soybean products

I believe in the wonders of soy. Yes, there is bad soy. Parts of the Amazon are being chopped down to grow it, and they are fed to livestock reared in the meat industry, but generally, if we buy organic and fermented non-GMO (see page 38) whole-bean soy products from reputable companies, there should be no problem. Most supermarkets now stock soybean products.

Miso: Traditionally a fermented soybean and grain product, miso has been produced for thousands of years in Japan and has a thick consistency and pungent aroma, ideal for flavoring soups, stews and sauces. Miso is naturally very salty. It is very rich in nutrients and vitamins and is good for calming the digestive system. The flavors of miso can range from nutty to winey and fruity. It can be gluten-free, but check the label to be sure.

Tamari: Just like soy sauce, but always produced in a traditional and healthy way. It has more flavor than most soy sauces and, when used properly, accentuates the subtle flavors in food. It is often gluten-free (but check the label).

Tofu: Probably the ultimate vegan food, tofu is versatile and often misunderstood. Tofu loves nothing more than soaking up flavors and marinades, and boasts a whole range of textures that can complement any dish, savory or sweet. That is part of its beauty: tofu can sneak effortlessly into a cheesecake, offering its wonderful smooth and rich texture and perfectly mingling with the flavors on offer. It has one of the highest levels of protein found in plant foods and is virtually cholesterol-free. To help firm tofu absorb sauce and flavors and to improve its texture, press it to remove excess moisture. Do this by wrapping it in a clean kitchen towel and putting it on a plate. Place another plate over it and balance a few books on top. The weight should be enough to gently press the tofu without splitting it. Leave it for an hour, draining the liquid once or twice.

Tempeh: Similar to tofu, but fermented. Tempeh uses whole beans and will generally be located with the tofu or in the freezer section. In this frozen form, I'd advise defrosting and steaming the tempeh for 10–15 minutes, which softens it a little and makes it more receptive to flavors. Then use as normal.

Seitan: This is a very meaty fella. Called mock duck by some, it is used throughout Southeast Asia to fool vegan tourists into thinking they're eating chicken! You can make your own seitan at home using a flour called vital wheat gluten. It's dead easy. Having some VWG in your cupboard means that you can add real texture to veggie burgers and sausages, and some swear by a couple of tablespoons in their bread. Seitan is the ultimate vegan trick up the sleeve, to impress people new to veganism. It's not just a crazy name for a food, but a delicious (dare I say it) meat substitute. Carnivore approved. It's basically pure gluten.

Pasta

Yes, have some. You already know your favorite shades and shapes and you know what I'm going to say. I like whole wheat pasta, etc., etc. Organic, etc., etc. Buy good stuff. There are also some pretty acceptable gluten-free pastas out there now, sans wheat. A simple plate of pasta, prepared with love, can change everything!

Cans, jars and cartons

I generally try to avoid canned goods. I know they are so much easier and sometimes cheaper, but the lining of tin cans is made of all kinds of nasty chemicals that can enter the food. I'd always opt for jars or fresh ingredients.

Coconut milk: Unless you have a decent supply of fresh coconuts, coconut milk is an essential pantry superstar, adding smooth, plant-based creaminess to dishes.

Milk: Plant-based, of course. I keep soy milk as a staple, but also love almond and oat milk. Even lentil milk is interesting. You can milk most things nutty or pulsy (see pages 38–41).

Capers: I always have them lurking some-where. Briny little buds that add so much piquant fruitiness to food – I don't know what I'd do without them. Stick them in the fridge once opened.

Mustard: Dijon, whole grain and English. The holy trinity of mustards can resurrect a sorry dressing. Some are gluten-free (check the label).

Jams, marmalades and chutneys: As you begin to approach middle age, friends and family no longer seem to buy you strange gifts, but offer jars of jams, marmalades and chutneys. The perfect gift in my eyes. Of course they are heaped with sugar, but

Sunday morning toast sessions are a must in the Beach House Kitchen.

Gherkins: Some call these cornichons, pickles, etc. I like gherkins. In fact, I love 'em. I eat them whole as my preferred late-night snack.

Pickled chilies/peppers: Called by many different names around the world, pickled chilies are a ready-made, ideal accompaniment to so many southern Mediterranean and Mexican dishes.

Margarine: In baking, it does add butter-iness, which vegans can miss out on. Find a good brand and avoid anything with strange-sounding fats in it.

Chipotle paste (or whole dried chipotle chilies): I always have some of these tucked away and they're getting quite popular – even my local shop is stocking them. Super smoky and sweet, chipotle is the taste of Mexican cooking, used extensively in the cuisine's soups, stocks and stews.

Sweeteners

Ethical, inexpensive sweeteners can be hard to find and normally cost a pretty penny. But there are options. Sugar is of course the cheapest, but sugar is sugar is sugar, no matter how we swing it. It just ain't doing us any good. I like to used dried fruits to sweeten things, and Jane regularly laments my lack of sugary tendencies (she has a supersweet tooth). I tend to use unrefined brown sugar to bake with, but admit that it will not produce as light and fluffy a cake as regular white granulated sugar.

Here are some sweeteners I use:

Unrefined brown sugar: Always look for organic fair-trade sugar if you can. Normally called soft light brown sugar in the UK, this is my staple baking sugar. Note that this is not the same sweetener referred to as "brown sugar" in the US. If you can't find unrefined soft brown sugar, you can try using turbinado, demerara, or sucanat (although the texture of these others isn't quite as fine). You can also always look online to source hard-to-find ingredients. For this, it might just be worth it – it's really the best.

Brown rice syrup: This is my staple liquid, gooey-style sweetener. It's relatively cheap and has a delicious caramel flavor ideal for dressings and cakes. It's also low GI (glycemic index) and even boasts a few minerals. It's naturally gluten-free, but check the label to be sure.

Maple syrup: Lordy, lordy! What a thing. Delicate, evocative, fragrant and scrumptious. Spend a bit more on maple syrup and you will be rewarded – just a dab here and there will light up cakes and desserts.

Pomegranate molasses: Sweet and sour, something like a southern Mediterranean tamarind/citrus substitute. Used almost exclusively for a special touch in dressings, and adds a surprise element to marinades and stews.

Date syrup: I love to use this rich, dark sweetener in dressings and dishes that have an exotic flavor. Makes a very mean muffin.

Molasses: Dark as tar, its potent stickiness is used mainly in marinades – especially good in barbecue-style sauces and some sticky Chinese-style marinades. I also like popping it into bread recipes.

Jaggery: An Indian version of unrefined sugar cane juice. Very sticky, like a fudge. I absolutely love it, and this is my exception to my sweetness scepticism. I use it in baking and chai teas. It has a very strong flavor, which can be a little domineering in the wrong place.

Muscovado sugar: Darker and stickier than soft brown sugar, muscovado is normally raw and unrefined, keeping all of that deep, dark molasses flavor. If you can't find it in the US, try substituting with unrefined dark brown sugar.

Barley malt extract: Cheap and cheerful, with a lovely malted flavor. Great in hot, milky drinks, and I love it in bread. Not quite as sweet as sugar, agave, etc., so add a little more.

Apple juice concentrate: Organic is always best here. Good apple juice concentrate is amazing for adding fruity sweetness to baked goods and dressings, and I even use it to flavor burgers and sausages.

Agave nectar: Made from the agave plant (of tequila fame). Some regard it as a wonder sweet elixir, and some folks with sugar intolerances can get away with enjoying it.

Baking

Flours: Whole wheat (staple), unbleached all-purpose flour (for a lighter touch), spelt (for bread and cookies; lower in gluten), buckwheat (no gluten, but can have great results when backed with a gluten flour), gram (chickpea) flour (a very healthy and ideal gluten-free replacement, with a strong flavor), rice (I use it mainly in baking; especially handy when making gluten-free bread), cornmeal (ideal for cornbread and for soft or baked polenta) and rye (for bread . . . gorgeous, dark bread).

Baking powder and baking soda: The main difference between these two is that baking powder makes things rise when paired with acidic ingredients, like lemon juice or vinegar. Baking soda is generally a better all-rounder, releasing carbon dioxide when combined with moisture, i.e., in soda bread. I always have both. I also brush my teeth with baking soda mixed with tea tree oil.

Vanilla extract: Costly, but lasts ages.

Nut extract: Almond and hazelnut normally do the trick.

Booze: You may need a little bit of liqueur when baking; one for the cake, two for the chef is the normal ratio in most kitchens! Whiskey, brandy and coffee liqueur especially can be added to cakes for that buzzed dimension. I always have a good bottle of malt for when Dad visits.

Oils and vinegars

Oils

Good fats and oils don't make you fat! If you eat too much of anything, it's not going to do you any good, but nutritionally, fats are essential. Our bodies love them. They need them, especially unsaturated fats, which are present in all plant-based foods. Without sounding like a smug tree-hugger, we vegans are very lucky to not have to monitor our saturated fat intake. There are hardly any bad fats present in the multifarious world of plants. Of course, eating a pound of Brazil nuts per day is still not cool for the body, but generally, we are free to munch away.

We all want a healthy heart and brain (they seem like good bits to look after). Fats can either assist or pollute these vital organs, depending on the types we choose to consume. Good fats, poly- and monounsaturated fats and some saturated fats (like lauric acid, found in coconuts), are filled with essential fatty acids and are the ones we want. They are easier for the body to utilize and less likely to be stored as fat. They also help our cells and nerves to function more efficiently, protecting them from nasty invaders; they keep our hearts healthy, actually lessening cholesterol in the blood; they make our skin bright with vitality, our hair shine. Good fats make us fuller for longer and help us to absorb the vitamin content in our foods and even protect us from things like strokes and high blood pressure.

You will notice quite a lot of oils being used in these recipes. I love the Mediterranean lifestyle and have taken on the idea that large glugs of oil lead to longevity. Good oils also give vegan food richness and shine. Please do not fear good oils – they are your friends. If we are regularly eating a vegan diet, we need the fat anyway; it is essential in maintaining a healthy body and mind.

- *Top 5 sources of healthy plant fats: Avocado, coconut, nuts and seeds (including nut and seed butters), olives.*
- *Top 5 healthiest oils: Hemp, grapeseed, flax, olive, canola.*

Here are the ones I use most often:

Coconut oil: Always buy high-quality, unrefined and organic if you can. Good coconut oil has outrageous health-giving properties; poor-quality coconut oil has the opposite. Used extensively in vegan and raw desserts and offers a subtle, shimmering coconut-ness to anything fried. You can now buy it unflavored.

Olive oil (light): You know the score. Good stuff, mechanically pressed, is the only way to go. I use olive oil a lot for frying, mainly because I love the flavor and it's really healthy. Olive oil should never be used at high heat; keep it at medium or low. Ideal for sautés.

Extra virgin olive oil: Only used for dressings and dipping warm bread into. It also adds a last-minute shine to sauces, stews, etc. Never use for frying or roasting: it is a shameless waste of the amber nectar.

Vegetable oils: Basic all-arounders that get the job done nicely. Good at high heat.

Canola oil: Increasingly popular and improving in quality. Canola oil used to be the standard option, but now it can be made using the same techniques as the finest olive oils. Dark golden and strongly flavored,

it doesn't suit every dish, but when married with bold flavors it can make all the difference. Operates well at high heat and smoking point if refined.

Toasted sesame oil: You can opt for untoasted, if you are not into the full-power flavor of toasted. Used in moderation, it adds a quintessential Asian twist to dishes that cannot be replicated (unless you sprinkle toasted sesame seeds on top). Best for marinades and dressings, not a fryer.

Vinegars

Balsamic, apple cider, sherry, red wine, white wine, rice, white, malt (for fries).

Herbs and condiments

Fresh is normally best, but sometimes, in baking especially, you're looking for that intense punch of thyme, not the delicate, fragrant thyme. Herb mixtures are quick and easy and can be very high quality. I am lucky enough to have a herb garden, but otherwise, I'd always keep at least two types of fresh herbs in the fridge to use as toppings or additions to salads.

Dried herbs

Thyme, mint, basil, dill, marjoram, rosemary, oregano, tarragon, sage.

Fresh herbs

Parsley, cilantro, thyme, mint, basil (weekly staples).

Condiments

I use some of the following ingredients regularly, but none could be classified as essential. Fortunately, they do last for a while.

Nutritional yeast flakes: In your average cupboard, few things sound more random than this vegan delicacy. "Nutritional yeast flakes? You're having a laugh." I'll have you know they impart a very savory, almost cheesy flavor to dishes and are also full of vitamin B. They do look like fish food, and cats are very interested in them, but apart from that, they are an irrefutable vegan classic. NYFs add a delicious, umami background to soups, salads, stews and even baked goods. Like a salt, with bells on.

Vegetable stock: It's better to make your own, but not always practical. There are some really decent stock cubes and bouillon out there. Several brands offer organic and low-salt options.

Others: Dried mushrooms, tamarind (paste or dried), rose water, orange blossom water, mirin, Chinese rice wine, pickled pink ginger (for sushi) . . . things you pick up along the way.

Spices

Where would we be without a little spice in our lives? Everything would taste like school lunches! Good spices are essential to a cook's repertoire, and our bodies love them, as they're a great way to boost the immune system.

There is a huge difference between a good spice and a not-so-good spice. Buy it fresh, keep it fresh, use it . . . fresh. I keep mine in the fridge, tucked away in a sealed container, far away from air or sunlight. I am lucky enough to travel frequently and have little pouches of special powders from all kinds of spice markets, from Marrakech to Delhi. Whenever I open them, it takes me right back to my first waft of spice in an alleyway somewhere in the world.

I sometimes use a coffee grinder at home to make my own spice mixes. Keeping spices in their natural state is a good idea – they can last for years at room temperature, but when ground will lose their essential oils (aka flavor, aroma . . .) very quickly. Grind small quantities, often. A pestle and mortar is also an essential tool in the true spice aficionado's cupboard. Once you've roasted and ground your own cumin and coriander, you'll never go back to the store-bought packets – it fills the house with such stunning aromas.

Due to the essential oils in spices, prolonged cooking is generally not a good idea. You'll lose some of the zing. Spice mixes like garam masala are usually added towards the end of cooking curries, and overcooking spices is anathema. Grind your spices just before cooking, just enough for that particular dish.

Spices don't just have to be used in cooking; they can make great infusions with wonderful health-giving properties. Try boiling anise seeds, caraway seeds, fennel seeds and coriander seeds together for a totally ancient take on an antacid. This is bound to awaken your digestive fire and soothe any stomachaches.

When using spices, it's a good rule to rub them between your finger and thumb or in your palms. This should get the oils going and a strong aroma should be wafting around your nose. If spices look and feel dry or crumbly, they are well past their prime.

Here is a quick shakedown of the spices that I generally have stashed away:

Ajwain seeds: Used extensively in Indian cooking, but rarely found in home spice collections. Ajwain is something you only need to keep in small quantities. I use it in a few recipes, but I am a curry nut. I find that dried thyme can be used as a reasonable substitute, as both contain the same essential oil.

Health benefits: *antifungal, antibacterial, rich in fiber and antioxidants. Used a lot in traditional medicine to treat indigestion, coughs and asthma.*

Allspice: Caution! This one is a live wire. It is very popular in Latin American and Caribbean food and is sometimes called pimento or Jamaica berry if you're on the road. If you like anything "jerked," allspice is the main flavor. Generally used in baking, but may also pop up in stews, curries and soups. Use sparingly; it packs a real punch.

Health benefits: *soothing, warming, increases digestive power, anti-inflammatory, anti-flatulent, high in vitamins and minerals (like vitamin C and iron).*

Anise seed/star anise: If you like ouzo or Pernod, you like anise. Used throughout the world, especially China, the exotic anise seeds are generally used in the US when tucked away in star anise (the rust-red husk). Anise has a fragrant, sweet aroma and a strong licorice-like flavor. It is stuffed full of antioxidants, which fight disease and promote good health. Mixed with hot water or served in a chai (see page 69), anise becomes a potent health elixir, great for treating colds, stomachaches and coughs. In India, it is a tradition to serve anise seeds at the end of a meal, especially a large cere-monial meal. The seeds are chewed and aid digestion.

Health benefits: *tonic, stimulant, antiseptic qualities, high in copper and iron, high levels of the B vitamins, decent for vitamins C and A, used to treat bronchitis, indigestion and asthma.*

Asafetida: Asafetida is the traditional Per-sian name for the spice that in India is referred to as "hing," and some people also call it "devil's dung." It has quite a savory flavor, reminiscent of onions, and for this reason is used in a lot of cooking, such as Jain or yogic, as a substitute for onions and garlic. Both of these are believed to be stim-ulants that stir up the mind. Asafetida must be kept in its own well-sealed container. It is a very strong spice and will corrupt the flavors and aromas of other spices it is stored near.

Health benefits: *antiflatulent, lowers blood pressure, antibacterial, aids digestion, sooth-ing.*

Bay leaf: The dark green leaves of the bay tree have been used since very early times as a subtly sweet and aromatic flavor addition to soups and stews. If you have access to a bay tree, you can use them fresh, but they are best dried out of direct sunlight (a dehydrator is very handy here). Bay leaves are a brilliant sub when making curries, if you can't get hold of curry leaves, for example. I use far too much bay and find it hard to cook lentils or beans without dropping at least one leaf in. It adds a subtle background flavor that you can build on.

Health benefits: *contains compounds that are said to fight cancer, and also boasts anti-septic, antioxidant and digestive qualities. Fresh leaves are a brilliant source of vitamins C and A, and are also high in minerals and folic acid. Bay leaves soothe the stomach, making them helpful when treating ulcers. Very high in iron.*

Black pepper: We sometimes toss black pepper into our meals almost without thinking, it's so commonplace on West-ern tables. Salt and pepper are our condi-ments of choice, but this has only caught on in our part of the world. I love to find freshly ground cumin on a North African restaurant table, or freshly ground Szech-uan peppercorns on a Chinese table. Tastes change all over the world, but black pepper, as a spice, is a sensation, especially when freshly ground or cracked. I love using it as the driving force of a spice mix, or pairing it with big bold flavors.

Pepper originated in Kerala, Southern India, and its use spread all around the world like wildfire. Sometimes known as the "king of spice," peppercorns are actually berries obtained from a tropical plant. They come in many colors, generally relating to the maturity of the peppercorn and how it has been treated. Black peppercorns are the most popular, picked when they're red and dried until they shrivel. Green peppercorns are picked early, and white peppercorns are soaked in a brine to remove the black color. Whole peppercorns keep for years at room temperature, but when ground, use them right away.

Health benefits: *anti-inflammatory, calm-ing, antiflatulent, stimulates digestion, great source of the B vitamins, good for vitamins C and A.*

Capers: Piquant, fruity little suckers, capers are the bud of a spindly plant, and are always picked early in the day. They are one of the essentials in every Mediterranean kitchen and I use them a lot as a sneaky treat in many of my recipes. The smaller or finer the caper, the better and more intense the flavor. Capers are generally sold in brine or vinegar, and this pickling process brings out their flavor. They can have high levels of salt added to them, which is well worth bearing in mind.

Health benefits: *powerful antioxidant qualities, promotes smooth circulation of blood, lowers bad cholesterol, decent levels of vitamins A and K. Capers have been used to treat rheumatic pain and stimulate the appetite.*

Caraway seed: A traditional European spice, caraway is a member of the parsley family. The seeds look a lot like cumin, but when sniffed they have a unique, peppery aroma. I don't use loads of caraway; it mostly crops up in Eastern European food and plays a major role in making borscht, one of the world's finest soups. I also sneak it into our homemade sauerkraut.

Health benefits: *speeds up digestion, high in dietary fiber, absorbs toxins, contains several powerful antioxidants, good for iron and zinc, used in remedies for IBS.*

Cardamom: Well renowned for its health-giving properties, cardamom comes in two colors, green and black. It's the little black, highly aromatic seeds we're interested in here – they have a "camphor-like" flavor that really comes to life when crushed (although the skins do contain beneficial essential oils). Cardamom is used almost equally in savory and sweet dishes and brings a whole new dimension to our traditional rice pudding.

Health benefits: *digestive, antiseptic, antispasmodic, calming, diuretic, general tonic, high in potassium, ridiculously high in manganese (helps clean out free radicals).*

Chilies: I could write a whole book on these feisty nightshades. I use lots of chilies in my cooking, both dried and fresh. Chilies come in many varieties and some recipes are much better made with specific chilies.

Health benefits: *capsaicin (an alkaloid compound) is what gives chilies their distinct flavor and spiciness. It has been shown to reduce cholesterol and to fight cancer and diabetes. Chilies have high levels of vitamin C and decent levels of minerals.*

Cinnamon: Very much one of those spices that is as much medicine as food. Cinnamon has the highest strength of antioxidants found in nature – one hundred times more than an apple. Generally sold as a ground powder or in "stick" form, cinnamon is the outer bark of *Cinnamomum* trees, which during the drying process rolls up into neat tubes. Cinnamon is so good for us, it makes sense that when winter comes it begins to appear in many traditional recipes. It has long been regarded as an excellent cold-beater.

Health benefits: *warming and soothing, antiseptic and with anesthetic qualities, helps against arterial diseases and strokes.*

Cloves: Little black dried flower buds, cloves have a strong, fragrant aroma and bring a good *biryani* to life. Cloves have well-known anesthetic qualities and I remember sucking on them as a child to get rid of toothache. Not my preferred serving suggestion.

Health benefits: *warming and soothing, antiseptic, anesthetic, kills stomach parasites. Clove oil is great for arthritis and aching muscles.*

Coriander seeds: Used since ancient times to treat ailments and in cooking, coriander seeds are one of the common spices in many kitchens. They have a strong, earthy orange flavor and I find they are best gently roasted and ground just before cooking, releasing all those crazy aromatics.

Coriander seeds are packed with healthy fatty acids and essential oils. When added to soups and stews, they can also act as a thickening agent, a nifty bonus feature.

Health benefits: *calming, digestive stimulant, very high in iron, generally high levels of minerals and vitamins. Coriander seeds can even help to combat bad breath!*

Cumin: There is no mistaking the distinct, pungent aroma and flavor of cumin seeds. Cumin is strong and warm, always best roasted and crushed before cooking. I like to sprinkle cumin onto curries and soups in place of pepper.

Health benefits: *high in dietary fiber, antiflatulent, aids digestion, very good source of iron, high in copper (good for the red blood cells) and calcium, high in carotenes and the B vitamins, helps colds and indigestion.*

Fennel seeds: Fennel has been revered in Britain since Anglo-Saxon times, when it symbolized longevity, courage and strength. These seeds are full of sweet and herby anise flavors and aromas. They are a little softer and greener than anise seeds, but they come from the same family, so are quite similar.

Health benefits: *great stores of vitamins A, E and C, and the B vitamins. Good levels of dietary fiber and a famed antiflatulent!*

Fenugreek seeds: Not one for the spice tourist, fenugreek is strongly aromatic and flavorful. Overdo the fenugreek at your peril! In their raw state they are very bitter, but mellow out when lightly roasted.

Health benefits: *helps get the bowels going, full of fiber, great for stabilizing blood sugar levels, laxative, given to mothers to aid milk production, helps coughs and bronchitis.*

Horseradish: You may know it as creamed horseradish, lathered over Sunday roasts, but there is more to horseradish than a mere condiment. Very pungent and hot, horseradish is a real eyebrow-raiser. It comes from the same family as cabbage, radish and mustard, and that unmistakable fiery flavor is present, at one level or another, in all these ingredients. Horseradish is best enjoyed for its one-off flavor contribution as opposed to its awesome nutrition. Fresh horseradish should be firm and young when bought – the older it gets, the less flavor it has and the more fibrous it is. Grate and serve fresh, combined with a little vinegar to keep the flames down!

Health benefits: *soothes the nerves, diuretic, anti-inflammatory, gastric stimulant (increasing appetite and stimulating digestion).*

Mustard seeds: I normally use the black or yellow mustard seeds, but they come in all sorts of colors: brown, white, etc. Mustard seeds are used throughout the world as a flavoring, be it in mustard (the condiment), mustard oil, or just the seeds on their own. Mustard seeds come to life when crushed and mixed with water or roasted. This kick-starts the essential oils and brings out the pungent nuttiness.

Health benefits: *high in niacin, riboflavin and thiamine, lowers cholesterol, plenty of good fats, helps with muscle pain and rheumatism, also has excellent levels of vitamin E (protecting our cells).*

Nutmeg/mace: Wars have been fought over nutmeg, which does seem a little over the top, but these aromatic seeds used to grow on only one small cluster of islands in Indonesia. Nutmeg and mace are basically the same thing, mace being the crimson outside skin of the nutmeg, with nutmeg being the seed of a little fruit. Each has a similar warm and sweet aroma and flavor. The only real difference is that mace will give a light, saffron-like tinge to food. Nutmeg has long been regarded as a potent aphrodisiac and is also, bizarrely, a relaxant. In Chinese and Indian medicine, nutmeg oil has been used to treat digestive and nervous ailments. You should not ingest large quantities of nutmeg in one sitting, as this sort of behavior may lead to hallucinations and delirium followed by death.

Health benefits: *antifungal, aids digestion, calming, antidepressant, jam-packed with antioxidants.*

Paprika: This is made from grinding dried red peppers into a powder. It is very popular in Spain and Hungary. Paprika comes in three main varieties: smoked, hot or sweet. I use smoked paprika quite a lot; it is so distinctive and unique. Sweet paprika is mainly a coloring spice; vibrantly red, it contains high levels of superbly body-friendly chemicals that give it its wild color.

Health benefits: *high levels of vitamin A, good for the eyes, heart and skin, decent levels of vitamin E to protect the nerves and organs.*

Saffron: The dried stigma or threads of a lavender-colored crocus flower, saffron is one of the most expensive ingredients in the world and rightly so. Saffron has an unmistakable, subtle flavor and adds a light amber color to food, not to mention incredible health-giving properties.

Health benefits: *contains chemicals that help fight stress, cancer and infection, boosts the immune system, therapeutic, antidepressant, helps the heart and digestion. Basically, it's a superhero!*

Tamarind: Tamarind fruit is encased in long pods, hanging from massive trees, and adds a lovely sweet/sour tang to dishes, especially condiments. Tamarind can be nibbled straight from the tree, but is generally sold as a paste or in dried, compressed blocks.

Health benefits: *powerful antioxidant, high levels of thiamine, vitamins C and A, iron and fiber, can be used as a laxative or digestive aid.*

Vanilla: Vanilla pods, traditionally from Central America, are extracted from an orchid that is only pollinated by hummingbirds. High-quality vanilla pods cannot be imitated, although there are some very good vanilla extracts out there. There are several different types of vanilla, and price is normally a good gauge to where you're heading quality-wise. Vanilla is a special-occasion spice and I use it as such.

Health benefits: *the Mayans used it as an aphrodisiac, but this is unproven. Vanilla is really all about the flavor!*

Nuts about nuts!

As a vegan you cannot avoid going a little nutty over our flexible, good-fat friends. Crammed full of richness and capable of adding a satisfying, creamy quality to dishes that just cannot be replicated in the vegan repertoire, nuts are indispensable. They are the plant world's nutritional powerhouses, and even just a small handful a day can keep us topped up with protein, minerals, vitamins and healthy fats.

Nuts are always best bought in the shell. They degrade when they are cracked open and most nuts, unfortunately, have been processed when bought without their hard jackets. Buying roasted nuts is fine if you plan on eating them soon, but roasting your own nuts at home can be a real giggle – check it out on page 147.

Let's give our nuts a closer inspection:

Almonds: Almonds come from a beautiful pinkish-white flower dangling off an equally lovely tree. Almonds are full of things called phytochemicals, which have incredible health-giving properties, and they contain high levels of monounsaturated fatty acids, which help to protect from coronary disease and strokes. Almonds also contain very high levels of minerals like manganese, calcium and iron (the list goes on) and are very rich in vitamin E, a potent antioxidant. Almonds make a great milk (see page 41) and are popular all over the world. I tend to soak almonds overnight and have half a handful in the morning for a turbo-charged boost. A handful of almonds a day keeps the grim reaper at bay!

Brazils: It's all in the name, really. Brazil nuts are from the Amazon, the seeds of the giant Brazil nut tree, which can grow to 160 feet tall and live for 700 years! Brazils are very high in energy and good fats, and the latter actually lower cholesterol levels in the blood.

Cashews: Without glorious cashews, I'd be a fifty-pound weakling! Delicately sweet, rich, totally delicious. I love 'em, and you can even eat the cashew "apple" that the nut hangs from. Cashews, like most nuts really, are high in good fats and dietary fiber. They are packed with minerals like zinc, which is great for tissue growth, along with helping digestion, and are also outrageously excellent sources of copper.

Chestnuts: Ye olde chestnut. Chestnut trees are native to North America. Members of the beech family, their nuts are a wonderful delicacy and relatively low in fat, from a nut perspective. I like to use chestnuts in purées and as a thickener in sauces or even desserts – they have a creamy, starchy, almost potato-like quality when broken down. Chestnuts actually have a nutritional profile more similar to a sweet potato than a nut. They should be stored like a vegetable and kept in the fridge.

Chia seeds: Chia seeds have been called the "ultimate superfood" for a while now. The Aztecs knew this and cultivated this low-growing herb, a member of the mint family. They are full of polyunsaturated fats, and contain a potent blend of vitamins, minerals, protein, antioxidants, dietary fiber, omega fatty acids . . . just a tablespoon per day contains much of your recommended daily allowance of many of these things. Scatter them on your fruit salad, morning cereal, smoothie or toast to add magnificence to your day.

Coconuts: This rough kernel of the coconut tree comes with an added bonus: water! Called a "complete food," one average-size coconut contains the energy, minerals and vitamins needed daily by your average-size person.

Hazelnuts: Sometimes called "filberts," hazelnuts belong to the birch family of trees. Very sweet, fatty and super-nutritious, hazelnuts are awesome sources of folate, a vitamin that battles anemia and is very good for expectant mothers. Added to this, hazelnut butter is one of the finest things you can spread on toast.

Macadamias: An Aussie nut. Super-sweet and über-luxurious (not to mention expensive), macadamias are a treat worth investing in. The gold bullion of the nut world yields not only supreme richness and crunch, but is very friendly to our hearts and has potent levels of the B vitamins. I use macadamias in many desserts, and when blended into a cream they are a dream.

Peanuts: These are actually a legume, but boast all the health-giving properties of a nut. The nutrient benefits of peanuts have been known since ancient times; they are a wonderful source of cheap plant protein and a supercharged snack (if the salted ones are kept to a minimum). Sometimes called groundnuts, like all legumes they actually enrich the soil and grow very quickly – in roughly one hundred days you could have a mature plant, laden with pea-nutty goodness.

Pecans: I've always wished for a pecan tree (a hickory) and a mango tree in my garden, but it'd mean a commute between North America and India. Coupled with incredible tastiness, pecans are a rich source of wellness, full of antioxidants, high in vitamin E and manganese, with a huge load of minerals to boot. Pecans are normally used in desserts, but I like to play with their bold flavors in salads and baking.

Pine nuts: Creamy, buttery, delicate and sweet, nothing beats a pine nut (except the price). Very high in monounsaturated fats and essential fatty acids. Manganese is there in spades and really helps us fight infections. When blended, pine nuts make one of the smoothest butters/purées around, especially good for lathering on the top of cakes or cookies.

Pistachios: Pistachios generally pop up in some of my favorite global treats. The finest pistachios, in my opinion, are Iranian; they are the size of large grapes, deep green and rich. In fact, that green color is a serious

attraction – it can really light up a plate of food. Like most of these nuts, one handful of pistachios a day will mean your protein, antioxidant, vitamin and mineral levels are all taken care of.

Walnuts: Walnuts contain the highest level of antioxidants in any nut. Quite a thing. These friendly chemicals scavenge our bodies for signs of disease and wipe them out. The oil of walnuts has excellent astringent properties, making the skin supple and shining – much, much better than overpriced beauty creams.

Soak your nuts:

Soak your nuts in water for 2–12 hours before use, as this will release enzyme inhibitors, making them more digestible and the nutrients better available to the body. Soaking also softens the nuts and makes them easier to blend, which is especially useful when making nut creams and butters.

Fruits

When you're trying to eat a decent quantity of raw food, juicing and smoothie-making becomes a good habit.

Buying local and seasonal fruits would be ideal, but it can be limiting. It is easy to be idealistic, but a world without mangoes is a bleak and hollow existence. We do, however, have many seasonal opportunities to forage for berries and fruits (see the Seasonality guides on pages 4–7). Hit the woods and gardens and freeze or make preserves with your bumper harvest. This will carry you through the leaner months of the year.

Many fruits contain plenty of vitamin C, which is a wonderful antioxidant. Try to keep fruits raw, or cooked to a minimum to preserve their vitamin and enzyme content. Enzymes are an integral part of a healthy diet and are killed by cooking.

Dried fruits

Great food for when you're on the go, the ideal pick-me-up snack, with the addition of a few nuts for good fats. Dried fruits keep wonderfully and are best when sun-dried or dried by other natural means.

Dried cherries, raspberries, the treat list goes on, but here are the staples: dates, figs, apricots or peaches (unsulphured), raisins, golden raisins, cranberries.

Vegetables

Vegans wouldn't get very far without them! Good vegetables are at the heart of every plant-based diet, and the fresher the better. Treat them with respect and you'll get the best out of them: scrub them tenderly, cook them with care and attention, savor their unique qualities . . . this may be getting into the realm of a romance novel, but it's true – love thy veggies!

I buy organic vegetables whenever I can, not because of the flavor (which I believe is generally better), but because of the ethics involved in growing them and the obvious fact that there are no harmful chemicals present. Organic generally means more nobbles, more lumps and more comical shapes, which is always a tell-tale sign of a real veggie. If they're covered in mud or leaves, even better.

Always scrub your vegetables with a little bristly scrubbing brush (it's the easiest way) and only peel when really necessary. When you peel, you lose all the vitamins and minerals trapped just below and in the skin. If you do end up peeling, think about making a stock or soup with the peelings.

A good way to wash nonorganic fruits and veggies is in a large bowl with half a cup of apple cider or white wine vineger and 1 tablespoon of baking soda. Leave them to soak for 15–30 minutes, then rinse well in water (filtered) and allow to dry naturally. This technique is said to remove more pesticides than scrubbing alone.

Veggies should never be overcooked. The best way to eat most vegetables, from a nutritional point of view, is raw, so be considerate in your cooking process.

A word on food waste: On average, a US household throws away over $600 worth of food each year. A "use by" date is a decent guide to the life span of foods, but I'd always opt for using common sense over following what it says on the package. A sniff, a feel and a little taste is normally a very good way of discerning the freshness of food. "Sell by" and "best before" dates are normally misleading, as the food will usually last longer than these stated times.

Mold is generally best avoided, but just because there is mold, it doesn't mean we need to trash something. Miso, for example, will form a light white mold, but in Japan it's perfectly normal and safe to skim it off and enjoy what lies beneath. This goes for most fermented products. There are, of course, good molds and bad molds. Bread with a bit of mold on it is still fine to eat, if the mold is cut off and the bread is toasted. If vegetables or fruits have gone slimy and rancid, they should be escorted to the compost bin. If there is just a little surface mold on a hard veggie, you can peel it off. With a little common sense and knowledge, we can easily minimize our food waste, especially if we are rotating and caring for our precious ingredients.

Americans throw away over 35 million tons of food per year, about half of which could be eaten. Food waste makes up almost 13 percent of what ends up in the trash in the US, but accounts for a much higher percentage of landfill-caused methane, a greenhouse gas that's at least twenty-five times more powerful than carbon dioxide. Good news, though – the USDA and EPA recently announced the first-ever national food waste goal initiative, calling for a 50 percent reduction in food loss by 2030.

Tips for cooking vegetables:

- *When boiling or blanching veggies, always add salt to the water. This slightly increases the water temperature.*

- *Vegetables that grow in the ground, i.e., roots, such as potatoes, must be cooked in lots of cold water brought to a boil. Leafy vegetables, i.e., greens, must be cooked in minimal hot water at a rolling boil for a short time. There should not be enough water in the pan for the greens to move around and bump into each other.*

- *When boiling your roots, make sure that the water is at a steady simmer, otherwise the outsides will begin to disintegrate before the insides are ready.*

What's up with dairy?

Cow's milk is the most popular milk in America, but what do cows go through to produce our daily pint? To produce milk, animals need to be lactating and therefore pregnant, stimulating their milk production. A few decades ago, your average cow used to produce 4,000 liters of milk per year. Due to modern production techniques this has risen sharply, to around 5,800 liters. Cows are milked three times daily; this intense regime leads to lameness and other diseases, and these are treated with high doses of antibiotics, which can be present in the milk of the animal.

The vast majority of calves that are born will not be allowed to suckle from their mothers, and financially useless male calves are normally killed within their first few weeks. Many cows are given fertility drugs to increase their pregnancy rate. Dairy cows' life expectancy is obviously dropping the more intensive the farming techniques become, and a quarter of all dairy cows are culled before they are thirty-nine months old. About half of these are sold to the beef trade.

In addition, many milk products contain the growth hormone rBST, which is very bad news and has been linked with a number of serious illnesses, such as breast and colon cancer.

Dairy farmers are also struggling in the current dairy industry setup. Overproduction has long been a problem in the dairy industry – famously, surplus milk used to be poured down the drains. Now, due to intensified production, animal welfare standards have slipped and smaller dairy farms cannot keep pace with the production levels, leading to many going out of business. This leaves the larger, industrial-scale dairy farms to monopolize the industry, potentially using genetically modified feed on their cattle.

Having said all this, I personally know some cow farmers who treat their cows like family members, knowing the entire herd by name. Buying organically, and especially locally, means you can make an informed choice for yourself. As a vegan, I can visit these farms and just enjoy the company of the happy heifers, knowing that any milk they produce will go in some part to raising a new generation of comfortable cows that will have a long and more natural life.

The transport of milk also clocks up the food miles. As with anything we eat, provenance is important, and generally, the further it's traveled the more difficult it is to be confident in your produce quality. The "keep it local" mantra seems ever more relevant.

From a nutritional point of view, we don't need milk in our diet, especially in the quantities in which many people consume it. The dairy industry has been promoting cow's milk for many years, and it's now the default milk of choice, but you may as well drink goat's, donkey's, llama's or ewe's milk. Even camel's milk, I have heard, has amazing properties, being very high in protein and low in fat. Our buying habits are directly affected by such promotion and advertising, and I can see, in the not too distant future, a shift away from dairy milks and more emphasis being placed on sustainably produced and organic soy, grain and nut milks. These can be a creamy treat and are perfect on your morning cereal. So let's leave the cow's milk for the calves and experiment with delicious plant milks instead. Surely milk is a commodity worthy of respect, something to be truly savored and enjoyed.

Homemade milks

"**S**o how do you milk an almond then?" says the cow-milk fan to the nut-milk nut. I've heard it all before . . . Milking beans and nuts is actually a breeze, and only takes a little know-how and hardware (a blender or food processor, a sieve, some muslin cloth and a pan). Soak, blend, strain and drink. It's basically as simple as that. These milks are all pure plant and therefore have no cholesterol or nasty saturated fats and boast an impressive array of health benefits. Did I mention that they also taste creamy and delicious? I like to call them milks, though many companies and other folks call them "dairy alternatives" or simply "drinks" – really it's all the same game.

You can't beat the flavor of a homemade milk and, best of all, you know exactly what has gone into your daily pint. Most store-bought milks are filled with preservatives and coagulating and thickening agents. Making plant milks also works out to be cheaper than buying good soy and nut milks. You will find that after soaking the beans or nuts, a few handfuls go a long way.

There are so many variations of nondairy milk alternatives that it can be overwhelming some-times. The basic guidelines when buying anything soy-related are to go for whole-bean and organic milks. Many soy milks are made with overprocessed and potentially GMO soy, which takes a wonderfully nutritious food and makes it potentially bad for us. Also, the flavor of whole-bean soy cannot be compared to the other stuff – it's much, much richer and creamier.

There are many sources of plant milks, and on page 41 I've even included a recipe for lentil milk (which, while one of the healthiest things that could touch your lips, is probably not ideal for splashing over your oatmeal), but I tend to stick to the basics: soy, oat, almond, coconut and cashew.

All these milks (bar the soy milk) are raw, meaning that all their essential enzymes and nutrients are not denatured by heating. Enzymes are as important as vitamins and minerals in our diet and are only present in raw foods. Enzymes are the catalyst that starts the essential chemical reactions that our body needs to thrive and develop. They are necessary for digesting food, stimulating the brain, providing cellular energy, and repairing all tissues, organs and cells. Drinking these raw milks means that we are getting a serious dose of nutrients and good fats, the perfect way to start the day and promote good health.

Almond and cashew milks are especially delicious, but are not everyday milks since they cost a little more. Switching to plant milks, especially on a daily basis, has a huge effect on our health in the long run. In fact, if you make one vegan change in your diet, opting to regularly use plant milk as opposed to dairy is a huge step in a good direction. I have been known to add a little dark rum, cinnamon and nutmeg to a warm pan of almond milk, transforming it into a winter cocktail that gets most vegans bleary round the edges and smiling. You may also like to try the healthy hot chocolate (see page 70) using your freshly made milks. Big yums!

The milk recipes that follow are quite creamy, and they may need thinning out using a splash more water. If you're a "creamline" type, maybe you'd like to add less for extra creaminess. Halve the water quantity and you will have something resembling a vegan half-and-half to be used on desserts and so on. Just up the sweetness a little. All these milk recipes are a blank slate for wonderful flavors – here are a few I love to add: vanilla extract, cinnamon, cardamom, soaked and puréed dried apricots/dates/figs, maple syrup, apple juice concentrate, nut butters, barley malt extract, cacao, banana, a shot of espresso, green tea, orange blossom water, elderflower, rose water, tahini . . . the list is completely open to the extent of your taste buds' imagination. I keep these milks in sealable containers or old (well-rinsed) cartons. They'll keep for a few days in the fridge or can be frozen if you are making a big batch.

Soy Milk

MAKES 1 QUART

The vegan's everyday milk of choice, great in a cup of coffee or tea, and loves nothing more than being poured over cereals. The leftover soy paste can be added as a binding agent to burgers and sausages.

THE BITS

2 cups (100g) dried soybeans (organic, non-GMO), soaked overnight

2 tablespoons brown rice syrup

a pinch of sea salt

½ teaspoon vanilla extract

DO IT

Drain and rinse the soaked beans. Place them in a pan with 1 cup (250ml) of filtered water and bring to a boil, then turn the heat down and cook for 15–20 minutes on a low simmer, skimming off any white foam that rises. Leave to cool.

Pour the beans and their cooking liquid into a blender and blitz for 2 minutes. Add the brown rice syrup, salt and vanilla extract plus another 1 cup (250ml) of filtered water and blend for another minute. Taste and adjust the salt/sweetness accordingly.

Pass through a sieve lined with muslin placed over a large bowl or pan. This is a slow process and the bottom of the sieve will need scraping with a spoon regularly to ensure a steady stream. Gather the muslin around the edges, then, once most of the milk is through, twist and squeeze out any more liquid. Pour in 2 cups (500ml) of water as you are scraping and stirring.

Cashew Milk

MAKES 2 CUPS

Rich, creamy and surprisingly refreshing. Very much treat territory, and not an "every-dayer" in the Beach House Kitchen. Best served in champagne flutes on special occasions.

Once you've strained the cashew milk, you will find some glorious plant cream in your muslin.

THE BITS

½ cup (80g) whole raw cashews, soaked overnight

1 – 1½ tablespoons maple syrup

DO IT

Drain and rinse the cashews, then place them in a blender with 1 cup (250ml) filtered water and blend for 3 minutes. Add the maple syrup and another 1 cup (250ml) of water and continue to blend for another minute. Taste and adjust the salt/sweetness accordingly.

Place a sieve lined with muslin over a pan or bowl and gradually pour in the cashew milk, stirring and scraping the muslin to ensure a steady trickle is coming through. Gather the muslin around the edges, then, once most of the milk is through, twist and squeeze out any more liquid.

Almond milk in almond rooibos chai, page 69

Almond Milk

MAKES 1 QUART

My mum likes to leave her almonds soaking for a couple of hours before straining – it makes the milk even creamier!

Blanching the almonds here does not result in a huge loss of nutrients. The almonds are still technically raw. You can dry the left-over almond paste and use it as almond flour (simply spread it out on a baking tray and place in the oven on low heat for 30 minutes). It is also ideal as a binding agent in vegan sausages and burgers, used instead of breadcrumbs – much tastier.

THE BITS

1 cup (150g) whole almonds
(blanched ones are best), soaked overnight

1½ tablespoons maple syrup
(or other sweetener of your choice)

a large pinch of sea salt

DO IT

If using unblanched almonds, boil a kettle or pot of water. Drain and rinse the almonds, then put them into a bowl, cover with boiling water and leave to sit for 10 minutes. Drain again. Now peel the skins off the almonds – they should just slip off.

Place the skinless almonds in a blender with 1 cup (250ml) of filtered water and blend for 3 minutes. Add the maple syrup and salt along with 2 cups (500ml) of water. Continue to blend for another minute. Taste and adjust the salt/sweetness accordingly.

Place a sieve lined with muslin over a pan or bowl and gradually pour in the almond milk, stirring and scraping the muslin to ensure a steady trickle is coming through. Gather the muslin around the edges, then, once most of the milk is through, twist and squeeze out any more liquid.

Add another 1 cup (250ml) of water to the milk (depending on how creamy you'd like it).

Sprouted Green Lentil Milk

MAKES 3 CUPS

I first tried this in a raw ayurvedic restaurant in Pondicherry, India, where it made the perfect accompaniment to a small plate of spiced coleslaw and a few crispy raw *vadas*. It was at this stage that I realized a vegan will milk anything!

This is one for the lentil fan – no question. You will be left with essence of lentil here, a savory flavor that can be challenging for the legume sceptic. A gentle warning: if you try this out on anyone but a full-blown lentil-lover you may put them off lentils for ever. You can use any legume/bean sprouts to make a milk. We also like to milk sprouting mung beans. The leftover paste here is perfect for thickening stews, curries or soups.

THE BITS

1½ cups (200g) sprouted green lentils

1 tablespoon brown rice syrup

a large pinch of sea salt

½ teaspoon garam masala and ½ teaspoon ground turmeric (spice-boosting options)

1 teaspoon wheatgrass or spirulina
(health-boosting options)

DO IT

Drain and rinse the sprouts, then place them in a blender with 1 cup (250ml) of filtered water and blend for 3 minutes. Add the sweetener and salt (plus the spices and funky green powder), along with 2 cups (500ml) of water, and continue to blend for 2 minutes. Taste and adjust the salt/spice/sweetness accordingly.

Place a sieve lined with muslin over a pan or bowl and gradually pour in the green milk, stirring and scraping the muslin to ensure a steady trickle is coming through. This takes some time. Gather the muslin around the edges, then, once most of the milk is through, twist and squeeze out any more liquid.

Breakfast

This is food that is sure to brighten up your day. Not only is it colorful and packed with fun flavor combos and textures, it also gives your body and belly a big gentle hug. Vegan food is light and densely nutritious, just what we need to get us off to a flying start. Our minds generally crave clean foods in the morning, the kind that give us clarity and don't overstimulate the mind like sugars and caffeine, but let us wake ourselves up steadily. Mornings are enough of a shock without a double espresso and doughnut added to the equation!

The best things to eat and drink in the morning are green. Our bodies have been basically starving for eight or so hours and are ready and waiting to fully absorb anything we put into them. We have our belly's full attention at this hour and it can't wait to get started. The number one way to start the day, and this is as old as the hills, is a glass of hot lemon water. It gets straight down to business, cleansing and stimulating our digestive tract and helping to detox our kidneys and liver. It gives all our internal organs a nudge and a tickle and reminds them to look lively.

Combine any of these breakfasts with a juice or a smoothie and you will hover to work in a cloud of peaceful well-being, radiating good health and sparkly eyes to everyone on your commute.

Raw-sli with Grated Apple, Blueberries & Macadamia Cream

FOR 4–6

I love muesli, but most store-bought brands are packed with things I don't want and a hefty helping of sugar to boot. I like making my own – I can put all my favorite bits into the mix and balance everything perfectly. I have kept this dish mostly raw, which means all the enzymes and nutrients are there, so it's really healthy. The dried fruits are not exactly classified as raw, but most raw food folk permit them. Remember to soak everything the night before. Even better, sprout the groats and seeds. To do this, soak them for 24 hours in cold water, then leave them at room temperature for 2–3 days, until little shoots start to appear. Rinse with fresh water twice daily.

The macadamia cream is not essential, but it does give the bowl a beautiful creaminess. Soy yogurt would be a good substitute. Use soaked buckwheat groats and quinoa in place of the oats and barley for a gluten-free twist.

THE BITS

½ cup (100g) oat groats (wheat groats are also fine), soaked overnight

generous ¼ cup (60g) barley or wheat groats, soaked overnight

generous ¼ cup (40g) whole almonds, soaked overnight

2 tablespoons pumpkin seeds, soaked for 2 hours

3 tablespoons sunflower seeds, soaked for 2 hours

½ a handful of walnuts

¼ cup (40g) sprouted mung or adzuki beans

2 tablespoons pecans, roughly chopped

2 tablespoons raw peanuts

2 tablespoons flaxseeds or chia seeds

2 tablespoons hemp seeds or sesame seeds

4 dates, finely chopped

½ a handful of raisins, chopped

a big handful of fresh blueberries, raspberries, blackberries, etc.

2 bananas, halved lengthwise and cut into small cubes

½ teaspoon ground cinnamon

For the macadamia cream

1½ cups (200g) macadamia nuts, soaked overnight

2 large dates, e.g., Medjool, soaked for 2–4 hours

1 teaspoon vanilla extract

a splash of almond or soy milk

For the topping

2 green apples, cored

juice of ½ a lemon

a large pinch of cinnamon

maple syrup, for drizzling

DO IT

Soak the ingredients for the stated times, as necessary, then rinse and drain well. Roughly chop the almonds and walnuts. Put them on a plate lined with paper towels with the rest of the soaked ingredients and dry as best you can. In a large bowl, toss all the muesli ingredients together and spoon into deep bowls for serving.

For the macadamia cream, simply blend the ingredients together until smooth. Grate your green apples for the topping and mix immediately with the lemon juice. Top each bowlful of raw-sli with a decent dollop of macadamia cream, a tall stack of grated green apple and a light sprinkling of cinnamon. Drizzle with maple syrup. You may also like to pour a little almond or soy milk on top to make it more like a traditional cereal.

Scrambled Tofu with Buckwheat Pancakes & Avocado Butter

FOR 6–8

A hybrid pancake/pizza that is an early morning feast for the eyes – worth getting up for! You can make these pancakes lighter and less intense (buckwheat has quite an earthy flavor) by replacing the whole wheat flour with unbleached all-purpose flour. Scrambled tofu is a wonderful morning meal and almost as simple as cracking an egg. It's comforting and vibrant and hearty, and you'll get a healthy amount of protein from the bean curd. Avocado is an excellent substitute for dairy products and is great on toast, but sometimes it's hard to get a good ripe one. If yours are like green bullets, place them beside the bananas in your fruit bowl and a day or two later you'll have a beautifully creamy, ripe avocado on your hands.

THE BITS

1 pound (500g) firm tofu, pressed (see page 18)

2 cloves of garlic, peeled and minced

1 red chili, finely diced (check for heat level – this is breakfast, after all!)

a large pinch of dried oregano

2 teaspoons tamari or a large pinch of sea salt

½ teaspoon ground turmeric

3 large ripe avocados, pitted and roughly chopped

juice of ½ a lemon

a large pinch of sea salt

4 teaspoons canola oil (as needed)

3 scallions, finely chopped, green parts included

For the buckwheat pancakes (makes about 14)

¾ cup (100g) buckwheat or unbleached all-purpose flour

1⅓ cups (200g) whole wheat flour

¾ cup + 2 tablespoons (200ml) unsweetened organic soy milk

½ teaspoon baking soda

a large pinch of sea salt

up to 2 cups (500ml) water, as needed

For the garnish

2 big handfuls of cherry tomatoes, thinly sliced

a big handful of fresh cilantro, chopped

DO IT

In a bowl, mash your pressed tofu with a fork and add the garlic, chili, oregano, tamari and turmeric; combine well. The tofu should transform into something resembling scrambled eggs.

In another bowl, mash the avocado, lemon and salt with a spoon or fork until smooth.

Put the flours into a large bowl and, with a metal whisk, stir in the rest of the pancake ingredients, except the water. As they combine, begin to whip them into a batter, adding water as needed. The consistency should resemble heavy cream. A few lumps are not a problem here; they will merge into the pancake.

Get two frying pans ready (one big, one smaller) and a plate with a clean kitchen towel (to wrap your pancakes in). In the big frying pan, heat 2 teaspoons of canola oil on medium-high and add the scallions. Fry for 2 minutes, then add the tofu mixture (draining off excess liquid before adding to the pan). Stir continuously and cook for 5 minutes – the tofu should start to color and the garlic will lose its raw flavor. Set aside and cover. You're almost ready to eat!

Heat the smaller frying pan on medium-high and add 1 teaspoon of cooking oil. When hot, add 2 tablespoons of the buckwheat batter. Spread it out quickly in even circular motions with the back of your spoon, forming a pancake that roughly meets the edges of the pan. Don't be too precious about holes; it will sort itself out.

Cook for 2–3 minutes, until the base is crisp and golden. Loosen the edges of the pancake with a flat spatula (some call this a duck's foot, which I like), then either flip the pancake over using your spatula (in one swift, graceful motion) or toss it like on Pancake Day. This will be exciting, and even if it sticks to the ceiling, you have more batter to play with.

Now that you're slightly more awake, cook the other side of the pancake for a minute or so and place it on your plate (form an envelope with your kitchen towel, snugly wrapping your pancakes). Repeat the pancake procedure until your batter runs dry.

Place a pancake on a plate, spread it thinly with 1 tablespoon of the avocado, scatter some tomato slices over it, then top with tofu and a sprinkling of cilantro. I think they look lovely like this, but if you are in a rush, you could "wrap and go." Eat any excess pancakes later for "breakfast dessert" (a new course I've added to breakfast – essential on Sundays, I find).

Extras

- Add some punchy sauce for a real wake-up call! Something like salsa verde (see page 139).

- If you are lucky enough to have avocado oil in your cupboard, drizzle 2 teaspoons over the tofu at the end of cooking.

Jane's Magic Bread

MAKES ONE LARGE LOAF OR TWO MEDIUM

Here we have the best toast loaf I know. Why is it magic? Well, it goes with everything, from savory to sweet; it loves to be toasted and is equally happy in a sandwich. The best way I've heard this bread described is "like a crumpet, crossed with a loaf."

The dough here is quite wet, but this leads to a nice dense loaf with a super-crispy crust. You can use any of the flour mixes below, but we normally make it with pure, unadulterated spelt. Spelt is lower in gluten than wheat-based flour and is a whole grain, so it retains loads of its health-giving nutrients. This is bread-making just like the Romans used to do it! Walnuts are great with spelt, so try adding a large handful, roughly chopped.

THE BITS

4 cups + 3 tablespoons (500g) stoneground spelt flour (or halve the amount of spelt and add 2 cups [250g] unbleached all-purpose flour or whole wheat flour)

½ teaspoon salt

1 teaspoon quick yeast

1 tablespoon brown rice syrup or barley malt extract

1⅔ cups (400ml) warm water

1 tablespoon olive oil

a large handful of seeds

½ a handful of golden flaxseeds

DO IT

Mix together the flour, salt and yeast in a large bowl. Dissolve the sweetener in the warm water and mix into gradually into the flour. The mixture will be slightly wet and sticky – don't worry, this is very OK.

Add the oil and seeds and continue to mix. Knead for a few minutes, then place in a large (9 x 5-inch/2 pound/1kg) loaf pan or two smaller (8½ x 4½-inch/1 pound/450g) pans. Cover loosely and leave to rise for 30 minutes.

Preheat the oven to 400°F (200°C).

Bake the bread for 40–45 minutes. The smaller loaves will take 5–10 minutes less to bake. Tap the bottom – if you're getting a nice hollow sound, it's done. Leave to cool on a wire rack for at least 20 minutes before slicing.

Apple, Jaggery & Walnut Breakfast Muffin

MAKES 6 MONSTER MUFFINS

Simple, tasty, hearty and robust, this is my ultimate breakfast muffin. It's based on a muffin I lived on for six very tough months when I was running a restaurant. It pulled me through many a 4:30 a.m. start. Jaggery is an unrefined Indian sugar, made by simply boiling sugar cane. It's my favorite sweetener and I use it in a lot of my baking. Some people say it's like a fruity fudge. It's a chewy, rich thing with a flavor like light molasses. The perfect sweet baking partner. If you can't find it in a store near you (an Indian grocery is probably your best bet), you can buy it online.

THE BITS

½ cup (85g) dates, soaked, pitted and roughly chopped

1½ tablespoons jaggery (or unrefined brown sugar, see page 20)

1 cup (120g) unbleached all-purpose flour

²/₃ cup (100g) whole wheat flour

1½ teaspoons ground cinnamon

1½ teaspoons baking powder

½ cup (45g) walnuts, roughly chopped

2 tablespoons toasted sunflower seeds

1 tablespoon poppy seeds

1½ tablespoons flaxseeds or chia seeds

¼ cup (40g) golden raisins

zest of ½ an orange

2 green apples (1 coarsely grated, 1 finely diced)

1 small carrot, scrubbed and finely grated

DO IT

Preheat the oven to 350°F (180°C).

In a bowl, combine the dates and jaggery. Add 1 cup (250ml) of water and mash them up together, making sure the jaggery is dissolved.

Sift the flours, cinnamon and baking powder into a large mixing bowl. Fold in the remaining ingredients and stir in the date mixture, combining well but not overdoing the mixing. It should be nice and sticky. Spoon into a nonstick jumbo six-hole muffin pan, filling each dimple with at least 2 tablespoons of batter. Don't attempt to bake these in muffin liners, as they will likely stick.

Bake for 25–30 minutes, until the muffins are golden (check out that smell!). Poke a toothpick into the middle of one of the muffins – if it's very sticky and wet, they need another 5 minutes. Because of the apple, these muffins are quite moist in the middle, so don't worry about a little wetness. Turn out the muffins and cool on wire racks.

Serve them warm (almost essential), although they're also good at room temperature. Jane is old-fashioned and likes a buttered muffin. Cut in half and lather on some sunflower butter, if you have similar feelings.

Muffins tend to dry out after a day or two. In this situation, I recommend toasting your muffin to revive it.

Raw Chia Seed Breakfast Bowl with Seasonal Berries

FOR 2

When the body wakes up it needs gentle, nutritious food. It craves a good start to the day, and chia seeds mixed with healthy berries are just the ticket. Use any berries you prefer – summer and early autumn are the finest times for making this breakfast bowl. Chia, a member of the Mexican mint family, is a hero of the plant world and can seed within days of planting. They have more omega-3 fats than salmon, are a complete source of protein, boast more fiber than flaxseeds and have a huge amount of antioxidants and minerals. You can add them to a cake/bread mix, sprinkle them on soups and salads, and pop them into smoothies.

I sometimes like to serve this kind of breakfast bowl with arugula. It's a real surprise to the taste buds, as you can imagine, but it completes the amazing nutritional properties of this dish and adds a dash of greenery.

THE BITS

½ cup (80g) chia seeds

2 tablespoons pumpkin seeds or hemp seeds (sprouted is best)

2 teaspoons brown rice syrup (adjust sweetness accordingly)

½ a handful of fresh mint leaves, finely chopped

4 tablespoons organic coconut milk or unsweetened soy yogurt

½ teaspoon vanilla extract

1 peach/nectarine/small pear, or 2 plums, finely diced

½ a handful of raspberries or strawberries

a handful of blackberries or blueberries

a handful of arugula leaves (optional)

DO IT

Put the chia seeds into a bowl and cover with about 1 inch (2.5cm) of fresh water. Leave to sit for 15–20 minutes. Make sure all the chia seeds are covered, and add a little more water if needed. The chia seeds should resemble a cold rice pudding crossed with frog spawn (YUM!).

Stir in the rest of the ingredients, sprinkling the berries and arugula on top last.

Plantain Breakfast Burrito
with Pico de Gallo

FOR 4

Most of us need a quick breakfast that is easy to prepare, and burritos are ideal. In Mexico, home of the burrito, breakfast differs from lunch in only minor details – restaurants serve dishes almost identical to any other time of day. *Pico de gallo* is a classic, and easy enough to assemble for breakfast – although having a bowl of pico de gallo in your fridge is never a bad idea at any time of day. It can be found all over Mexico and Central America and bizarrely translates as "beak of rooster." If you're not serving your burrito with pico de gallo, I recommend mixing some fresh cilantro leaves and tomatoes into the filling. Salsa verde (see page 139) is also amazing lathered over burritos or served on the side. Serve these warm, with fresh chilies or chili sauce. *¡Qué rico!*

THE BITS

2 large green plantains

2 tablespoons cooking oil

1 onion, finely diced

1 red bell pepper, deseeded and finely diced

8½ ounces (240g) firm tofu, pressed (see page 18), or tempeh, mashed with a fork

3 cloves of garlic, peeled and crushed

½ teaspoon ground cumin

½ teaspoon ground coriander

½ teaspoon ground turmeric

½ teaspoon sweet paprika

½ teaspoon oregano

1–2 green chilies, deseeded and finely sliced (jalapeños would be perfect)

a large pinch of sea salt

4 large whole wheat tortillas (must be fresh – stale tortillas will crack when rolled – and they dry out very easily, so keep them covered; gluten-free tortillas are available)

1 x pico de gallo (see page 140)

DO IT

Make the pico de gallo. Peel the plantains with a vegetable peeler, then halve them lengthwise and chop them into 1cm chunks. In a large frying pan, heat half the oil on high heat, then add your plantains and toss well. They will become nicely caramelized. Stir them regularly to prevent sticking and remove when they have some nice crisp brown bits – roughly 5–7 minutes. Set aside, uncovered.

Add the rest of the oil to the pan. On high heat, sauté your onions and peppers and stir well. After 5 minutes, when they are beginning to caramelize, add the tofu, garlic, cumin, coriander, turmeric, paprika, oregano, chilies and salt. Cook and stir for another 5–7 minutes, adding 1 tablespoon of water to ensure the spices are not sticking to the pan. Now stir in the cooked plantains and check the seasoning. Remove from the pan, cover and set aside.

Wipe out the frying pan with a paper towel and warm your tortillas for a minute on each side (or you can warm them beforehand in an oven set to the lowest temperature). They should be just warmed through, fragrant and still soft and pliable. If they are too toasted, they break when wrapping.

Spoon 3 tablespoons of plantain filling into the center of each tortilla and top with 2 tablespoons of pico de gallo. Fold in two edges, pressing gently down, then roll the whole thing over. A burrito is like a tucked-in wrap, a fat tortilla parcel if you like.

Tostada con Tomate
(aka Spain on Toast)

FOR 4

This dish is one of the best things about eating in Spain, and can be found in every sleepy café. Few dishes could represent Spain more. It's light and packed with nutrition; tomatoes are a great way to start the day, as they contain loads of antioxidants and nutrients. Everyone has their favorite way of preparing *tostada con tomate* – a sprinkling of herbs here, a scrub of garlic there. I regularly spread the toast with tofu ricotta (see page 114) before spooning on the tomato, to give it some bulk and creaminess. Black olive tapenade (see page 308) spread on the toast is lovely, too, and I also like to add a few capers to the tomatoes, negating the need for salt. The permutations are as wide as the plains of La Mancha!

Keep in mind that Spanish tostadas are different from the tortilla-based tostadas you find on the menus at Mexican restaurants. *Tostada* literally means "toasted" in Spanish and, as such, the tostada recipes in my kitchen (and in Spain) call for toasted bread.

GF folk, you know the score: reach for your favorite delicious sans-gluten loaf.

THE BITS

4 medium-sized, awesomely fragrant and ripe tomatoes

4 slices of spelt, sourdough or whole wheat bread (or treat yourself to a fresh baguette – whatever's your favorite bread, basically)

1 clove of garlic, peeled and halved lengthwise

a small pinch of dried mixed herbs (optional)

glugs of fruity olive oil

a good sprinkling of sea salt

a scant pinch of freshly cracked black pepper

DO IT

Coarsely grate your tomatoes into a sieve over a bowl. Allow them to drain, pressing the pulp lightly through the sieve with the back of a spoon (drink the juice chilled – it's delicious). Place the drained tomato pulp in a bowl.

Toast your bread and, straight out of the toaster or oven, rub it all over with the cut side of the garlic. Spoon a good layer of grated tomatoes on top. Serve immediately, sprinkled with a few herbs, drizzled with olive oil and seasoned with a little sea salt and cracked black pepper.

¡Buen provecho!

Banana & Almond Toast with Strawberry & Maple Syrup

MAKES 6 SLICES

This is my twist on French toast, with the added wonder of almonds and bananas (not to mention strawberries). I can't resist maple syrup at breakfast time, and in this recipe the strawberries help rein in its outrageous sweetness. Maple syrup contains decent amounts of zinc and manganese, and it also boasts fifteen times more calcium than honey. I sometimes use it to flavor tea or coffee as a treat.

Gluten-free option: use GF bread.

THE BITS

2 large ripe bananas

1 teaspoon brown rice syrup
(or other sweetener of your choice)

1 cup (240ml) oat or soy milk

½ teaspoon vanilla extract

6 tablespoons almond meal

2 tablespoons flaxseeds (golden look best)

3 tablespoons rolled oats (gluten-free)

a small pinch of sea salt

⅛ teaspoon ground cinnamon

1 tablespoon coconut oil or vegetable oil

6 slices of whole wheat, sourdough, spelt or rye bread (your favorite toast)

For the strawberry & maple syrup

3 handfuls of strawberries, trimmed and roughly chopped

½ cup (120ml) maple syrup

For the garnish

a handful of sliced almonds

DO IT

Blend the bananas and the rest of the ingredients (apart from the bread) in a food processor until smooth. Pop into the fridge for 20 minutes.

Put the ingredients for the strawberry and maple syrup into the food processor or a blender and blitz together, adding a splash of water if needed. This syrup can be served hot or cold. I don't have a rampant sweet tooth – maybe you'd like to add more maple syrup. Have a taste.

Toast one side of the bread under the broiler or in a toaster oven. Flip the slices over, give them a good layer of the lovely banana mix and toast until golden brown.

Serve the toast fresh from the oven, with a good drizzle of the syrup and topped with some sliced almonds

Smoothies, Juices & Hot Drinks

Smoothies and juices are the first port of call for the dedicated nutrition-seeker and offer an intense spot of detox in daily life. We don't need to go crazy to grab a superbly healthy start to the day – a green smoothie will more than do.

Most days I skip breakfast altogether and feel bursting with energy from just one glass of smoothie or juice. The nutrients, vitamins and minerals are all there, easily accessible to the body and absorbed very quickly, so the benefits are felt after only a few minutes.

Go to town with your smoothies and juices and make them special. Dig out some cocktail glasses or dust off those champagne flutes. The glassware will make all the difference – everything tastes good out of a champagne flute!

Frozen bananas and berries are ideal for all things smoothie. Just chop bananas that may be past their best and freeze them in a sealable container. Berries can be bought frozen or saved from a summer glut. In late summer and early autumn the price of berries and fruit in general drops – take advantage of this and stock up the freezer with gorgeous fruits. Come a dark chilly December morning you'll be delighted to find a bag of bright red strawberries waiting for you to make smoothie magic.

Tropical fruit can be a bit hit and miss – you can caress a mango all you like, it may have fragrant skin and be soft to the touch, but often you cut it open and there's no flavor. One more reason to stay local and seasonal, but who can resist a little tropical sun sometimes? Life would be dull without pineapples.

I am not a huge fan of food supplements – I believe it's all there for us if we eat a balanced and varied diet. I do, however, appreciate the addition of what I call the "funky green powders" to juices and smoothies, things like spirulina, wheatgrass and barley grass. They are concentrated hits of chlorophyll, calcium, protein and other wonderful nutrition. They can be a little expensive, but you don't need much. Try them out and I'm sure you'll feel and see the difference. I remember when I was in India once, eating a pretty meager diet of lentils and rice, a friend bought me some spirulina and after a week I noticed that my nails were really strong. I also had more energy, and I have been a funky green powder convert ever since.

We use brown rice syrup a lot in smoothies – it's one of our favorite vegan sweeteners. Barley malt extract is also lovely, although neither are as sweet as honey or sugar. If you find any of these smoothies and juices too sweet, balance them out with a little celery or lettuce. Sounds strange, but it works wonders and adds minerals to the mix.

Your juicer may prefer it if you chop harder root vegetables into chunks first. I have killed a juicer by trying to force a beet through it. Use the lower setting first for the softer, less dense bits, then ramp up the power for your tough roots. The pulp left over from juicing can be added to soups and works well in burgers and salads. I've even heard of a pulp sorbet!

I like a good thick smoothie, so add a little more water if you'd prefer it thinner. These recipes make large glasses, around 10 ounces (300ml), normally with leftovers. Some of these recipes do require a juicer, but who's to say that you can't make a perfectly amazing juice into a perfectly amazing smoothie. Try them out in your food processor/blender. The higher power the kit, the smoother things get.

There are so many awesome nut and other plant-based milks that can make rich and superbly comforting hot drinks. You will never, ever, miss your saturated-fat-laden cappuccino or sugar-laced mocha frappé something-or-other.

There is so much variety when preparing a vegan milk (see pages 38–41). I recently tried sprouted green lentil milk, which was surprisingly delicious. Not one for making hot chocolate with, but ideal for adding to smoothies, curries or soups.

Vegans are generally an unassuming, health-conscious lot, and this mentality filters down into everything we eat and drink – treating ourselves to a satisfying hot drink does not necessarily mean lacing ourselves with bags of nasty fats and sugars. There is another way to treat yourself, and here it is . . . hugs in a mug just got a whole lot nuttier!

All these steaming beauties can be chilled in the fridge and reheated, or even enjoyed chilled over ice. And all are gluten-free.

Peaches &
Cream Smoothie

FOR 4 GLASSES

This is like dessert in a glass. Not your everyday smoothie, and quite filling for the mornings, with all those nuts. A smoothie to savor in its sweet, fruity decadence and richness. Try this one out on a lazy Sunday morning. It's the perfect breakfast-in-bed smoothie. If you can't get hold of good peaches, then nectarines or even apricots will suffice. I have used dried apricots, too – soak them in water for a few hours and they're ready to blend. This smoothie can also be frozen into a wonderful ice cream – just follow the chilling techniques for the chocolate and maple ice cream on page 290.

THE BITS

1 cup (150g) macadamias, soaked for
2 hours or more

7 ounces (200g) peaches, pitted and sliced

½ a vanilla pod, insides scraped out,
or 1 teaspoon vanilla extract

1 cup (240ml) filtered water

3 large dates (Medjool are best),
soaked for 20 minutes in warm water

DO IT

Pop it all into a blender and blitz until nice and smooth. Eat with a spoon.

Strawberry
Ice Cream Smoothie

FOR 2 GLASSES

Frozen bananas make anything taste like ice cream – it's an easy vegan cheat. Strawberries are outrageously healthy and a potent healing food. Add to that a whole host of beneficial minerals and you're looking at a wonder berry (aren't they all?!). Strawberries are calming for the liver and joints, and our bodies generally love 'em.

For a slightly more refined smoothie, you may like to juice the strawberries and pear beforehand and then add the juice to the smoothie.

THE BITS

¾ pint/9 ounces (260g) strawberries,
chopped

1 large ripe pear, cored

3 bananas, chopped and preferably
frozen beforehand

a drizzle of soy milk (if needed)

DO IT

Place it all in a blender and blitz until it looks thick and ice-creamy, adding a drizzle of soy milk if needed.

Peaches & cream
smoothie

Green banana
detox smoothie

Green Banana Detox Smoothie

FOR 4 GLASSES

After drinking this smoothie, you are officially ready for anything. Scale tall mountains, climb a tree, or just go to work with loads of energy. Full of green things and a helpful banana boost, this is shining health in purée form. If you drink one of these every morning, you'll probably live until you're a hundred!

THE BITS

2 bananas

2 celery stalks

3 handfuls of spinach or kale leaves

1 apple, cored and quartered

½ cucumber, seeds and skin removed

1 inch (2.5cm) fresh ginger, grated

juice of ½ a lemon

²/₃–¾ cup (150–200ml) filtered water (depending on
whether you prefer a thick or thin smoothie)

a handful of ice

1 tablespoon funky green powder
(i.e., spirulina, wheatgrass, barley grass, etc.)
or a small handful of fresh parsley

DO IT

Pop it all into a blender and blitz until smooth.

Spiced Apple & Pear Juice

FOR 2 GLASSES

If you're going to juice, it's best to get green. The broccoli here adds a lovely savory edge and the fruits are the perfect combo for autumn and winter, the time of year when we need to be reaching for our green friends. Cinnamon is one of those medicinal spices that we regularly use and seldom realize their incredible healing potential. Drinking smoothies like this in the winter months can ward off any nasty colds and other unwanted sniffles – proper medicine!

THE BITS

3 apples

2 pears

3 large florets of broccoli

1-inch (2.5cm) cube of fresh ginger, peeled

juice of 1 lime

2 pinches of ground cinnamon

DO IT

Juice all the fruit and veggies. If your juicer is up to it, juice the lime with them. However, I normally use a manual squeezer to get at the lovely citrus juice, negating the potential bitterness of the seeds. If you are blending, core the apple and pear first.

Pour into two nice glasses and top with a light dusting of cinnamon.

Mango, coconut &
lime smoothie

Mango, Coconut &
Lime Smoothie

FOR 2 BIG GLASSES

Straight out of *Castaway*! All you need is a tropical island and a hammock.

Fragrant, ripe mangoes will make all the difference here. I know a guy who knows a guy who can get me something resembling what you munch on in Thailand or the Philippines. It's always that kind of deal, as the supermarkets just don't cut the mustard, mango-wise. Coconuts, however, can be easier to get and are a real treat. Ideally we'd use young coconuts here, but the old husky varieties are fine. The milk is actually more flavorful and better to use in smoothies, I find.

THE BITS

1 large mango, peeled and chopped

2 green apples, chopped

juice and zest of 1 lime

scant 1 cup (225ml) coconut water
(normally the water from one big coconut
is enough) or coconut milk

2 large dates, pitted and soaked
in warm water for 20 minutes

To serve

2 tablespoons chia seeds
(for an even healthier smoothie)

1 tablespoon grated coconut

DO IT

Pop it all into a high-powered blender and blitz until smooth, stirring the chia seeds in afterwards, then sprinkling with grated coconut and hopping into your hammock!

Green Dream
(Watercress, Kale &
Sunflower Seeds)

FOR 2 GLASSES

The ultimate green juice. There is no better detox . . . it's an elixir for the real high life. All those green things, with the added bonus of supercharged seeds. This juice is best topped with alfalfa sprouts for that final, supersonic touch. If you are a home sprouter, using sprouted sunflower seeds in this smoothie is quite wonderful, too.

THE BITS

5 large kale leaves (any type is good,
and dark green cabbage also works well)

a handful of fresh flat-leaf parsley

2 handfuls of watercress (or spinach)

1 apple

3 carrots

3 celery stalks

juice of ½ a lemon

²/₃ cup (80g) sunflower seeds, soaked in cold
water for 1 hour or sprouted beforehand

1 tablespoon chia seeds (optional)

For the garnish

a handful of alfalfa or mustard seed sprouts
(or any other sprouts)

DO IT

Juice all the veggies and the apple. (Always juice your leaves first, followed by the harder stuff, as this will help to flush the juicer out. A drizzle of water also helps to extract all the juicy bits hiding in the pith and the leftover cellulose.)

Blend all the juice with the seeds in a blender. Sprinkle with some sprouts and you're all good!

Raw Cucumber Mojito

MAKES 1 BIG PITCHER (ENOUGH FOR 6 GLASSES)

One of the best things I consumed in Mexico, and there were many, was a cucumber juice. Mixed with a little sugar, it was sensational. Cucumber is very soothing for the body and mind, an ideal way to start the day, especially if stress is on the horizon. Of course, this can be enjoyed at any time of the day and can be made rather boozy with the addition of white rum or tequila/mezcal. You're looking for a strong sweet-and-sour kick here, a decent balance of syrup and lime. Best served in something resembling a cocktail glass, with a thin slice of cucumber sitting on the rim.

THE BITS

1½ cucumbers, juiced
juice of 3 limes
a handful of mint leaves, finely sliced
2–3 teaspoons brown rice syrup (to taste)
2 cups (480ml) sparkling water
crushed ice (optional)

For the garnish
2 sprigs of fresh mint

DO IT

This mocktail is best when all the ingredients are shaken in a cocktail style, but they can also be mixed in a pitcher and poured over crushed ice. Make sure the syrup is well mixed in, as it tends to dwell in the bottom of the glass.

Garnish with mint leaves. You may prefer to strain the cocktail (use a sieve) if you don't like the idea of mint leaves floating around in your drink.

Avocado "Red Eye" Smoothie

FOR 2 GLASSES

We all occasionally wake with the dreaded "red eye," for a variety of reasons (I hope they were fun!). This is the vegan Bloody Mary. The raw, super-savory smoothie that is going to drag you back into the land of the living (or get you out of bed and down to the kitchen at the very least). This smoothie has been rigorously trialed and tested, and I can confirm that this green delight could resurrect Tutankhamen himself!

THE BITS

5 ounces (140g) soy yogurt or silken tofu
1 avocado, pitted and peeled
½ a red bell pepper, deseeded
2 large handfuls of spinach leaves
or kale leaves
juice of ½ a lemon
½ a red chili, finely diced,
or a dash of Tabasco
scant 1 cup (225ml) soy milk
a small handful of cilantro leaves

DO IT

Pop it all into a blender and blitz until smooth. Scrape down the sides of the blender a few times, as the spinach leaves will try to climb out. Enjoy in moderation.

Raw cucumber
mojito

Almond Rooibos Chai

FOR 4-6 CUPS

Chai is the finest beverage for a chilly winter's night. Nothing comes close. It's basically a potion of warming spices wrapped up in a cloak of steaming creaminess. It's equally great when chilled and served ice cold, and can easily be made boozy with the addition of some rum or brandy. I use the richness of almond butter in the decaffeinated rooibos tea to make this almost guilt-free treat truly spectacular, but if you prefer you can use Assam tea leaves, which give it a more traditional appearance. Loose-leaf rooibos infuses better and seems to pack more of a punch flavor-wise. If you are using bags, split them open and pour the leaves in.

THE BITS

1½ inches (4cm) fresh ginger, scrubbed and grated

7 green cardamom pods, seeds removed and crushed with a pestle and mortar, or just cracked

4 black peppercorns

1 cup (240ml) water

4 rooibos tea bags, cut open, or 3 heaped teaspoons loose-leaf rooibos

1 cinnamon stick, broken into 3 pieces

4 cloves

2 star anise

generous 3 cups (740ml) almond milk (why not make your own? – see page 41)

2 teaspoons almond butter

sweetener of your choice

DO IT

With a pestle and mortar, mash up your ginger, cardamom and black peppercorns.

In a small pan, bring the water to a boil and add your tea and spices, then lower the heat, cover and simmer for 10 minutes. Leave to infuse, the longer the better.

Using 2–3 tablespoons of almond milk, thin out the almond butter into a loose paste. Add this, along with the rest of the almond milk, to the pan and bring back slowly to a boil (keep your eye on the pan, as this has a habit of bubbling up all over your lovely sparkling stovetop). Allow to simmer vigorously for 10–15 minutes.

Strain the chai using a sieve (a small one is perfect) when serving, which is easiest done with a ladle. Add a sweetener of your choice – I like to let people add their own sugar. Remember, chai is normally enjoyed sweet, sweet, sweet.

Chai is usually served in small cups – think slightly larger than espresso. You can always come back for seconds! Though as you can see, our mugs are a bit bigger.

Healthy Hot Chocolate

FOR 6–8 CUPS

Raw cacao powder is seriously dark and flavorful, nothing like cocoa powder, which can be laden with quite a few freaky ingredients and non-vegan nasties. Raw cacao powder is pure, with incredible health-giving properties – it has a wickedly potent chocolate flavor, to be used sparingly when compared to standard cocoa. It can be found in health food stores, and you'll probably find cacao butter on the same shelf. If cacao butter is hard to track down, try nut butters such as cashew, almond or Brazil. I love using almond milk, which adds great richness to a plant-based potion like this one and, as we all know, nuts and chocolate are always a brilliant pairing. This hot chocolate can also be chilled in the fridge and used as a chocolate sauce. If it's a little bitter, sweeten it up, but we love the contrast between a sweet dessert or ice cream and a bitter chocolate sauce.

THE BITS

3¼ cups (750ml) unsweetened almond milk (or vegan milk of your choice)

½ cup (45g) raw cacao powder (or vegan cocoa – check the package!)

1½ tablespoons cacao butter (for optional gorgeous richness)

3 tablespoons unrefined brown sugar (or other sweetener of your choice; see page 20)

DO IT

Warm the almond milk in a pan until it is just steaming, then whisk in your cacao and cacao butter, which will give the hot chocolate a nice frothy look. If you are using raw cacao, take care not to heat the milk above 104°F (40°C), as this can decrease the nutrient content. But if you like it hot, go for it! Now sweeten as you like and wrap yourself around a hearty mug.

Cacao is quite bitter, so you may need to add a little more sweetness than usual.

Lavender, Rosemary & Lemon Infusion

FOR 4 CUPS

Great for an early morning detox/herbaceous pick-me-up, this is more like a health tonic than merely a tasty beverage, and it takes just minutes to make. A zesty infusion to lift spirits, steeped in well-being. I don't use boiling water, as it would kill all the vitamins and the subtle aromas of the herbs. Leaving the boiled water for a couple of minutes before you use it means you don't scorch the herbs, but have just the right amount of heat to convince them to release their fragrant oils. I like to drink this out of a small bowl, or a large wide mug – this way you get to see the herbs in all their glory.

THE BITS

2 big handfuls of mint leaves

3 sprigs of fresh rosemary

8 thin slices of lemon (2 per mug)

2 sprigs of dried lavender

3 sprigs of fresh thyme

sweetener of your choice (as needed)

DO IT

Place an equal amount of the bits into each small bowl or large mug.

Boil a kettle of water and leave to sit for a couple of minutes, then pour the hot (but not boiling) water over the herbs.

Allow it to infuse with a saucer over the top for 5 minutes, then serve. Enjoy the revitalization!

Warm Apple Mull

FOR 4 CUPS

For me, this is the quintessential taste of winter splendor, all steaming and golden in a mug. There is something intoxicating, and almost alchemical, about the combination of apple and cinnamon. Try to source some nice apple juice for this magical mull, as it makes all the difference. Try the cloudy stuff out for size. Adding glugs of dark rum to the finished mull can only lead to a wonderful sense of merriment and rosy cheeks. As with most of these hot drinks, I make a double batch of this and have it the next day as well.

THE BITS

2 cinnamon sticks, broken
into small pieces

6 cloves

3 star anise

1½ inches (4cm) fresh ginger,
peeled and finely grated

5⅓ cups (1.25 liters) apple juice

sweetener of your choice
(I like a dark unrefined sugar for this),
if the apples aren't sweet enough

DO IT

Place all the spices in a mortar, add the ginger and give it all a decent bashing.

Put all the ingredients into a small pan and slowly bring to just below boiling. Pop a lid on the pan and simmer on a very low heat for at least 1 hour. Leave to sit and infuse.

Sweeten, then strain into cups and serve steaming.

Soups

I could happily eat soup for every meal. Starter, main and dessert could easily be covered (I recently had an incredible papaya and mango soup). The potential for variation in texture and flavor is seemingly endless, and with the backbone of a decent stock, you can hardly fail.

Everywhere you travel around the globe, there is the great soup constant. We all seem to love a good slurp! From the depths of winter in Wales to the bubbling *pho* stands of Ho Chi Minh City, we're all face down over bowls of steaming broth. I have even eaten a form of chickpea soup in the middle of the Sahara, with smiling Bedouins, cups of mint tea and desert-baked bread (bread buried and baked in the sand). The cooling and restorative qualities were amazing. I make many of my soups at lunchtime in a little retreat center that I work in at the foot of Mount Snowdon, overlooking a tranquil lake with its own verdant biodynamic vegetable garden. It's one of the most spectacular places in the world to cook.

Soup takes us up in its simmering arms and whisks us off to a place of healing and nourishment. Why is it that after eating soup we feel lifted? A bowl of soup is like a prolonged hug that only ends when the last dunk of bread or gulp of noodle has disappeared. Soup changes things! It's either alchemy or the fact that soup can boast so many concentrated flavors, sometimes from humble and, let's be honest, past-their-best ingredients. The finest soups don't always come from the finest cuts of carrot or the most perky bunch of spinach.

Slurping is a very important part of eating soup; people who eat soup in a polite, genteel fashion are always worrying and probably hiding something. Call me a savage, but the louder the slurps, the greater the enjoyment.

Here is a selection of mainly simple soups that covers a decent wedge of the supping-sphere.

Braised Pumpkin & Butter Bean Soup with Orange Chili Oil

FOR 6-8

This is a beautifully creamy soup, if I may say so myself. It's the kind of soup that pleases everyone – meat-eaters especially like the hearty richness that the pumpkin-and-beans combo brings to the bowl. Toasting and grinding your own coriander seeds is essential here. I like to make the orange chili oil the day before and keep it sealed in a cool place. You may have some left over, in which case don't worry, it keeps for a couple of days and can be used on salads and mixed into stews. Try it stirred into some mashed potatoes!

THE BITS

generous 1 cup (200g) dried butter beans, soaked overnight

3 teaspoons coriander seeds

1 tablespoon olive oil

1½ pounds (700g) sugar/pie pumpkin, peeled and cut into 1-inch (2.5cm) cubes

3 teaspoons toasted sesame oil

2 onions, roughly chopped

¼ pound (125g) white cabbage, roughly chopped

1½ inches (4cm) fresh ginger, finely diced

2 bay leaves

6⅓ cups (1.5 liters) vegetable stock (or bean cooking liquid)

2 large pinches of freshly grated nutmeg

sea salt to taste

a big handful of fresh cilantro (optional)

For the orange chili oil

3 teaspoons coriander seeds

a pinch of sea salt

zest of 1 orange

2 red chilies, deseeded and finely chopped

5 tablespoons olive oil

DO IT

Drain the soaked beans and rinse with fresh water. In a small pan on medium heat, toast all your coriander seeds (6 teaspoons) for a minute until fragrant and occasionally popping. Grind together with a pestle and mortar or food processor. Enjoy the aroma! Reserve half for the soup, half for the orange chili oil.

Put ½ tablespoon of olive oil into the same pan, on high heat, and roast your pumpkin for 8 minutes, until slightly caramelized. Set aside. Put the sesame oil into a large heavy-bottomed pan and warm on medium heat. Add the onions and cook for 5–7 minutes, then add the cabbage, ginger, half the ground coriander seeds and the bay leaves and cook for 2 minutes. Add the stock or bean liquid, followed by the butter beans and pumpkin. Bring to a boil and pop a lid on the pan. Cook for 25 minutes at a steady simmer.

To make the orange chili oil, blend the other half of the ground coriander seeds with the salt and orange zest with a pestle and mortar or food processor until you have a chunky paste. Add the chilies, then gradually add the olive oil while crushing or blending the ingredients together. Check the seasoning – there should be a nice orange kick to the oil.

The soup should now be ready, so stir in the nutmeg and pick out the bay leaves. Season with sea salt. Using an immersion blender, whiz the soup in the pan until smooth and thick and creamy. It should not resemble baby food, so dilute with warm water or more stock if needed. Serve topped with a good drizzle of your orange chili oil or a scattering of cilantro leaves.

Fennel, Dill & Saffron Soup

FOR 4

This soup combines some pretty wonderful flavors in one pan. Fennel is something I cannot get enough of – we buy ours from a local farm. I tend to stockpile saffron when I'm in Spain and then hoard it for no apparent reason. It's a precious commodity and is so labor-intensive to harvest. It really cannot be replicated and adds an element of luxury to everything it graces. The more flowers in food the better, I say. The cauliflower adds a lovely smoothness without the weightiness of potatoes – it's a little trick I like to use. And tofu adds a creamy richness to any soup. You won't believe this is all plant!

THE BITS

1 tablespoon olive oil

1 onion, chopped

3 medium bulbs of fennel, cut into chunks

1 small cauliflower, roughly chopped (including the stem)

1 teaspoon curry powder

¾–1 teaspoon saffron threads, soaked

in 1 tablespoon warm water

scant ½ cup (100ml) white wine (vegan)

3¹/₃–4¼ cups (800ml–1 liter) vegetable stock

5 ounces (140g) silken tofu

½ a handful of fresh dill or fennel fronds, chopped

DO IT

Heat the olive oil in a large pan on medium-low and add the onions. Cook them for 10 minutes, until soft. Add the fennel, cauliflower and curry powder, stir and cook for 5 minutes, then add the saffron (with its soaking water) and white wine. Bring to a boil and pour in the stock, then cook at a low simmer with a lid on for 25–30 minutes, until the fennel is tender.

Add the tofu and most of the dill, and allow to warm through. Then, using an immersion blender, blitz the soup until smooth, loosening the consistency with more stock if needed.

Serve topped with a light scattering of dill or fennel fronds.

Smoked Cuban Black Bean Soup with Avocado & Lime Salsa

FOR 4

This is made in a similar way to the Portuguese/Brazilian *feijoada*, a stew/soup that is normally served with lots of pig parts, smoky and fatty. To add richness here I've used diced smoked tofu and the wonderful chipotle pepper. The recipe came about after Jane returned from a visit to Havana with an array of dried beans and one giant avocado. I like to cook this in the oven, like a good old feijoada – it seems to taste better that way, although you can also make it on the stove. If you can't track down smoked tofu, just use firm tofu instead or leave it out. The protein in the beans will keep you charged for a long time. For added richness, try topping this with creamy cashew cheese sauce (see page 303).

THE BITS

1⅓ cup (250g) dried black beans, soaked overnight

2 tablespoons coconut oil

1 large onion, peeled and finely diced

5 cloves of garlic, peeled and minced

2 celery stalks, finely diced

1 red bell pepper, deseeded and diced

2 bay leaves

2 carrots, scrubbed and finely diced

3 large smoked chipotle peppers, roughly chopped, or 2 teaspoons chipotle paste, or 2 teaspoons smoked paprika

3 teaspoons balsamic vinegar

1 teaspoon dried thyme

3 cups (700ml) vegetable stock or water

9 ounces (250g) smoked tofu, cut into 1cm cubes

sea salt and freshly ground black pepper to taste

For the avocado & lime salsa

2 avocados, peeled, pitted and diced

2 scallions, finely sliced

3 tablespoons chopped fresh cilantro

juice of 1 lime

a pinch of salt

DO IT

Drain the soaked beans and rinse them in fresh water. Heat a large cast-iron oven dish (or something like that) on the stove on medium-low, and when warm add the coconut oil, followed by the onion, garlic, celery, red pepper, bay leaves, carrots and chipotle or chipotle paste (if using paprika, see below). Cook through, stirring frequently, for 10 minutes, until soft.

Preheat the oven to 350°F (180°C).

Add the balsamic vinegar to the veggies and allow a moment for it to evaporate. Then pop in the drained beans, paprika (if using) and thyme, stir, and add the stock or water. Cover and place in the oven for 1¼ hours. The slower it cooks, the more flavor you can expect! The beans are tough and can take longer in the oven. Check the beans by tasting one, and pop the dish back in for another 15 minutes if necessary. Meanwhile, make the avocado salsa by putting all the ingredients into a bowl and mixing well.

When the soup is ready, pick out the bay leaves, then ladle out roughly a third of the soup and blend it in a food processor (or pop an immersion blender into the soup and give it a few whizzes). Return the blended soup to the pan and stir in the smoked tofu. Season well with sea salt and black pepper. Serve topped with a couple of spoonfuls of avocado salsa.

Adzuki Bean & Oat Soup

FOR 6

This soup reminds me of the rustic origins of vegan food, on the periphery since the sixties, when vegan restaurants were tucked away in alleys. It's got loads of soul and there's hardly any preparation required. Adzuki beans are one of the most health-boosting beans going, and combined with oats they produce a potently healthy concoction of robust flavors and nutrition. I enjoy popping a handful of oats into soups, as they add substance and a little creaminess.

I like this soup chunky, but you can blend it into a nice smooth soup with an immersion blender if you like. If you choose chunky, make sure you cut your vegetables neatly – there is nothing worse than an uneven celery chunk!

Gluten-free option: use GF oats, miso and tahini.

THE BITS

7½ cups (1.75 liters) water (use the bean cooking liquid)

1 cup (175g) dried adzuki beans, soaked overnight

2 bay leaves

1 large onion, finely diced

2 celery stalks, finely diced

1 large carrot, scrubbed and finely diced

1½ handfuls of oats (steel-cut or rolled are fine, but use the traditional/old-fashioned style, not quick-cooking)

2 tablespoons brown miso

1 tablespoon tahini

1 teaspoon ground coriander

⅔ teaspoon dried thyme

1 teaspoon sea salt, if needed

DO IT

Put the water, drained adzuki beans and bay leaves into a large pan and bring to a boil, then cover the pan and simmer for 30 minutes.

Add the onion, celery, carrot and oats, followed by the miso, tahini, coriander and thyme. Reduce the heat to low and cook, still covered, for another 30 minutes. Check that the carrots are tender, then remove the bay leaves and add the salt. Thin down the soup with more hot water as needed, check the seasoning, and add more miso (or salt) as needed.

Zen Noodle Broth

FOR 4

Food plays a large role in the daily life of a Zen monastery. It is not merely about nutrients, but about energy to replenish and nurture the spirit. I try to think about this whenever I cook, putting as much positive energy into my cooking as possible. (Fortunately this is easy, as I love bashing pots and pans.) The idea for this Zen-style broth first came about because a friend lived on it while practicing to be a Zen Buddhist monk, and it stayed because it's really simple to prepare and yet almost infinitely complex. A pleasant paradox.

Soba noodles are made primarily with buckwheat and are generally much better for the body and digestion than other noodles. They have a wonderfully full texture. Sometimes I will add a splash of sake or mirin to the frying vegetables, which adds even more flavor to the stock.

Still the mind, feel the love, stir the soup. Enjoy the whole process (including washing up).

Gluten-free option: use 100 percent buckwheat noodles and GF miso.

THE BITS

6¾ cups (1.6 liters) water

3 carrots, halved lengthwise and finely sliced into half-moons

2 onions, very finely chopped

3 large green cabbage leaves, finely shredded (kale/cavolo nero works well)

1 red chili, finely diced

½ tablespoon cooking oil

3 strips of dried wakame (seaweed)

12 dried shiitake mushrooms

3–4 tablespoons brown miso

5½ ounces (150g) soba noodles

For the garnish
3 scallions, finely sliced at an angle

DO IT

Bring the water to a boil in a large pot, then reduce the heat and let it gently simmer while you fry the vegetables.

In a wok on a high heat, flash-fry the carrots, onions, cabbage and chili in the oil for 3–4 minutes, then add the vegetables to the simmering water. Add the wakame, shiitake mushrooms and miso (diluted in 4 tablespoons warm water) and simmer uncovered on low heat for 15 minutes.

Place your noodles in a separate pot of boiling water and cook for 4 minutes (or see package instructions). Drain, then refresh with cold water.

Taste the soup and add extra miso if more saltiness is needed. Add the cold noodles to the soup and warm through for a minute.

Serve right away, topped with slices of scallion.

Zucchini, Cumin & Mint Soup

FOR 4

This was a traditional Turkish-style soup until I got my hands on it. Zucchini grow like wild-fire, and each summer we are inundated with wheelbarrows full of them. The kitchen at work suddenly becomes like an industrialized processing plant – barrels of zucchini enter at one end and come out the other puréed, roasted, pickled and poached. This soup is best served in the sunshine, but is also perfect for lunch on a bright, crisp November day. It is traditionally made with lots of yogurt, but the silken tofu steps in and adds wonderful creaminess to the proceedings. No need to be too precious with the prep here, as it's all going to be blended!

THE BITS

2 tablespoons olive oil

1 onion, sliced

1½ teaspoons cumin seeds

1 teaspoon salt

4 cloves of garlic, peeled and diced

4 zucchini, chopped

2 celery stalks, sliced

1 large potato, peeled and cubed

¼ of a white cabbage, chopped

1 teaspoon dried mint

⅓ teaspoon freshly ground black pepper

4 cups (950ml) good vegetable stock or water

5½ ounces (150g) silken tofu or unsweetened soy yogurt

a handful of fresh mint, finely chopped

For the garnish

½ a handful of fresh mint leaves

½ teaspoon freshly ground cumin seeds

a glug of fruity olive oil

DO IT

In a large thick-bottomed pot, warm the olive oil on medium heat. Add the onions, cumin seeds and salt and sauté for 10 minutes, until beautifully golden. Add the garlic, zucchini, celery, potatoes and cabbage, and continue to sauté and stir for 5 minutes. Add the dried mint and black pepper and stir well.

Pour in the stock and bring to a boil, then cover and simmer for 25–30 minutes, until the potatoes are nice and tender.

In a bowl, whisk up your silken tofu with a fork and stir it into the soup. Blend it all together with an immersion blender – I like to leave it slightly chunky. Sprinkle in the chopped mint and stir.

Garnish with fresh mint leaves, a sprinkle of freshly ground cumin and a good drizzle of olive oil.

Raw Avocado & Lime Gazpacho

FOR 4-6

This is a simple summer cooler with the richness of avocado and all the wonderful flavors of a bright and breezy summer's day. Raw soups can be spectacular, and all you really need to do is gather and blend. Without a food processor, however, preparing raw soups and stews is pretty tough. Although I don't like the term "processing" – it's a little industrial for my liking – a food processor is an essential kitchen tool for the modern cook with hungry mouths to feed and a head full of ideas.

You may like to serve this chilled soup in nice glasses with spoons, or in glass bowls.

THE BITS

3 large ripe tomatoes, diced

1 cucumber, peeled, deseeded and diced

3 scallions, sliced

1 small green bell pepper, diced

2 avocados, peeled, pitted and diced

1 cup (250ml) tomato passata or tomato purée

scant ½ cup (100ml) water

1 teaspoon unrefined brown sugar (see page 20)

juice of 1 lime

zest of ½ a lime

1 teaspoon sea salt

a large pinch of cayenne pepper

2 handfuls of fresh cilantro leaves

For the garnish

½ a handful of cilantro leaves

DO IT

Put all the ingredients into a large bowl or pan and combine well.

Place two-thirds of the mixture in a blender and blitz until smooth. Stir the chunky mixture together with the smooth, then taste and season accordingly. Refrigerate until cool.

Serve slightly chilled (remove from the fridge 15 minutes before serving), topped with a few fresh cilantro leaves.

Apple & Beet Borscht
with Horseradish Sour Cream

FOR 6–8

This is one of the simplest soups I know – no messing, just all into the pot and boil. And I really think that borscht is the finest thing to come out of the Russian kitchen. It's the color that gets you with this one: deep purple. Horseradish works in perfect harmony with borscht – I wouldn't serve it with anything else. The soup can be served cold or hot and has untold health benefits.

THE BITS

4 beets, peeled or scrubbed, and cubed

3 cloves of garlic, peeled and minced

2 onions, thinly sliced

2 tablespoons tomato paste

5¼ cups (1.25 liters) vegetable stock or water

¼ of a red cabbage, thinly sliced, hard stems in the compost bin

2 carrots, thinly sliced

1 potato, peeled and diced

2 green apples, peeled, cored and diced

3 tablespoons apple cider vinegar

2 tablespoons molasses (not blackstrap) or brown rice syrup

3 tablespoons cream sherry

2 tablespoons tamari

1 tablespoon caraway seeds

½ a handful of fresh dill

For the horseradish sour cream

14 ounces (400g) silken tofu

2 tablespoons grated horseradish

1 tablespoon lemon juice

1 teaspoon rice vinegar

½ teaspoon salt

1 small clove of garlic, peeled and well crushed

For the garnish

½ a handful of fresh dill, chopped

DO IT

Place all the soup bits, except the dill, in a large pot and bring to a boil, then reduce the heat and simmer for 2 hours.

Meanwhile, make the horseradish sour cream by placing the ingredients in a food processor and blending until smooth and creamy.

With an immersion blender, smooth most of the soup. Some lumps are good. Add the dill, check the seasoning and add sea salt if needed.

Serve topped with more chopped dill and a large spoonful of the horseradish sour cream.

Salads

The majority of people think vegans live primarily on salads, which I think I've proven isn't really true. And everyone who thinks salads are just "rabbit food" should get a load of these recipes!

For me, salads are simply a way of arranging beautiful, complementary, eye-catching ingredients on a plate. Normally they're raw. I don't mind if they're vegetable or fruit, nut or leaf, legume or preserve; all are welcome in my salad realm.

What is a salad anyway? We thought we knew: something to do with icebergs and salad dressing. Jeez, we've come a long way, brothers and sisters. My parents remember when olive oil could only be procured from the pharmacy!

These are vibrant, evolving times. Our diets are shifting and keeping pace with this rapidly changing world. Technology and science are steaming ahead and this is leading to huge advances in all things nutrition. We know now that you can actually live on leaves (although admittedly it wouldn't be that interesting). We can certainly live on plants: fresh plants, bursting with life force. Nowhere else is this freshness and crispness better shown off than in a colorful platter of vegetation.

The very best salads are easy to arrange. They can get the Jackson Pollock treatment, scattering chopped mint here, flicking some sweet paprika over there, as your imagination runs wild. Your seasonal produce and spice rack form a palette of sorts, a handful of nuts adds richness, a squeeze of lemon lightens the tone. This is art on a plate. Don't overarrange – go wild!

The ultimate rule with salads is fresh, fresh, fresh. If it's limp, it fails the audition and should be utilized in something cooked or shown to the compost bin. No food goes to waste in the Beach House Kitchen – either we eat it or the worms do.

Couscous Salad with Tempeh, Preserved Lemons, Yellow Zucchini & Almonds

FOR 6

Tempeh is like chunky, funky tofu, with a slightly fermented taste and a little bit more substance. It stands up to the full flavors of the preserved lemons in this dish admirably. If you can get your hands on yellow zucchini, they look great in any dish. There is no difference in flavor from their green buddies; they just make a refreshing change sometimes and have some good nutrients in their skins. Preserved lemons are becoming more common-place in supermarkets and can also be found in the corners of Middle Eastern shops around the land.

Gluten-free option: use quinoa or millet instead of couscous, and GF tahini.

THE BITS

1¾ cups (300g) couscous

2¼ cups (525ml) boiling water or vegetable stock

½ tablespoon olive oil

7 ounces (200g) tempeh (well drained, then cut into thin 2-inch [5cm] slices)

1 teaspoon cumin seeds

2 red chilies, deseeded and finely diced

3 cloves of garlic, peeled and crushed

3 tablespoons finely chopped preserved lemons

a handful of sliced almonds, toasted

⅓ cup (60g) dried apricots, roughly chopped

a handful of green olives, piited and chopped

sea salt and freshly ground black pepper

3 small yellow zucchini, sliced lengthwise into thin strips

½ a handful of fresh mint, finely chopped

a handful of fresh parsley, finely chopped

For the dressing

scant ½ cup (100ml) extra virgin olive oil

2 teaspoons tahini

juice of ½ a lemon

1 clove of garlic, peeled and well crushed

½ tablespoon white wine vinegar

DO IT

Pour your couscous into a large bowl and cover with the boiling water or stock. Pop a lid on immediately and leave for 15 minutes. Fluff up with a fork a couple of times when ready to use, otherwise leave covered. You have to love that simplicity!

Grab a large frying pan and warm ½ tablespoon of oil on medium-high heat. Add the tempeh and sauté for 5–7 minutes, to get a little color on the chunks. Add the cumin seeds, followed by the chilies and garlic, and cook for 5 minutes, stirring well. Pop in the preserved lemons, most of the almonds, the apricots and olives and season with salt and pepper, warming everything through. Remove from the heat and cover.

Warm a small grill pan, then brush the zucchini strips with a little oil and grill in batches. Thin strips should take only 1–2 minutes per side. The strips should still have a little spring to them. Whisk the dressing ingredients together in small bowl.

Fluff up the couscous and gently mix in the tempeh, dressing and most of the fresh herbs, followed by the zucchini (try not to break them up too much). Sprinkle the rest of the almonds and herbs over the top. Serve in a large shallow bowl or on a large plate.

Fennel, Walnut & Celeriac Salad with Caesar-ish Dressing

FOR 4

Here is an untraditional Caesar salad, without the unmistakable anchovy, but with the positively pokey caper and a decent dab of mustard, all invoking something along the lines of the classic dish. Good enough for me! It's nice to use the salad leaves to help with the scooping and eating of this salad – Caesar salad was traditionally eaten this way. The dressing should cling to the leaves. You want crisp leaves here, so maybe reserve any softer outer leaves for another salad, wrap, etc.

THE BITS

a large handful of toasted walnuts

1 fennel bulb, finely sliced lengthwise, fronds and all

3 celery stalks, halved lengthwise and cut into ¾-inch (2cm) dice

½ a red onion, finely diced

⅓ of a medium celeriac, peeled and grated

2 green apples, cored and cut into ¾-inch (2cm) dice

6 radishes, finely diced

½ a handful of raisins

3 tablespoons nonpareil capers, well rinsed and drained

2 tablespoons toasted pumpkin seeds

2 small romaine lettuces, outer leaves placed in the fridge to crisp up, hearts thinly sliced

For the Caesar-ish dressing

4 tablespoons cashews, soaked for 4 hours, then drained

2 cloves of garlic, peeled and crushed

scant ½ cup (100ml) olive oil

2 teaspoons nonpareil capers, rinsed and well mashed

juice of 1 lemon

sea salt and freshly ground black pepper to taste

For the garnish

a handful of fresh dill, chopped

For a decadent touch

pine nut Parmesan (see page 313)

DO IT

To make the Caesar-ish dressing, place all the ingredients in a food processor, drizzling in the olive oil as the blades are running, to give you a shimmering, thick dressing. Check the seasoning – I like it with a good kick of pepper and garlic.

Roughly chop the walnuts and set aside half for sprinkling over the salad at the end. Put the rest of the walnuts and all the other salad bits, including the shredded romaine hearts, into a big bowl. Add the dressing and combine well. Arrange the crisped-up lettuce leaves in a big circle around the edge of a large serving plate. Mound the dressed salad in the center, then sprinkle with dill and the reserved walnuts, or, if you're feeling frisky, some pine nut Parmesan.

Hazelnut, Buckwheat &
Greens Salad with Watercress Oil

FOR 4-6

Buckwheat, we salute you and your impressive range of nutritional benefits. You are a gluten-free grain, you are a tasty sucker and you take as much effort and thought to cook as couscous (which is actually easier than toast).

THE BITS

2 cups (400g) raw buckwheat groats

1–2 tablespoons balsamic vinegar (to taste)

1 teaspoon sea salt

½ teaspoon freshly cracked black pepper

½ a small head of broccoli

5½ pound (150g) runner beans, sliced in half diagonally

a handful of fresh dill, finely chopped

½ a handful of fresh parsley, finely chopped

½ a handful of fresh chives, finely chopped

½ a red onion, finely diced

5 cups (100g) baby spinach leaves (if larger leaves, roughly chop)

a handful of raisins, soaked and roughly chopped

a handful of roasted pumpkin seeds

a large handful of roasted hazelnuts, roughly chopped

For the watercress oil

4 tablespoons olive oil

1 clove of garlic, peeled and crushed

2¼ cups (80g) watercress

a large pinch of sea salt

DO IT

On medium-high heat, dry roast the buckwheat in a pot for 7 minutes, until it begins darkening. Cover with 1 inch (3cm) of cold water and bring to a boil, then cover, turn down to a very low heat and cook for 20 minutes.

Pour the balsamic vinegar over the warm buckwheat and season with salt and pepper, fluff with a fork, then leave to cool.

Bring a large pot of salted boiling water to a steady simmer. Blanch your broccoli for 2 minutes, then remove and place in a large bowl of very cold water. Leave for a few minutes, then drain. Set aside, covered with cold water. Using the same pot, repeat this process with the runner beans. Make sure both the broccoli and beans are cold – if not, dunk them in cold water again. They should be nice and firm, crisp, with a good crunch. Vibrant greens!

Put your watercress oil ingredients into a blender and blitz until nice and smooth.

Combine the remaining ingredients with the broccoli and beans in a large bowl (saving some hazelnuts and herbs for topping). Sprinkle the buckwheat on top with your hands (making sure it's well broken up). Toss well and turn out onto a lovely serving platter.

Drizzle with the watercress oil and garnish with the rest of the hazelnuts and fresh herbs.

Seaweed, Fennel & Avocado with Udon Noodles

FOR 4–6

This salad is best served chilled. It's hearty yet light, full of zing and vitality. A perfect salad for a contemplative, lazy summer lunch. If you live by the coast, you can try foraging for your own edible seaweed. Otherwise you can just head to the supermarket or health food store and look for some Japanese sea greens – here I have used one of my favorites, wakame, which is packed full of life-giving properties.

Gluten-free option: use brown rice noodles instead of udon noodles, and GF sake.

THE BITS

9½ ounces (270g) udon noodles

2 handfuls of ice cubes

2 ounces (60g) wakame seaweed, sliced into thin strips

2 teaspoons toasted sesame oil

2 tablespoons rice vinegar

1 teaspoon unrefined brown sugar (see page 20)

2 teaspoons tamari

3 teaspoons lime juice

4 teaspoons sake (mirin or even dry sherry will do)

1 avocado, peeled, pitted and cut into small cubes

½ a medium bulb of fennel, fronds trimmed, pitted, chopped very finely lengthwise

1 small cucumber, peeled, deseeded, halved lengthwise and chopped

1 small carrot, peeled and cut into thin batons

For the garnish

1 tablespoon lime zest

3 tablespoons all-natural pink pickled ginger

DO IT

Bring a pot of water to a rolling boil and cook your noodles for 4–5 minutes (see the package for the best cooking time noodle-wise, as they can vary). Drain and run under cold water until cool.

Put the ice cubes into a large bowl, fill with water, then plunge your noodles and wakame seaweed into the seriously chilled water. Leave for a few minutes to ensure the noodles are nice and cold (you can pop them into the fridge for a while, too). Drain well and toss them in a bowl with the sesame oil.

Whisk the vinegar, sugar, tamari, lime juice and sake together. Taste and add more tamari if necessary. Lightly toss the avocado, fennel, cucumber and carrot with the dressing.

On a large plate, make a shallow bed of the noodles and scatter your green salad on top. Garnish with a sprinkle of lime zest and the pink pickled ginger.

Mediterranean Tofu Tostada
with Murcian Salad

FOR 4–6

Jane and I spend a lot of time in Spain, down in the wild red deserts and craggy mountains of Murcia where we raid the local Sunday farmers' market, with its year-round abundance of fresh, seasonal produce. Our friend Fey, who came up with the dressing used here, lives in a beautiful valley not far from our little casita. This is a "rustic" salad, so don't bother chopping the vegetables too finely. I use three big slices of whole wheat bread, cut into triangles, though a traditional Spanish tostada uses the whitest of white bread.

Gluten-free option: use your favorite GF bread.

THE BITS

12 small pieces of bread

1 head of soft-leaf lettuce (such as oak-leaf), roughly chopped

2 Little Gem lettuces, quartered lengthwise

½ a small red onion, finely chopped

½ a cucumber, quartered lengthwise and diced

1 carrot, quartered lengthwise and diced

3 tomatoes, quartered and roughly diced

½ a zucchini, quartered and roughly diced

2 handfuls of high-quality black olives, pitted and halved widthwise

5 piquillo peppers or 1 red bell pepper, finely sliced

3 tablespoons nonpareil capers, well drained

a handful of fresh parsley, finely chopped

1 teaspoon sea salt

½ teaspoon freshly cracked black pepper

For the Mediterranean tofu

14 ounces (400g) firm tofu, pressed (see page 18)

1 large clove of garlic, peeled and minced

1 small celery stalk, finely diced

2 teaspoons sweet paprika

½ teaspoon smoked paprika

½ teaspoon dried thyme

½ teaspoon dried oregano

¼ teaspoon dried dill

a pinch of dried rosemary

8 sun-dried tomatoes, soaked, then finely chopped

4 tablespoons chopped green olives

2 tablespoons fresh parsley, finely chopped

½ tablespoon tomato paste

2 tablespoons olive oil

1 tablespoon nutritional yeast flakes (optional)

sea salt (if needed)

1 x Fey's parsley and lemon dressing (see page 303)

DO IT

Toast your bread – the crisper the better. Let it cool on a wire rack. To make the Mediterranean tofu, place all the ingredients in a food processor and blend until smooth. It should be a thick, rich and creamy paste. Check the seasoning – you should only need a little salt. Now make Fey's dressing.

Arrange your salad in a large flat bowl or on a serving platter. Start with your soft leaves, then arrange your quarters of Little Gem around the edge of the bowl. Scatter the rest of your vegetables on top, leaving the piquillo peppers and capers until last, then sprinkle with the fresh parsley.

Spoon a big helping of the tofu on each of your cooled tostadas. Place the tostadas all over the salad, tucking them in a little bit. Season and serve in a sunny spot, with smiles.

Braised Cauliflower & Puy Lentil Tabbouleh

FOR 4–6

Tabbouleh is a proper southern Mediterranean classic. Combined with a great olive oil and sweet roasted cauliflower, it makes a substantial salad. I love the spice mix baharat – if you can find it, substitute it for the ground spices. I like to use pomegranate molasses in the dressing, as it gives a fun reddish tinge and has a sticky tang all of its own.

Gluten-free option: replace the bulgur wheat with millet.

THE BITS

½ cup (100g) Puy (petite French green) lentils

1 bay leaf

1¼ cups (220g) uncooked bulgur wheat, rinsed in cold water

about 2 cups (450ml) boiling water or vegetable stock

1 small cauliflower, cut into small florets, roughly ¾-inch (2cm) in size, stalks finely diced (waste nothing!)

a large pinch of ground cumin

a large pinch of ground coriander

a large pinch of sweet paprika

a large pinch of ground turmeric

a small pinch of ground cinnamon

½ teaspoon sea salt

4 scallions, finely chopped

½ a cucumber, deseeded and finely diced

2 ripe tomatoes, deseeded and finely diced

1 tablespoon high-quality olive oil

½ a handful of dried apricots, soaked for 2 hours, then drained and finely chopped

a handful of fresh flat-leaf parsley, finely chopped

½ a handful of fresh mint leaves, finely chopped

seeds from 1 small pomegranate

1 tablespoon toasted sesame seeds

1 x pomegranate dressing (see page 304)

For the garnish

4 tablespoons pomegranate seeds

a handful of chopped fresh parsley and mint

DO IT

Put the lentils into a pot and cover with water. Leave for 5 minutes, then pick out any floating lentils. Drain, cover with fresh water, and add the bay leaf. Bring to a boil, then reduce the heat and simmer for 30 minutes, stirring and adding more water if needed. The lentils should be springy but cooked through. Drain if necessary, though there should be very little liquid left.

Put the bulgur wheat into a large heatproof bowl and pour in the boiling water or stock, enough to cover it by about ¾ inch (2cm). Cover and leave for 30 minutes. Once cooked, fluff with a fork and cool.

In a frying pan, heat the oil on high, then add the cauliflower. Stir regularly and cook for 10–12 minutes. Once the cauliflower has softened and the edges are slightly charred, sprinkle in the ground spices and salt and cook for another 2 minutes, stirring well. Cover and leave to cool. The cauliflower should be evenly coated with the spices.

Make the pomegranate dressing. Add three-quarters of the lentils to the bulgur wheat, along with the cauliflower, herbs and the rest of the ingredients, then pour the dressing over and mix gently together with your hands until well combined. Place in a wide, shallow serving bowl and spread out evenly. Sprinkle the remaining lentils on top and garnish with pomegranate seeds and herbs.

Charred Fig & Arugula Salad with Lemon Tofu Feta

FOR 4

I struggle to eat vegan in France. However, when we were visiting Sancerre, and sipping our way around the surrounding countryside, we stopped in a tiny little place where the kindly chef offered to roast me some figs in balsamic vinegar and served them with arugula salad. The natural sweetness of the figs and the sharp arugula lit up my mouth. Here I've added a little fragrance with the basil and a good dollop of tofu "feta," which makes it into a light lunch salad.

THE BITS

3 handfuls of arugula leaves

a handful of fresh basil leaves

6 ripe figs, quartered

2 tablespoons balsamic vinegar

3 tablespoons toasted pine nuts

For the lemon tofu feta

1 tablespoon nutritional yeast flakes

juice of ½ a lemon

½ teaspoon lemon zest

1 tablespoon olive oil

14 ounces (400g) firm tofu, pressed (see page 18) and crumbled

1 clove of garlic, peeled and crushed

a large pinch of sea salt

a pinch of freshly cracked black pepper

For the dressing

1 tablespoon lemon juice

1 teaspoon brown rice syrup

½ tablespoon balsamic vinegar

a pinch of sea salt

1 tablespoon extra virgin olive oil

DO IT

To make the tofu feta, put the nutritional yeast flakes into a bowl with the lemon juice and zest and leave to dissolve. Heat the oil in a small frying pan on medium and add the tofu and garlic. Panfry until slightly golden, then add the lemon mixture, salt and pepper, bring to a boil and cook until the lemon juice has evaporated. Spoon into a bowl and allow to cool. Check that it's just a little too salty, like feta.

To make the dressing, whisk together the lemon juice, brown rice syrup, vinegar, salt and olive oil in a small bowl.

Mix the arugula and basil leaves together in a bowl. Drizzle 1 tablespoon of the dressing over the leaves and toss together. Keep the rest of the dressing for further dipping and drizzling.

Warm a grill pan on high heat and brush with a little oil. Just as the oil begins to smoke, place your figs widthwise in the pan. Allow to cook for 2 minutes, basting them with balsamic vinegar as you go. Turn them when well caramelized, then remove the now sticky figs from the heat.

Scatter the leaves artfully on plates, and top with the warm figs, a couple of spoonfuls of the tofu feta and a sprinkling of toasted pine nuts.

Fragrant Wild Rice, Curly Kale & Pistachio Salad

FOR 4-6

I was raised on rice – I grew up in the Philippines, and rice is a 24/7 constant for Pinoys. I went back there recently and clambered up some very impressive rice paddies in the mountains of Luzon. I was pleased to see that many of these ancient steplike structures are still being used, stretching and winding across many miles of verdant valleys, hugging the most gravity-defying crevices and nooks. This is a simple salad that combines some wonderful ingredients. There are a lot of flavors going on here: the occasional sweetness from the raisins, the hunk of saltiness from the sun-dried tomatoes – it's a feast of a salad. It's also very tasty served warm; just leave the rice to cool for 20 minutes, rather than cooling completely. You can transform it into a wonderful big plate by adding panfried tempeh, cut into chunks.

THE BITS

1⅔ cups (250g) wild rice

1 carrot, grated (if you have any carrot greens, finely chop them and add)

5 leaves of curly kale, de-stemmed and very finely sliced

3 tablespoons raisins, soaked for 2 hours and roughly chopped

½ a handful of roasted pistachios, roughly chopped

6 radishes, trimmed and finely diced

6 sun-blushed (semi-dried) or sun-dried tomatoes, including any oil, finely chopped

4 scallions, finely sliced

½ a handful of fresh dill, chopped

½ a handful of chives, finely sliced

a handful of sprouted mung beans or green lentils

For the dressing

2 cloves of garlic, peeled and crushed

3 tablespoons olive oil

juice of 1½ limes

zest of ½ a lime

½ teaspoon sea salt

½ teaspoon freshly ground black pepper

For the garnish

a handful of roasted pistachios

3 tablespoons chopped fresh dill

DO IT

Rinse the wild rice in cold water a number of times until the water runs clean. Place in a pot, pour in enough water to cover by 1 inch (3cm), then bring to a boil and put a lid on. Reduce the heat to its lowest possible setting and cook for 45–50 minutes, until the rice is soft and all the water has evaporated. Fluff up gently with a fork and allow to cool fully. Spreading the rice out on a plate will help here.

To make the dressing, whisk the ingredients together in a small bowl.

Combine the rest of the ingredients in a large bowl and toss well to mix evenly (using your hands here is amusing). Add the dressing, spoon in the rice and combine well.

Serve in shallow bowls, garnished with the extra nuts and herbs.

Trigonos Retreat Center,
Nantlle Valley, Wales.

Charred Pumpkin with Salsa Verde, Butter Beans & Piquillo Peppers

FOR 4

This is one of my favorite salads to make when I'm in Spain. The salsa verde cuts through the sweet pumpkin and rich beans nicely and you're left with happy mouth tingles. Adding cubes of tofu or tempeh to the salsa verde and leaving it to infuse overnight is a nice idea, and turns the dish into main course material. Chargrill your pumpkin on a grill pan to get best results. *Piquillo* peppers are small, roasted Spanish sweet peppers and can often be found at specialty food shops or Hispanic grocery stores. Regular roasted red peppers are a great substitute. Or, if you like, you can grill red bell peppers with the pumpkin for a similar flavor and effect.

THE BITS

1 small sweet pumpkin, scrubbed, deseeded and quartered, then cut into 1cm thick half-moon wedges

12 cloves of garlic, unpeeled

2 tablespoons olive oil

sea salt

5 handfuls of baby spinach (slice larger leaves into thick green ribbons)

⅔ cup (120g) dried butter beans, soaked overnight, cooked and drained

2 ripe tomatoes, diced

1 x salsa verde dressing (see page 139)

For the garnish

5½ ounces (150g) piquillo peppers, cut into thick slices

3 tablespoons toasted pumpkin seeds

a handful of fresh cilantro

½ teaspoon sweet paprika

2 teaspoons fruity olive oil

DO IT

Preheat the oven to 400°F (200°C), and put a grill pan on the stove over high heat.

Put the pumpkin and cloves of garlic into a large bowl and add the oil and 1 teaspoon of sea salt. Rub the oil into the pumpkin, then place the chunks on the hot (probably slightly smoking) grill pan. Leave them for at least a minute without moving them, then turn them over and do the same on the other side. You're looking for pronounced black lines. This is probably best done in batches.

Place the pumpkin chunks on one half of a large baking tray and the garlic on the other. Pour any leftover oil on top. Place in the oven and roast for 20 minutes, until the garlic is soft and gooey. Using a spatula, remove the garlic and place it on a plate to cool. If the pumpkin is not quite soft yet, return it to the oven for another 7–10 minutes.

Make the salsa verde. Sprinkle the spinach leaves over a large serving platter. Scatter the beans, roasted garlic (skins on), pumpkin chunks and diced tomato on top, then drizzle with some of the salsa verde. Be creative here, go wild! Splatter sauce and toss beans around – the freer you are, the better it looks.

Top with the sliced piquillo peppers and a sprinkling of pumpkin seeds and fresh herbs. Drizzle with a little more salsa verde, sprinkle with sea salt and sweet paprika and add a good glug of fruity olive oil.

Superhero Sprouted Salad with Cashew Hummus

FOR 4–6

One of the finest examples of converting pennies into supercharged fuel for the body and mind, sprouting is a wonderful way to feed yourself cheaply with incredible wonder foods.

This salad can be made to great effect with most sprouts – I call for mung beans, green lentils and adzuki beans here. You can try your hand at sprouting your own, or you can purchase your sprouts at the grocery store or local farmers' market. The most widely available sprouts in the US are alfalfa, mung bean and broccoli.

Very rarely does a plate of food scale such heady heights of vitality and potent nutritional value. This salad is a head-turner, a gob-smacker, a lip-tickler and a full-on riot of plant power.

THE BITS

2 handfuls sprouted mung beans

2 handfuls sprouted green lentils

2 handfuls sprouted adzuki beans

1 large carrot, scrubbed and grated

1 beet, peeled and grated

1 apple, cored and finely diced

6 brussels sprouts or ¼ of a small cabbage, very finely sliced

1 celery stalk, finely diced

½ a red onion, finely diced

1 yellow bell pepper, finely diced

2 handfuls of broccoli, chopped

3 tablespoons pitted and finely sliced black olives, or nonpareil capers

a handful of toasted sunflower seeds or pumpkin seeds (these can also be sprouted in the same way you sprout beans)

1 tablespoon chia seeds or sesame seeds

1 big handful of fresh parsley, finely chopped

romaine lettuce leaves, or any big lettuce leaves, for making a "nest" (endive leaves work well for smaller portions)

1 x superhero dressing (see page 303)

1 x cashew hummus (see page 144)

For the garnish

a handful of sprouted alfalfa

sprinkles of wheatgrass, spirulina, etc. (optional "superhero" topping)

DO IT

First make your superhero dressing and cashew hummus. Put all the salad ingredients, except the lettuce leaves, into a large bowl and add the dressing. Toss together, making sure everything is lightly coated.

Form a nest with the lettuce leaves in a large salad bowl, then scoop in the salad and sprinkle in the alfalfa and funky green powder (spirulina, etc.) if you have any. Alternatively, you can use the individual salad leaves as "boats" for your sprouts, spooning neat piles onto individual leaves. If the leaves you are using are soft and pliable, why not make some raw wraps?

This salad is magical with the cashew hummus. Avoid bread this time – the ridiculous amount of nutrients in this salad will keep you full for a long, long time. Give it around 20 minutes to digest and do its thing and you'll be well sated.

Beet, Apple & Raspberry Salad with Herb Millet

FOR 4–6

Millet is a magnificent whole grain and makes a delicious, gluten-free, low-carb alternative to potato, rice, wheat and all those other things we eat loads of. I've had millet as porridge for breakfast in villages in the Himalayas, where the ground grains are also made into roti (flat-bread). It is used in many communities around the world, especially Africa – in the places where wheat has not yet heavily infiltrated.

Raspberries and beets are two powerful allies that add serious nutrition, color and flavor to this salad. I sometimes like to throw in tofu (which I've done here) – it bulks it out and gives a nice well-rounded, protein-packed feel to the plate.

THE BITS

3 beets with leaves on

1 carrot, scrubbed and grated

1 sour green apple, cored and roughly grated

½ a small red onion, peeled and roughly grated

7 ounces (200g) firm tofu, pressed (see page 18) and diced into small cubes

a handful of raspberries

a handful of toasted walnuts or hazelnuts

For the millet

generous ¾ cup (175g) uncooked millet

1¼ cups (300ml) water

1 tablespoon olive oil

2 teaspoons fresh thyme leaves

½ teaspoon salt

3 tablespoons finely chopped fresh parsley

1 x raspberry dressing (see page 304)

DO IT

Cut the leaves off the beets, keeping them whole. Cut the stems into ¾-inch (2cm) pieces, and scrub and roughly grate the roots.

In a small pot, toast the millet for 7 minutes, until it starts to become golden, shaking and swirling the pot frequently to keep the millet moving. Add the water, lower the heat to the lowest setting and cover. Cook for 30 minutes. Fluff up the millet gently with a fork, and heat a little longer if it is still damp. Turn out onto a plate and leave to cool.

When the millet is just warm, stir in the olive oil, thyme, salt and most of the parsley. The millet may be sticky, which is fine. Break it up with your hands – the olive oil and parsley will help with this.

Make the raspberry dressing. Place all your grated bits in a large bowl and stir in most of the dressing, along with the chopped beet stems.

Arrange the sliced beet leaves around the edge of a serving plate and spoon the millet in the center. Scatter the grated bits and tofu chunks over the top, followed by the raspberries and nuts, then drizzle on a little more dressing and sprinkle with the rest of the parsley.

Sides

As a vegan, you get used to dining out on side dishes. We recently went to a top seafood restaurant for my dad's sixtieth birthday and I ate brussels sprouts for a main course. They were delicious! A few chestnuts and a little Madeira and the potential of a side dish was made very evident to me.

Side dishes are an added detail to a meal, the little touch that shows you care and have plenty of skills. There is absolutely nothing wrong with a plate of simple steamed veggies, but you hardly want to read a book about them! Here we have sides to tantalize and sometimes even steal the thunder of the main dish.

Sides are like the string section to a seventies rock band – they can be utilized wonderfully, enhancing the overall effect of the experience (see "Kashmir" by Led Zeppelin), or they can be mismatched and hopelessly out of place (see all of ELO's releases bar "Mr. Blue Sky," which is a bona fide belter and makes me happy). These are no shrinking violets, so pairing them with an appropriate main course is essential. Like the Small Plates on page 132, these dishes can be gathered together into a wonderful little selection for a tapas-style meal.

Turkish-Style Spinach with Creamy Tofu Ricotta

FOR 6 AS A SIDE DISH OR 4 AS A BIG PLATE

Turkish food is stunning – I love the eclectic mix of influences. This delightful Turkish dish may seem heavy on the spinach, but you know what it's like – it just disappears into a pile of gorgeous green. You can use any suitable greens here – kale works beautifully, beet leaves are brilliant, and even the greener shades of thinly sliced cabbage will do. This dish can easily be made into a bigger plate by adding sliced cooked potatoes and cherry tomatoes to the spinach. You will have better results if you make the tofu ricotta a day ahead and keep it in the fridge.

THE BITS

1 tablespoon olive oil

4 cloves of garlic, peeled and crushed

½ teaspoon ground allspice

2¼ pounds (1kg) spinach

2 large pinches of freshly grated nutmeg

a big handful of fresh dill

a good pinch of salt

For the tofu ricotta

1½ pounds (700g) firm tofu, pressed (see page 18)

½ teaspoon sea salt

2 cloves of garlic, peeled and crushed

1 tablespoon lemon juice

1 tablespoon nutritional yeast flakes

1 teaspoon dried basil or oregano

For the topping

a good pinch of sweet paprika

olive oil, for drizzling

DO IT

Put the oil and garlic into the largest pan you have, on medium heat, and fry for a minute. Then add the allspice and fry for a moment, stirring constantly. Add the spinach in big fistfuls and stir to help it to wilt. You will need to do this in batches; covering the pan helps a lot. Once all of the spinach has wilted down, stir in the nutmeg and dill with a pinch of salt and cook uncovered until most of the liquid has disappeared. Remove from the heat and cover the pan.

Place the ingredients for the tofu ricotta in a blender and blitz until smooth.

Preheat the oven to 400°F (200°C).

Spread out the spinach in a medium baking dish and press it into the corners to make a solid layer. Top with the tofu ricotta, spreading it in a thick layer until it meets the edges. Sprinkle with the paprika and drizzle some olive oil on top, then place in the oven for 25–30 minutes, until the tofu is browned.

Serve warm with flatbreads, roasted veggies, or maybe a nice glass of "lion's milk" (the turkish apéritif raki – don't worry, it's vegan!).

Sweet & Sour Eggplant

FOR 4

Over a billion Hindus and thousands of years' worth of tradition have resulted in a beautiful array of vegetarian fare in India; from north to south, east to west, the food varies so much in this fascinating country. I ate something like this dish on my first night in Delhi, many years ago, wondering why they didn't serve this kind of Indian food in my local curry house.

To make this dish more authentic, try to get some smaller eggplants. Baby eggplants would work perfectly. Leaving the top of the eggplant intact adds to the look. If you'd like a thicker sauce, add a couple of chopped tomatoes when you add the water. The tomato and basil pilaf on page 127 would be lovely with this dish.

THE BITS

1 teaspoon salt

8 baby eggplants, quartered lengthwise, keeping the stem intact

3 tablespoons gram (chickpea) flour

2 teaspoons cumin seeds

2 teaspoons coriander seeds

1 tablespoon finely grated fresh ginger

2 cloves of garlic, peeled and crushed

½ teaspoon cayenne pepper

1 teaspoon sweet paprika

a handful of fresh cilantro leaves, finely chopped

3 tablespoons coconut oil (or vegetable oil)

juice of ½ a lemon

3 teaspoons unrefined brown sugar (see page 20)

For the garnish

a handful of fresh cilantro leaves, chopped

DO IT

Rub ½ teaspoon of salt into the eggplants and leave them to drain in a colander for 30 minutes.

Put the flour, cumin seeds and coriander seeds into a heavy-bottomed frying pan and toast on medium heat until the seeds pop and the flour becomes darker. Place them into a mortar and roughly crush the seeds. Add the ginger, garlic, cayenne, paprika, cilantro and ½ teaspoon of salt to the mortar and mash into a thick, sticky paste.

Pat the eggplants dry with a kitchen towel or paper towel, then rub the paste into them, giving them a good, tasty coating.

Put the oil into a large frying pan or wok (or an Indian *karhai* if you have one handy) and heat on medium-high. When it is hot (test with a little of the paste), add the eggplants and begin to fry, browning them on all sides for around 3–4 minutes. Add 3 tablespoons of water. Pop a lid on the pan and leave to simmer gently for 15 minutes, depending on the size, until the eggplants are nice and tender.

Take the lid off, then whisk the lemon and sugar together and pour over the eggplants. Continue to cook for a few minutes, turning them once, until there is a thick sauce and the eggplants are almost falling apart.

Serve warm, topped with chopped cilantro.

Tamarind & Coconut
Mashed Sweet Potatoes

FOR 4

Sweet potato and tamarind are such good bedfellows, and the addition of coconut milk takes these mashed potatoes to intergalactic levels! This dish is so bursting with flavor, you'll probably want to serve something simple with it. It is perfect alongside roasted vegetables (with a little spice added) and some wilted greens for a wonderfully balanced meal. If you use tamarind paste instead of pulp, halve the quantity. We've all added butter and milk to mashed potatoes; now try this for a change.

THE BITS

1 pound (450g) baking potatoes, peeled and cut into chunks

1 pound (450g) sweet potatoes, peeled and cut into chunks

1½ teaspoons salt

2 tablespoons tamarind pulp, soaked in 3 tablespoons of warm water for 2 hours

1 tablespoon coconut oil

a big handful of cashews

1 teaspoon cumin seeds

1 teaspoon fenugreek (methi) leaves

1 teaspoon mustard seeds

1 lemongrass stalk, halved, or 2 teaspoons lemon zest

1–2 teaspoons red pepper flakes (to taste)

generous 3/4 cup (200ml) coconut milk

For the topping

a handful of fresh cilantro, finely chopped

2 tablespoons cashews (optional)

DO IT

Place all the potatoes in a pot, cover with water, add 1 teaspoon of salt and bring to a boil. Simmer until tender – around 25 minutes. Drain, saving the liquid for a soup or stew (it's delicious). Leave for 5 minutes to steam dry, then pop back into the pot and put the lid on.

While the potatoes are cooking, pass the tamarind through a sieve, pressing down with a spoon. Make sure most of the pulp passes through and none of the seeds. Heat the coconut oil in a frying pan on medium and add the cashews, cumin seeds, fenugreek and mustard seeds. Allow to cook and pop for a minute, but be careful not to let them burn. Add the lemongrass and red pepper flakes and cook for less than a minute, then stir in the tamarind pulp. Pour in the coconut milk, bring to a slow boil, then simmer gently for 15 minutes. Cover and leave to sit for a while, letting the flavors have a party.

Pour two-thirds of the coconut sauce into the potatoes (picking out the lemongrass stalk) and get your mash on, mashing well until smooth and adding more sauce as needed. Zero lumps are tolerated. Check the seasoning and add the rest of the salt if necessary.

Sprinkle with fresh cilantro and a few more cashews, if you are so inclined.

Kasha with Rosemary, Apricots & Walnuts

FOR 6

Kasha is just another name for roasted buckwheat, but it sounds so much more exotic! Buckwheat is superbly nutritious and is actually completely gluten-free. This method of roasting buckwheat before steaming it really brings out its earthy flavor and is the way to go for me. The grains hold their shape and it becomes less of a mush. You don't have to soak the apricots – it just plumps them up and makes them a little softer, which I like.

THE BITS

2 tablespoons olive oil

1½ cups (360g) raw buckwheat groats

1 large red onion, finely diced

generous 2 cups (500ml) warm vegetable stock or water

2 large sprigs of fresh rosemary

⅔ cup (125g) dried apricots, soaked in 2 tablespoons of water for 1 hour, then roughly chopped

a large pinch of freshly ground black pepper

1–2 tablespoons tamari (to taste)

¾ cup (70g) toasted walnuts, roughly chopped

a handful of fresh parsley, finely chopped

½ a handful of pumpkin seeds

For the garnish

a handful of toasted walnuts, roughly chopped

DO IT

Heat 1 tablespoon of oil in a large heavy-bottomed pan on low and roast the buckwheat gently for 5 minutes, stirring regularly. When its color changes to a darker brown, it is ready.

Add your onions and continue to cook, stirring frequently, for 6–8 minutes, then add the warm stock and the rosemary sprigs. Cover, lower the heat to the lowest setting, and simmer for about 15 minutes.

Remove the rosemary sprigs, fluff up the buckwheat with a fork, then stir in the rest of the ingredients and add 1 tablespoon of olive oil. Check the seasoning, pop the lid back on, and leave to mingle for 5 minutes. Serve warm, sprinkled with toasted walnuts.

Kimchi

MAKES ONE LARGE CONTAINER

Kimchi is currently taking the world by storm. It's made by fermenting cabbage with flavorings, a process called lacto-fermentation, in which a salty brine kills all bad bacteria. I omit the fish sauce and shrimp paste that is traditionally used and substitute kelp and some shiitake-flavored stock, adding a decent dose of umami taste to the proceedings. The most important step is to taste the kimchi each day – it should be fiery and salty. Remember, a little goes a long way. It keeps well in the fridge. I serve it with simple wok-fried vegetables flavored with tamari and ginger and rice or noodles, but if you're a real kimchi fiend, grab yourself a spoon and eat it straight out of the jar!

THE BITS

2¼ pounds (1kg) Chinese (napa) cabbage

½ cup (140g) sea salt

8 cups (1.9 liters) spring water

2–4 tablespoons red pepper flakes (depending on desired heat)

1 apple, cored and peeled

1 inch (2.5cm) fresh ginger, peeled and finely sliced

1 white onion, peeled and roughly chopped

4 tablespoons tamari

5 cloves of garlic, peeled

2 tablespoons cooked potato – leftover white rice can also be used

6 scallions, cut into 2-inch (5cm) pieces

1 large hot red chili, sliced into thin rings, seeds left in

1 tablespoon sesame seeds

For the stock

2 large pieces of kelp

6 dried shiitake mushrooms (or 1 mushroom stock cube)

2 cups (500ml) water

DO IT

Cut the cabbage in half lengthwise and remove the thick stems. Cut widthwise into 2-inch (5cm) strips. Put the salt and cabbage into a large bowl and massage the salt into the cabbage – once it begins to release some liquid, cover with the spring water and press down with a plate, making sure all the leaves are submerged. Leave for 2 hours.

Put the stock ingredients into a pot and bring to a boil. Allow to cook down until roughly ¾ cup (175ml) of liquid remains. Strain and allow to cool. Rinse the cabbage and leave to drain in a colander for 15 minutes. Put the red pepper flakes, apple, ginger, onion, tamari, garlic and potato into a food processor, add the stock, and blend to a smooth paste.

Gently squeeze out any excess moisture from the cabbage. Put it back into the large bowl with the scallions, fresh chili and sesame seeds. Pour in the vivid red paste and massage it into the leaves, making sure they're all well covered (you may like to use gloves here; the chilies can be rough on the hands and whatever you choose to scratch next).

Place in a sealable container or a large clean jar or two. Leave about 1 inch (2.5cm) of space between the kimchi and the top of the container. Place the container on a plate; it may bubble over when left to ferment. Leave at room temperature in a safe place for 1–5 days (3 days being the average). Taste daily and press the leaves back down into the brine. Store in the fridge once you're happy with the tang and kick.

Winter Roots Braised in Porter

FOR 4-6

This is a full-power way of roasting your winter roots with one of my favorite winter things: jet black and intoxicating porter beer. Licorice meets deep espresso while flirting with a smidgen of cacao in a heady brew. This dish is especially nice made with baby carrots and little parsnips, roasted whole, but if you can't find the little versions of these veggies, just use their big brothers chopped into similarly shaped chunks. The mini versions do retain their flavor better when roasted. This makes a delicious main course when served with kasha (see page 119), or serve alongside a hearty dish like parsnip rumbledethumps (see page 186) or nut roast (see page 179).

THE BITS

¼ pound (100g) parsnips

¼ pound (150g) carrots

¼ pound (150g) rutabaga

4 celery stalks

7 ounces (200g) small onions (such as pickling onions), peeled

2 tablespoons canola oil

3 cloves of garlic, peeled and crushed

¾ cup (175ml) porter

1 sprig of fresh rosemary

1 tablespoon tomato paste

1 cup (250ml) vegetable stock

1 tablespoon unrefined brown sugar (see page 20)

½ teaspoon sea salt (or to taste)

½ teaspoon freshly cracked black pepper (or to taste)

DO IT

Peel or scrub the parsnips, carrots, rutabaga and celery as necessary and cut into small, similar-sized batons.

Bring a small pot of salted water to a boil, drop in the onions and cook for 10–15 minutes, until they are tender when stabbed with a sharp knife. Drain well and pat them dry.

Heat the canola oil in a pot on medium, add the onions and celery and cook until lightly golden – roughly 10 minutes. Add the garlic and cook for 2 minutes, then add the carrots, rutabaga and parsnips. Stir, then pour in the porter. Add the rosemary, tomato paste, vegetable stock and sugar and bring to a boil. Cover the pot and cook until the vegetables are tender, checking after 10 minutes.

The cooking stock should now be nice and thick. If not, remove the vegetables with a slotted spoon and keep warm, then continue to cook the stock until it has thickened. Put the vegetables back into the pot, pick out the rosemary sprig, and season as needed.

Catalan Spinach

FOR 4-6

This side dish makes a great starter, or can even be served as a main course with a hunk of bread or some couscous. I love tapas and ate this a lot in Cataluña – it can be tough being a vegan in Spain, and this traditional spinach dish was an utter savior.

THE BITS

⅓ cup (50g) golden raisins

1 tablespoon olive oil

1 onion, finely chopped

2 cloves of garlic, peeled and finely chopped

1¾ pounds (800g) spinach, roughly chopped

4 tablespoons toasted pine nuts

sea salt and freshly cracked black pepper to taste

DO IT

Soak the golden raisins in a bowl of warm water for 30 minutes, then drain and set aside (drink the water – it's lovely and sweet).

Heat the oil in a large heavy-bottomed pan on medium. Add the onion, stirring and cooking for 6–8 minutes, then add the garlic and cook for 2 minutes more. Throw in your spinach leaves, stir, then cover the pan and continue to cook for another 4–5 minutes, until the spinach has wilted down. You may need to do this in batches.

Add the golden raisins and most of the pine nuts to the pan and season with salt and pepper.

Warm through and serve with a few more pine nuts on top.

Sesame & Sweet Corn Pancakes

MAKES 10 SMALL PANCAKES

Lovely little pancakes to soak up your favorite stew or curry. The gram (chickpea) flour adds unmistakable earthiness and plenty of nutrition and the regular flour helps to bind things together nicely. A great pancake partnership. If you'd like to go for full-on nutrition, add buckwheat flour instead of the normal flour. If you leave it to cool, it may even turn pink (a strange habit of buckwheat). Enjoy with anything in the curry section (pages 196–219) or make a flame-grilled vegetable and chermoula wrap (see page 142)!

Gluten-free option: use buckwheat flour instead of regular flour.

THE BITS

¾ cup (100g) unbleached all-purpose flour

¾ cup (100g) gram (chickpea) flour

2 teaspoons baking soda

2 tablespoons sesame oil (cold-pressed and not toasted)

2 teaspoons tamari

1½ cups (360ml) unsweetened soy milk

¼ cup (30g) sesame seeds, toasted

2 handfuls of fresh sweet corn kernels (or 1 small can)

2 scallions, finely sliced

a little vegetable oil, for frying

DO IT

Sift the flours and baking soda into a large mixing bowl. In a separate bowl whisk together the sesame oil, tamari and soy milk until well combined. Now fold the dry ingredients into the wet ingredients until a batter is formed. Stir in the sesame seeds, sweet corn and scallions. Cover and place in the fridge for 20 minutes.

Lightly oil a small frying pan and heat on medium-high. When it's hot, add roughly 3 tablespoons of the mixture at a time and fry until one side is brown, 2 minutes max. Flip over and fry the other side for slightly less time. This should leave you with a nicely cooked pancake to enjoy. You may need to add a little more oil to the pan as you go along. Wrap the pancakes in a clean kitchen towel when cooked, to keep warm.

Mujaddara with Crispy Onions

FOR 4

This dish is Arabic in origin, but I think many countries would consider this legume and grain combo their own, and rightly so, as it's a surefire winner. My version sees lentils and wheat teaming up to make a flavorful side and a base for many wonderful additions. Just add a dressing, chopped herbs and vegetables and you're looking at a very special pilaf. I've left it plain here for you to play with. If you feel up to it (bearing in mind this is a side dish), the crispy onions finish this dish perfectly. Ideal teamed up with seeded lentil falafels (see page 159) and dollops of cashew hummus (see page 144).

For a gluten-free option, replace the bulgur with millet or brown rice (more traditional).

THE BITS

⅔ cup (115g) dried green or brown lentils

2 cups (480ml) vegetable stock

scant ⅔ cup (110g) uncooked fine bulgur wheat

1 tablespoon olive oil

2 teaspoons cumin seeds

1 onion, finely chopped

sea salt and freshly ground black pepper to taste

a large pinch of chili powder

a large pinch of ground cinnamon

For the topping (optional)

vegetable oil

2 onions, very finely sliced

a handful of fresh parsley, finely chopped

DO IT

Cover the lentils with cold water and soak for 5 minutes, picking out anything dodgy that floats to the top. Drain, then place the lentils in a pot with the stock, bring to a boil and simmer for 35–45 minutes, until tender. Stir in the bulgur and add enough water to cover by about ¾ inch (2cm). Cook on very low heat for 5 minutes, then remove from the heat, cover and let stand for 10 minutes.

Heat the oil in a frying pan and sauté the cumin seeds for a minute. When they begin popping, add your onions and sauté for 6–8 minutes, until soft. Stir the onions into the pilaf with a fork and season with salt, pepper and the chili and cinnamon. Fluff up the mujaddara with a fork and cover, keeping it warm.

To make the topping, heat a decent amount of vegetable oil in a heavy-bottomed frying pan – we are shallow-frying these onions until very golden and crispy. Turn the heat to medium and make sure the oil is hot. When it's shimmering (and a piece of onion frizzles when dropped in), add your onions and fry for 15 minutes, until deeply golden and sweet. Drain well using a slotted spoon, and place on a plate covered with paper towels. Pat the onions with more paper towels to remove any excess oil.

Serve the mujadarra topped with the crispy onions and chopped parsley. Best served hot, but also great cold.

Tomato & Basil Pilaf

FOR 4-6

This is a decidedly European twist on pilaf. A delicious rice side dish that can be easily served as a big plate. In late summer, basil grows wild on our window ledges and works its fragrant way into most of my dishes. It's so pungent and intoxicating you can barely believe it's legal! I like to use brown basmati rice for taste and health reasons, but white basmati will also do. Just take 10 minutes off the overall cooking time. Stir in cooked beans or chickpeas and more veggies to make a more substantial main course dish, or serve with a gorgeous curry of your choice (see pages 196–219 for inspiration).

THE BITS

2 cups (400g) uncooked brown basmati rice (white basmati is also fine)

4 tomatoes, coarsely chopped

2 big handfuls of fresh basil leaves

scant 1 cup (225ml) vegetable stock

2 tablespoons olive oil

10 peppercorns

1 cinnamon stick (about 3 inches [8cm])

6 cloves

2 bay leaves

1 medium onion, finely chopped

1 teaspoon sea salt

½ teaspoon chili powder (if you like things spicy)

DO IT

Wash your rice, cover it with water and swirl with your hand. Continue until the water is clear when drained. Leave to soak in fresh water for at least 45 minutes. Drain well.

Blend the tomatoes and basil in a food processor and mix with the stock in a large bowl. There should be roughly 2½ cups (600ml) of liquid, so make up the amount with water if you need to.

Now pour the oil into a large heavy-bottomed saucepan and heat on medium-high. When the oil is hot, add the peppercorns, cinnamon, cloves and bay leaves, stir a few times, then add the onion. Keep stirring for 5 minutes, then add your rice. Stir gently, scraping the bottom and coating the rice with the oil.

Now stir in the tomato mixture and salt, and the chili powder if using, and bring to a boil. Cover the pan and cook on very low heat for 35–40 minutes. Never lift the lid on your rice – it needs the steam.

Fluff up the rice with a fork and serve.

Cauliflower "Rice"

FOR 4-6

This is a brilliant alternative to rice – gluten-free, very simple and something really quite different. It's just like rice, but with loads more nutrition, fewer carbohydrates and, dare I say it, more flavor. This is ideal for serving with curries. I like to add the turmeric for a little color, but it can easily be omitted to have pure white rice instead.

THE BITS

    1 large cauliflower, very finely chopped
    1 tablespoon olive oil or vegetable oil
    1 teaspoon ground turmeric
    1 tablespoon water
    1 teaspoon sea salt

DO IT

Make sure that your cauliflower is very well chopped – the easiest way is to put it into a food processor and pulse about five times, until it resembles rice. Any big bits can be picked out and kept for a later pulsing.

Heat the oil in a frying pan on medium-high and begin to fry your cauliflower. Stir it regularly, and after 5–7 minutes, when the cauliflower is getting a little color, add the turmeric and water. Continue cooking for another 5 minutes, until the cauliflower has become tender but still has a bit of bite to it.

Season with salt and serve.

Braised Fennel, Pear & Radish
with Toasted Almonds

FOR 4

This is a robust cold-weather side that can light up a dark night. The fennel and pears work brilliantly together, and the radish adds its unique pink sphere of charm. Use firm sweet pears here, or they'll end up in a mush.

THE BITS

2 tablespoons olive oil

a pinch of sea salt

1 tablespoon red wine vinegar

1–2 tablespoons whole grain mustard

1 teaspoon unrefined light brown sugar (see page 20)

2 large fennel bulbs, sliced lengthwise into 1cm thick slices

6 cloves of garlic, peeled

2 handfuls of radishes, washed and trimmed

3 sprigs of fresh thyme, leaves only, or 1 teaspoon dried thyme

¼ cup (50ml) dry white vermouth (i.e., Noilly Prat or dry Martini), or ⅓ cup (75ml) white wine (vegan)

2 ripe pears, cut lengthwise into thick slices

For the garnish

a handful of toasted almonds, roughly chopped

DO IT

Whisk together ½ tablespoon of olive oil, a pinch of sea salt, the red wine vinegar, mustard and sugar to make a dressing. Set aside.

Warm the rest of the oil in a wide heavy-bottomed frying pan on high heat. Add the fennel and fry for 3 minutes, then add the garlic and radishes and toss in the oil for another 4 minutes. Now add the thyme and vermouth and lower the heat, covering right away to trap the steam. Leave to braise for 10 minutes, shaking the pan regularly, until everything becomes beautifully browned and sticky.

Add the dressing and cook uncovered for 5 minutes longer, stirring and allowing the flavors to intensify. Add the pears and gently toss together, warming everything through, and remove from the heat.

Serve on a warm platter, topped with toasted almonds.

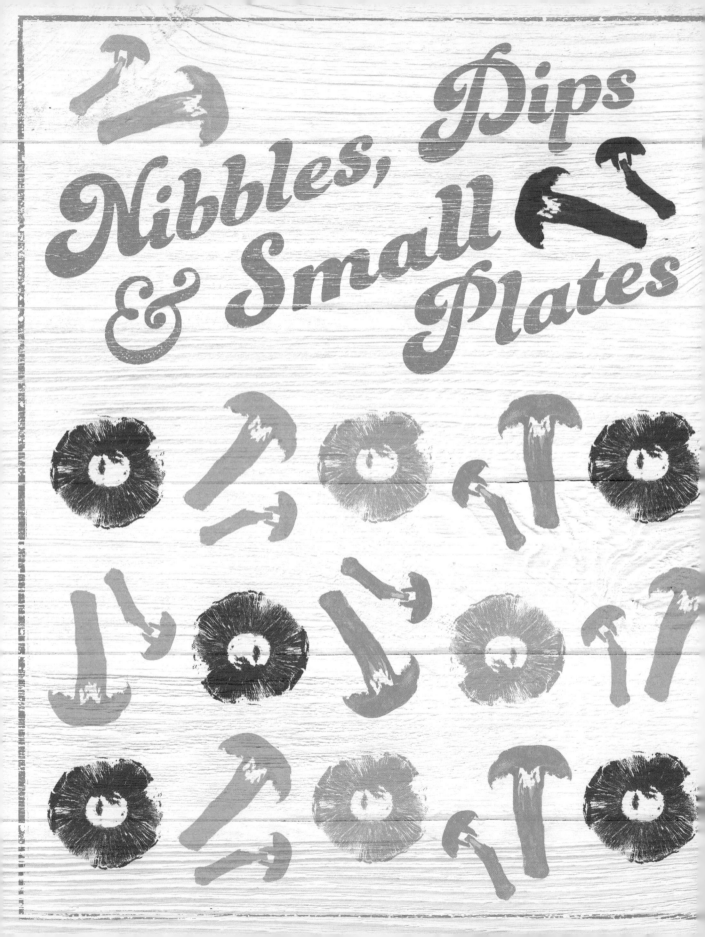

Nibbles, Dips & Small Plates

Small but perfectly formed. Modest explosions of flavor set to tantalize the palate, sparking the imagination. A prelude to a perfect main course or maybe a table full of these tasty little critters, variety being the spice of life and all.

These plates balk at "size matters" and concentrate on intensity instead. My favorite food cultures in the world do not eat off massive platters with piles of things mounded on them. I like little plates, in the middle of the table, and plenty of openhearted sharing. Bits and pieces, bites and morsels, plenty of chatting and sipping, everyone trying everyone else's food and then their own!

Serve these dishes as starters or gathered together into a smorgasbord of joyous goodness. Let's face it, it's party time! We rarely make special nibbles without having something to celebrate. Making your own nibbles is fun and, importantly, a lot cheaper than what you'll find in the supermarket. A few vegetables, a gentle fry and you have a large bowl of vegetable chips! Little things like this make me happy.

Homemeade always means more – your guests will really appreciate it, and you'll get a lot more holiday cards (most probably mentioning your spicy maple pecans). Here we have some roasted bites and perfect purées that are anything but store-bought, and the best part about them is they are comparatively very healthy! Plus they have gone nowhere near a factory, which I think is hugely important.

These recipes are not too vexing to make and are the perfect excuse to get a party started. You'll love sharing the results with your friends and loved ones. People won't even realize that you're feeding them vegan fare.

Salsa verde, page 139

Fava bean & avocado dip, page 137

Artichoke & almond purée, page 138

Vegetable Chips

MAKES ONE LARGE BOWLFUL (ENOUGH FOR 8–10 NIBBLERS)

So simple you'll stop buying the overpriced store-bought varieties. The great thing about these crispy beauts is that you can moderate the amount of salt – and eat them warm. A warm chip is a thing of deep and meaningful wonder. You can use most vegetables here, but the starchier the better. I like adding an apple to the mix as it's something a bit different.

Using a mandoline is very dangerous, so take it easy and always use the protective guard that's provided. You can use a thin blade on your food processor, although this has varying results. Most will be fine, but you'll probably be left with some chunks. Just cut these as thin as you can.

THE BITS

1 beet
1 parsnip
1 potato
1 carrot
1 small sweet potato
1 apple
cooking oil, for deep-frying
sea salt to taste

DO IT

Preheat the oven to 300°F (150°C).

Scrub all the produce, peeling any that are marked or bruised, and slice them very thinly, using a mandoline if you have one (be careful!) or the fine blade on a food processor. Fill a large, flat pan one-third full with oil and heat to 350°F (180°C), or until a slice dropped in sizzles immediately – this takes about 4 minutes.

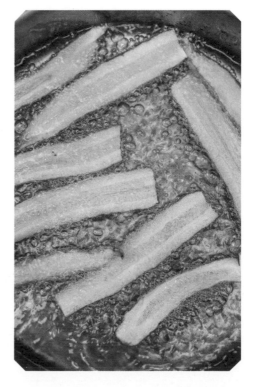

Dry off your veggies in batches, pressing them quite firmly between kitchen towels or paper towels to remove as much moisture as possible, then fry them. They all take different times to cook, so keep them separate – don't mix potato with apple, for example. Give them a little stir, making sure they don't stick together. Fry the beet and carrot first, as they can become soft after frying and need longer in the oven to crisp up.

When the chips are golden, they are ready. Drain each batch on paper towels to remove excess oil, then place on a baking tray and put them in the oven. Bake for 10–15 minutes, until they are all crispy.

Serve warm, sprinkled with sea salt.

Fava Bean & Avocado Dip with Lemon & Thyme

MAKES ONE LARGE BOWLFUL

Superbly green and full of rich, smooth, fresh flavors, this dip makes the ideal accompaniment or spread for sunshiny weather. The fava bean harvest is one of my favorite times of year. I love podding them – it's very therapeutic, although many of the beans end up in my mouth. I have found that many people prefer fava beans cooked a little, so we are going to blanch them here. If the beans are not freshly picked or it's getting late in the season, I'd recommend you peel the sometimes leathery coats off them. Otherwise, just blend them up to a vibrant bowl of vivid green and enjoy with some sliced veggies – the ubiquitous carrot works well, but you could also try beet batons or kohlrabi shards, green apple chunks or even endive boats.

THE BITS

10 ounces (300g) fava beans, shelled and blanched

2 ripe avocados, peeled and pitted

2 cloves of garlic, peeled and minced

a big handful of fresh mint, chopped

3 sprigs of fresh thyme, leaves only

juice of 1 lemon

zest of ½ a lemon

½ teaspoon sea salt

a large pinch of freshly cracked black pepper

2 tablespoons olive oil (or to taste)

DO IT

Cook the shelled fava beans in salted boiling water for 5 minutes. Drain well and cool.

Put all the ingredients except the olive oil into a food processor, and trickle in the oil while blitzing. Use enough oil to give a shimmering appearance – 2 tablespoons should do nicely, but add a bit more if necessary.

Serve with long dippers of your choice.

Artichoke & Almond Purée

MAKES ONE BIG BOWLFUL

A purée that really highlights the potential of plant-based creaminess. The richness of the almonds balances the sharpness of the artichokes and lemon, a magical match made in the Mediterranean. It's a tried-and-true "carnivore friendly" dip. In fact, some people have said that this is the highlight of a meal, and I guess if the dip overshadows the rest, you know you're doing something right. I normally buy fresh artichokes if I have time to treat them with the care they deserve. But I also use jarred ones – they're much better than canned.

THE BITS

14 ounces (400g) artichoke hearts
(jarred is fine)

2 big handfuls of almonds, soaked overnight, skins peeled off (blanched almonds are fine)

2 cloves of garlic, peeled and minced

1 teaspoon dried mint

juice of ½ a lemon

½ teaspoon sea salt

3 tablespoons olive oil

For the garnish

any leafy green fresh herb
(parsley, mint or even chives will work)

a large pinch of sweet paprika

DO IT

Place all the ingredients in a food processor and blend until creamy.

Garnish with a sprinkle of fresh herbs and paprika. Note: Normally I'd serve this with some seeded breadsticks or, if the occasion is slightly fancy, in hollowed-out cherry/small plum tomatoes (striking to look at, but admittedly a little fiddly). Easier to thinly slice a carrot, cucumber, green apple, etc., spoon a small amount of purée onto each slice, and top with herbs and paprika. Stunning!

Watercress & Butter Bean Purée

MAKES ONE BIG BOWLFUL

If you are short of time, you can use canned beans in this delicious dip, though I much prefer to soak and cook my own. Anything canned just doesn't have the same flavor or texture, and you also don't get the heavily flavored cooking stock, which can be used in all sorts of ways. If needed, add it to this purée to thin it out. Think of nutritional yeast flakes as very nutritious vegan Parmesan – they are ideal when a little cheesy savoriness is required.

THE BITS

6 large handfuls of watercress

1⅓ cup (250g) dried butter beans, soaked and cooked, or 4 cups canned, drained

2 large cloves of garlic, peeled and crushed

3–5 tablespoons olive oil

juice of ½ a lemon

1 teaspoon sea salt

For the garnish

a handful of dandelion leaves
(fresh young leaves only)

2 tablespoons nutritional yeast flakes
(optional)

DO IT

Wash the watercress and trim off the very ends of the stalks if necessary. In a small pot of salted boiling water, blanch the watercress for 1 minute and drain well in a colander.

Place all the ingredients in a food processor and blend until thick and creamy. Add a little water (or bean cooking liquid) to thin it out.

Serve on seeded crackers with some chopped dandelion leaves and sprinkled with nutritional yeast flakes.

Pinto Bean Pâté
with Walnuts & Raisins

MAKES ONE BIG BOWLFUL

This is a hearty vegan pâté, nice and chunky, with a smoky paprika twang. I generally make it during the colder months, as it's quite filling. It's perfect to serve with drinks, since it's almost a meal in itself, allowing happy hour to stretch long into the night. Note that smoked paprika can vary in quality and will age badly. If you're using the good stuff, one teaspoon will suffice in this recipe. This dip is awesome served on pumpernickel toast or any German-style heavy bread, such as Schwarzbrot (black rye bread), the daddy of all German baked goods.

THE BITS

1½ cups (285g) pinto beans, soaked and
cooked, or 4½ cups canned, drained

½ a small red onion, finely diced

3 cloves of garlic, peeled and crushed

2 tablespoons fresh thyme leaves

a handful of fresh parsley, finely chopped

3 tablespoons olive oil

½ cup (75g) roasted pumpkin seeds

¾ cup (70g) walnuts, roughly chopped

3 tablespoons raisins, roughly chopped

1 teaspoon smoked paprika

1 teaspoon sea salt

½ cup (120ml) water

For the optional garnish
a drizzle of olive oil
a pinch of smoked paprika

DO IT

Place all the ingredients except the water in a blender and drizzle in the water while blending, until a thick, chunky consistency is achieved. Don't overdo the blitzing. This is not a smooth pâté. You may like to drizzle a little more oil on top and add a sprinkle of paprika to round things off.

Salsa Verde

FOR 6

The party has not started until salsa verde lands on the canapé table – the ultimate expression of zest, herbs and fiery chili, all mingling in some form of green gorgeousness. Green sauce ("salsa verde") is made all over the world, from Italy to Mexico. Most people have their favorite balance of flavors. This is a really simple recipe – a few warm tortillas and you're on your way. If you can't find green tomatoes, just use red ones instead. Slightly unripe is probably best for this salsa. Tomatillos also work well and have a lovely tart and citrus twang, taking things in a proper Mexican direction.

THE BITS

4 large green tomatoes or tomatillos

2 big handfuls of fresh cilantro

a big handful of fresh parsley

1–2 fresh red chilies, finely diced (to taste)

2 cloves of garlic, peeled and crushed

juice of 1 large lemon or 2 small limes

zest of ½ a large lemon or 1 small lime

½–1 teaspoon sea salt (to taste)

DO IT

Place all the ingredients in a food processor and blitz until well combined, adding water as needed. Sometimes you want a thin salsa, sometimes you want something thicker. It depends on the occasion. For dips, go thick! This can be served at room temperature or cold.

Pico de Gallo

MAKES A DECENT BOWLFUL

I love this salsa – it's greater than the sum of its parts. Pico de gallo adds freshness and zing to every plate and can be served with all sorts of dishes, from burgers to burritos. It also makes a wonderful topping for soups and stews. I spent some time working on a banana farm in Nicaragua and we ate pico de gallo with every banana-based meal. The finest tomatoes will shine in this dish – the sweeter, the better. You can add a little sugar to brighten things up a bit.

THE BITS

3 ripe tomatoes, finely chopped

½ a red onion, finely diced

a big handful of cilantro leaves,
finely chopped

juice of 1 lime

1 chili, deseeded and finely chopped

½ teaspoon salt

½ teaspoon unrefined light brown sugar
(see page 20), if the tomatoes are
not sweet enough

DO IT

Combine all the ingredients in a bowl and allow to settle for half an hour.

Sweet Sake Sugar Snaps

FOR 4

You could use any other green peas or beans, like snow peas or string beans, for this lovely combination of crisp beans and sweet and salty sauce. Sake is well worth having around – it's a light, wine-like alcohol made with rice. It is delicious served warm and is also very handy to use as a substitute for mirin in Japanese-style cooking.

THE BITS

1 pound (450g) sugar snap peas

½ teaspoon sunflower oil

1 inch (2.5cm) fresh ginger, peeled
and finely grated

2 tablespoons sake (gluten-free, if needed)

2 teaspoons brown rice syrup

2–3 teaspoons tamari (to taste)

2 teaspoons toasted sesame seeds,
for topping

DO IT

Bring a pot of water to a rolling boil, then drop in the peas and cook for a minute. Drain, cool thoroughly under cold water, and drain again. Put them on a plate covered with paper towels and make sure they are nice and dry, ready to be fried.

Heat the oil in a heavy-bottomed frying pan on high. When it's very hot, add the peas and ginger, sauté for 2 minutes, then add the sake and brown rice syrup. Let the liquid reduce for a minute, then remove from the heat.

Season with tamari, sprinkle with the sesame seeds and serve immediately.

Pico de gallo

Flame-Grilled Vegetables with Chermoula & Cashew Hummus

FOR 4

Barbecues can sometimes be a lackluster affair for vegans, but these veggies are perfect for a summer grill-out – the punchy *chermoula* and creamy hummus make up for the lack of cremated sausage. I love the zest and vibrancy that chermoula brings to the party. Piles of light fluffy couscous finish this dish perfectly. Alternatively, serve as a wrap with sesame and sweet corn pancakes (see page 125).

THE BITS

1 red bell pepper, deseeded and cut into chunky strips

1 yellow bell pepper, deseeded and cut into chunky strips

1 medium eggplant, cut into ¾-inch (2cm) chunks

2 medium zucchini, cut into ¾-inch (2cm) chunks

3 small red onions, quartered

2 bulbs of fennel, fronds trimmed, cut into 1cm slices lengthwise

4 tablespoons high-quality olive oil

2 teaspoons cumin seeds

2 teaspoons caraway seeds

sea salt and freshly ground black pepper

2 handfuls of cherry tomatoes

1 x cashew hummus (see page 144)

For the chermoula

1 teaspoon coriander seeds, or ½ teaspoon ground coriander

1 teaspoon cumin seeds, or ½ teaspoon ground cumin

1 cup (100g) fresh cilantro leaves

½ cup (50g) fresh parsley

2 cloves of garlic, peeled and crushed

2 tablespoons lemon juice

2 teaspoons lemon zest

8 tablespoons olive oil

DO IT

Heat a grill pan or barbecue to high heat. Toss all the vegetables (except the tomatoes) in a large bowl with the oil, then grill for around 10 minutes, turning every so often, to char all over. You may need to do this in batches. Keep the cooked veggies covered and warm.

Preheat the oven to 400°F (200°C). Place all the vegetables, except the tomatoes, on a baking tray with the cumin and caraway seeds, then drizzle any leftover oil from the bowl on top. Season with salt and pepper. Bake the vegetables for 25–30 minutes, turning them twice and basting them with the juices. Add the tomatoes 5 minutes before the end. Meanwhile, make the cashew hummus.

To make the chermoula, dry roast the coriander and cumin seeds in a small frying pan on medium-high heat for about 1 minute (they will pop). Keep them moving and make sure they don't burn or they will become very bitter. Grind the seeds in a mortar into a powder. Add all the ingredients (except the oil) to the mortar and continue pounding, then drizzle in the oil. The chermoula should resemble a thin sauce, so add more oil if needed. Put into a bowl and set aside.

Serve the vegetables on large warmed plates, drizzled generously with chermoula and with the cashew hummus on the side.

Cashew Hummus

MAKES ONE BIG BOWLFUL

Most vegans have a long and committed love affair with the cashew – it has such a gorgeous, silky-smooth feel and subtle, creamy flavor. Soaking nuts unlocks the enzymes within and allows the nutrition of the nut to be better utilized by the body. Soaking also makes them nice and soft, which is ideal when blending these precious little gifts. I like a decent amount of tahini in my hummus. It boosts this recipe into the stratosphere of outrageously healthy and delicious. This hummus is quite rich, and you only need a small spoonful. Enjoy it responsibly! Sometimes I mix two handfuls of fresh basil leaves in here.

THE BITS

2 cups (300g) cashews, soaked overnight

1–2 big cloves of garlic (to taste), peeled and crushed

juice of ½ a lemon

½ teaspoon sea salt

3 tablespoons tahini (gluten-free, if needed)

½ teaspoon freshly ground cumin seeds

scant ½ cup (100ml) olive oil, plus extra for drizzling

⅓ cup (75ml) water

DO IT

Place the cashews, garlic, lemon juice, salt, tahini and cumin seeds in a food processor and blitz, turning off the machine and scraping down the sides regularly.

Once combined, blitz continuously and drizzle in the olive oil. When you are getting towards the right consistency, add the water (this lightens the hummus a little). Keep blitzing and drizzling in oil until the desired texture is achieved. Cashews don't thicken up in the fridge like chickpeas, so don't make it too thin.

Serve drizzled with olive oil, with long celery stick dippers and a smile.

Oven-Baked "Gigglebeans"

SERVES 6

Superbly simple party food and homemade nibble goodness. Gigglebeans are what our German brothers and sisters call their *Kichererbsen,* or chickpeas. They're very nutritious and more wallet-friendly than buying loads of cheap chips. Healthy nibbles are far too rare, and most chickpea snacks are deep-fried. The vast amounts of oil tend to negate the shining health properties of your gigglebeans. Granted, there is a hefty glug of oil in these chickers, but you can always add less and they still turn out wonderfully. You can do all sorts of things with these roasted chickpeas – I normally like to add some warm, smoky spices.

THE BITS

1¾ cups (350g) dried chickpeas, soaked overnight

1 cup (250ml) sunflower or peanut oil

1½ teaspoons sea salt

½ teaspoon smoked paprika

¼ teaspoon cayenne pepper

¼ teaspoon ground cinnamon

DO IT

Preheat the oven to 350°F (180°C).

Drain your chickpeas really well and pat them dry with a kitchen towel. Combine the chickpeas and oil on a baking tray, allowing enough space for the chickpeas to spread out. You don't want them stacked up. Bake for 20 minutes, give them a good stir, then bake for 10–15 minutes more. They should be golden and very crispy at this stage.

Pour them onto a large plate covered with lots of paper towels to absorb any extra oil, then put them into a serving dish. Mix the salt and spices in a small bowl and sprinkle over the hot chickpeas.

Reserve a few of the gigglebeans for yourself, because these suckers don't last long in the wild. Serve immediately.

Spicy Maple Pecans

FOR 4

This is a great way to spice up your nuts – I love the combination of sweet and spicy. Pecans and maple are Canada's answer to chapati and chai, tequila and nachos, black coffee and a slab of dark chocolate. This is a special-occasion snack, a full-on celebration nibble. You can use any nut you like with this recipe and the results will be similarly spectacular. Real maple syrup is costly, but I always recommend keeping some stashed in your cupboards. Less is more with maple syrup, and you cannot replicate that flavor.

THE BITS

2 cups (200g) pecans

2 tablespoons unrefined brown sugar (see page 20)

1–1½ teaspoons sea salt

⅓ teaspoon cayenne pepper

a large pinch of ground cinnamon

1 teaspoon sweet paprika

a large pinch of ground ginger

3 tablespoons maple syrup

1 tablespoon water

2 teaspoons cooking oil

1 teaspoon orange zest

DO IT

Heat a large heavy-bottomed frying pan on medium, then throw in your nuts and gently toast, stirring almost constantly and making sure they don't burn. After 7–8 minutes you should be getting gorgeous aromas of toasted nuttiness. Add the rest of the ingredients to the pan, then heat through and stir for 2–3 minutes on low heat.

Spread the nuts out on a baking tray or a large plate – the coating should be clinging to them. Leave to cool slightly, and serve warm.

Mixed Nut Cheewra

FOR 6

Now this is a real nut-fest! A spicy one at that. Indians know how to nibble and are experts at producing savory snacks, or *namkeen*. Most of these salty snacks are deep-fried and they come in piles of glorious colors and varieties. It seems that all grains and legumes, all shapes and sizes, are given the namkeen treatment. In the traditional version of this dish, the focus is on rice. *Cheewra*, also known as *poha*, is magnificent served with grated onion, tomato and fresh cilantro (don't forget the healthy pinch of spices). In winter, you may like to add chestnuts to the mix.

THE BITS

3 tablespoons vegetable oil

1 teaspoon cumin seeds

2 teaspoons black mustard seeds

3 tablespoons unrefined brown sugar (see page 20), or sugar of your choice – jaggery works well

2 teaspoons garam masala

½ teaspoon ground turmeric

a large pinch of cayenne pepper

a large pinch of freshly ground black pepper

1–1½ teaspoons sea salt (to taste)

a handful each of raw almonds, walnuts, peanuts, cashews and raisins

2 handfuls of plain puffed cereal (rice is traditional, but anything puffed up will do; choose a gluten-free option if you need to)

DO IT

Preheat the oven to 350°F (180°C).

Heat the oil in a large frying pan on medium for a minute, then add the cumin and mustard seeds and allow them to splutter and pop for 30 seconds. Add the sugar and wait for it to melt a little, then add in the spices and salt. Stir constantly and let it bubble for a minute, making sure the sugar doesn't burn. You don't want a full caramel here, just slightly melted sugar.

Add the nuts to the pan and give them a good coating of the sticky spice mix. Spread the nutty goodness out on a foil-lined baking tray and bake for 15–20 minutes, until golden brown. Stir a few times during the baking, and keep your eye on them.

Set aside and let them cool slightly on the tray, then place in a bowl and mix in the raisins and puffed grains.

Serve warm, to "oohs" and "aahs" from your guests.

Young Leeks, Watercress & Asparagus with Tofu Gribiche

FOR 4–6

Some of my most magical memories are of camping in the Côte d'Or in France during *le vendange* (the grape-picking season). By 10 a.m. we had already munched our first whole baguette, the grape-pickers' version of an express lunch, containing lashings of butter, marinated artichokes, local cheese and slabs of chocolate (this was in pre-vegan times of rampant indigestion). I returned home like an overweight lump of salted *beurre*, with Beaujolais-tinted cheeks and a smile painted on my face. Many things have changed since then, but my love of old-fashioned romance, good French wine and *gribiche* are undiminished. I have tampered in a vegan fashion with the traditional recipe, while keeping the tangy herbiness of this condiment that I love so much.

THE BITS

1 pound (500g) young leeks, trimmed and cleaned

14 ounces (400g) young asparagus, trimmed

10½ ounces (300g) watercress, washed well and dried

1 tablespoon olive oil

3 tablespoons toasted pine nuts

For the tofu gribiche

8½ ounces (240g) firm tofu, pressed (see page 18)

3 teaspoons capers, drained and roughly chopped

2 tablespoons chopped fresh tarragon leaves

1 tablespoon chopped fresh chervil or parsley

sea salt and freshly ground black pepper to taste

3 tablespoons olive oil

½ teaspoon unrefined light brown sugar (see page 20)

1 tablespoon lemon juice

1 teaspoon Dijon mustard

DO IT

Make the gribiche first. Put the tofu into a bowl and break it down using a fork – it should resemble hard-boiled eggs. Add the capers and herbs and season well. Mix together the oil, sugar, lemon juice and mustard in a small bowl and stir it into the tofu mixture. Cover and pop into the fridge for at least 30 minutes (2 hours is ideal).

Fill a medium saucepan two-thirds full with water, add a little salt, and bring to a rolling boil. Dunk in your leeks and cook for a couple of minutes, then remove with a slotted spoon and set aside to cool. Allow the water to come back to a boil, plunge in your asparagus and cook for a couple of minutes, then remove and set aside. Bring the water back to a boil again, blanch the watercress for 30 seconds and set aside. (Keep this water: it is awesome stock.)

When cooled, dry the asparagus and leeks (the leeks may need a gentle squeeze). Put a grill pan on high heat and brush with a little olive oil. When very hot, chargrill the leeks and asparagus for 1 minute on each side. This will bring out even more of their flavors.

Once the vegetables are cool, place them on a shallow serving plate with the watercress. Spoon the gribiche on top and garnish with a scattering of pine nuts. It's a green feast!

Toasted Sourdough with Roasted Zucchini, Tomatoes, Marjoram & Almond Cream

FOR 4

Here's a shining summer starter, or lunch, that takes advantage of glorious fresh seasonal produce and bread that is slightly past its prime. This is the kind of thing I imagine Italians tucking into on their leisurely afternoon break. I don't often eat bread, but when I do, sourdough is my preference. As for the tomatoes, I actually rarely skin mine since I'm lazy!

Gluten-free option: use your favorite GF bread.

THE BITS

12 ounces (350g) ripe tomatoes

2 small green zucchini, trimmed and cut lengthwise into 1cm strips

plenty of extra virgin olive oil

3 cloves of garlic, peeled and crushed with 1 teaspoon sea salt

a handful of fresh marjoram leaves

a large pinch of salt and freshly cracked black pepper

3 thick slices of sourdough bread (slightly stale will work)

a handful of fresh basil leaves

1 teaspoon lemon juice

For the almond cream

a big handful of almonds (soaked, with skins slipped off or blanched)

¼ cup (50ml) unsweetened almond milk (soy will do)

1 teaspoon nutritional yeast flakes

a pinch of sea salt

½ tablespoon extra virgin olive oil

DO IT

Preheat the oven to 400°F (200°C). If peeling the tomatoes, bring a small pot of water to a boil, then cut an "X" in the base of your tomatoes and drop them into the water. Blanch for a minute, then take them out and place them in a large bowl of cold water. Once cool, peel them.

Rub the zucchini slices with olive oil and place them on a baking tray. In a small bowl, mix together the garlic, marjoram leaves and 2 tablespoons of olive oil and season with salt and pepper. Drizzle this mixture over your zucchini and roast for 15–20 minutes.

Meanwhile, tear your sourdough into roughly 2-inch (5cm) cubes, place them on another baking tray and drizzle with a good glug of olive oil. Toss the bread with your hands to coat with the oil. Pop in the oven for 5–7 minutes, then toss again and put back into the oven for 3–4 minutes. The bread should be crisped on the outside, but still chewy in the middle.

To make the almond cream, put the soaked almonds into a food processor and blend until creamy – you should have something resembling a loose peanut butter. You will need to scrape the sides of the processor a few times. Add the rest of the ingredients and blend until a smooth sauce forms.

On a large serving platter, lay out your warm sourdough pieces. Cut all the tomatoes in half horizontally and squeeze the juice and seeds from half of them over your bread. Roughly chop the flesh of the squeezed tomatoes and sprinkle on top. Lay your zucchini slices on top in a lattice fashion and scatter on the rest of your halved tomatoes. Gently tear your basil leaves and shower them over the dish, then sprinkle with the lemon juice. Spoon your almond cream on top and serve immediately.

Beet & Cumin Fritters with Horseradish & Dill Yogurt

MAKES 8–10 FRITTERS

These little fritters are bursting at the seams with flavors, and the herbaceous horseradish yogurt tops things off very nicely. A punchy, zesty sauce is perfect with any fried food, lighting up the palate. The sweet earthiness of the beet and the fragrance of cumin were, very simply, made for each other. I'll use any green peas or beans for this, but the edamame probably have the edge due to their nice crunchy texture, which adds an almost nutty bite to the fritters. Use any flour you like, but I prefer to keep them gluten-free. Gram (chickpea) flour would work well.

THE BITS

1 large potato, scrubbed and cut into cubes

4½ ounces (125g) firm tofu, pressed (see page 18) and well mashed

⅓ cup (40g) buckwheat or whole wheat flour

a handful of fresh mint leaves, finely chopped

zest of 1 lemon

1 teaspoon sea salt

¼ teaspoon freshly ground black pepper

10½ ounces (300g) beets, scrubbed and coarsely grated

a handful of edamame/green peas/fava beans

1½ teaspoons cumin seeds, toasted and roughly ground

vegetable oil, for frying

1 x horseradish & dill yogurt (see page 306)

For the garnish

a big handful of watercress or spinach leaves

2 scallions, thinly sliced

DO IT

Put the potato into a small pot, cover with water, add a pinch of salt and bring to a boil. Cook for 25 minutes, until soft. Drain in a colander, mash well and leave to cool.

Make the horseradish and dill yogurt. This can be done well in advance.

Once the potato has cooled to handling temperature, mix with the mashed tofu, flour, mint leaves, lemon, salt and pepper. Now gently mix in the grated beet and peas, until well combined – using your hands is best. We'd like these fritters to be chunky and packed full of texture.

In a large heavy-bottomed frying pan, dry toast your cumin seeds on medium-low heat for a minute. They should pop and give off a lovely aroma. Put them into a mortar and mash them up a little, then stir them into the fritter mix.

In the same pan, warm ½ tablespoon of oil on medium heat, ensuring that the bottom of the pan is evenly covered with a film of oil. Spoon in 2 heaped tablespoons of fritter mixture per go, pressing it down a little with the back of the spoon until it's roughly 1cm thick. Cook for 3–4 minutes on one side and slightly less on the other. Repeat until you have a few fritters cooking at the same time, and continue to cook in batches. Drain on paper towels and keep them warm in a low-temperature oven.

Serve warm and crispy on a bed of vibrant green watercress or spinach leaves, garnished with the scallions and with the horseradish and dill yogurt on the side.

Muhammara (Syrian Roasted Pepper & Walnut Dip) with Warm Black Olives

FOR ONE SMALL BOWLFUL

This dish goes above and beyond the call of a dip. The combination of flavors are quintessentially southern Mediterranean, which is some kind of Eden for the vegan-leaning foodie. Many cultures call *muhammara* their own, and I'm not weighing on to that debate. I just know that all is good in the world when warm pita encounters muhammara and the salty twang of good olives.

Gluten-free option: swap the bread for your favorite GF variety.

THE BITS

2 large red bell peppers

2 tablespoons fruity olive oil

1 teaspoon red pepper flakes

2 slices of whole wheat bread, crusts removed (stale bread works best)

2 big handfuls of walnuts

1½ tablespoons pomegranate molasses (add the juice of ½ a lemon if you can't get this)

1 teaspoon unrefined brown sugar (see page 20)

½ teaspoon smoked paprika

4½ ounces (125g) firm tofu

½ teaspoon sea salt

For the warm olives

2 tablespoons olive oil

½ teaspoon cumin seeds

½ teaspoon fennel seeds

½ teaspoon red pepper flakes

1 clove of garlic, peeled and crushed

1¼ cups (200g) high-quality black olives, pitted

zest of ½ a lemon

2 tablespoons fresh parsley

For the garnish

a glug of olive oil

½ a handful of fresh parsley, finely chopped

a large pinch of smoked paprika

DO IT

Preheat the oven to 425°F (220°C).

Using your hands, rub the peppers with a little of the olive oil and place on a baking tray. Roast them for 15–20 minutes, turning them over once, until the skins are slightly blackened and the peppers are very tender. Place in a bowl and cover to allow them to cool. Once cooled, cut the peppers in half and scoop the seeds out with a spoon. Peel the bitter skin off – it should slip off easily.

Place the peppers and all the other muhamarra ingredients in a food processor and blitz until creamy.

For the warm olives, place the oil, cumin seeds, fennel seeds, red pepper flakes and garlic in a small pan and fry for 30 seconds, then add the olives and lemon zest and bring to a gentle simmer. Remove from the heat and stir in the parsley. Cover and set aside until you're ready to serve.

Serve the muhammara in the center of a large serving platter, drizzled with olive oil and sprinkled with parsley and smoked paprika, with toasted pita bread around the edge and a bowl filled with the warm olives.

Greek Filo Parcelettes with Creamy Pesto

MAKES 24

Greece made a huge impression on my palate when I was a young fellow. The main attractions on many Greek menus are of course the fresh seafood and hearty meat dishes, but like many great food cultures, once you scratch the surface, a whole host of vegan options pour in. I love dolmades (stuffed grape leaves), but struggled to locate vine leaves in rural Wales. I reached for the filo instead, and a very, very minor part of food history was made. This has all the flavors of dolmades, surrounded by crispy filo and served fresh from the oven.

THE BITS

½ cup (125ml) olive oil + 1 tablespoon for frying the onion

1 large red onion, finely sliced

scant 1 cup (175g) uncooked long-grain brown rice (white is also cool, and millet is very cool indeed!)

1 teaspoon ground allspice

1 teaspoon sea salt

½ teaspoon freshly ground black pepper

3 tablespoons lemon juice

1 tablespoon lemon zest

3 tablespoons currants, roughly chopped

½ a handful of mint leaves, finely chopped

a handful of fresh dill, finely chopped

3 tablespoons toasted pine nuts

12 sheets of filo pastry

1 x creamy pesto (see page 312)

For the garnish

1 lemon, cut into wedges

DO IT

Heat 1 tablespoon of oil in a large saucepan and add the onion. Fry gently for 3–4 minutes, then stir in the rice, allspice, salt and pepper, along with half the lemon juice. Pour in enough cold water to cover by 1 inch (3cm) and bring slowly to a boil. Cover tightly with a lid, and simmer gently for 35–40 minutes. Remove the lid and fluff the rice up with a fork, gently mixing in the remaining lemon juice and zest, currants, mint, dill and pine nuts. Season if needed and allow to cool. Meanwhile, make your creamy pesto.

Now you need to make a bit of space. The quicker and more organized you are, the easier the next step will be. Be gentle with the filo, as it breaks very easily. On a well-oiled surface, lay out a sheet of filo and brush well with olive oil. Lay another sheet of filo on top, being as exact as possible (this is not easy!). Brush with olive oil, add one more sheet and – you guessed it! – brush more olive oil on it. This gives the filo its richness; otherwise it would be a bit of a dried-up affair.

Now cut the filo rectangle into six squares, using the tip of a sharp knife. Spoon 1 tablespoon of filling into the center of each square and brush the outer edges with a little oil. Gather all the edges into the center and pinch them above the filling to form a small, taut money-bag shape. Brush with olive oil, especially the random frilly edges that stick out. Continue with vigor and nimble fingers, making many tasty parcelettes.

Preheat the oven to 325°F (170°C). Using a spatula, gently place the parcelettes on an oiled baking tray (you may need two). Bake for 10 minutes, then swap and turn the trays (so they are evenly browned) and bake for another 10 minutes, until very golden and crisp. Serve the parcelettes with a bowl of the creamy pesto for dipping and a scattering of freshly cut lemon wedges.

Shiitake Tempura with Wasabi Mayo

FOR 4–6

There's an art to frying tempura so that it results in the lightest of batters, crispy and retaining very little oil. This form of deep-frying is actually healthier than most shallow-frying. It's all about the temperature – if that's right, the food doesn't absorb so much oil. It just happily fizzes and bubbles away towards golden perfection. Tempura is only good when the oil is very hot and the batter is chilled. If you have any of this batter left over, just fry it on its own – it makes a great little snack. If you can't get your hands on shiitake mushrooms, any mushroom will do and can be cooked in the same way.

THE BITS

2 cups (500ml) cooking oil (or enough for deep-frying)

4 tablespoons unbleached all-purpose flour,
for dusting

10½ ounces (300g) fresh shiitake mushrooms
(oyster mushrooms are also rather nice)

For the batter
scant 2 cups (240g) unbleached all-purpose flour

2 cups (475ml) cold (iced) water

½ teaspoon sea salt

For the wasabi mayo
9 ounces (250g) silken tofu

juice of ½ a lemon

3–4 tablespoons wasabi

2 tablespoons olive oil

sea salt to taste

For the garnish
3 handfuls of watercress or spinach leaves

DO IT

To make the mayo, blend the tofu, lemon juice and wasabi together in a food processor. Drizzle in the olive oil. Check the seasoning and spoon into a small bowl for dipping purposes.

Lightly whisk together your batter ingredients in a shallow bowl. Don't worry about lumps (they make the tempura even lighter). Pop it into the fridge for 20 minutes to chill.

Warm the oven on its lowest setting. Heat the oil to between 320°F (160°C) and 350°F (180°C) in a heavy-bottomed pan – a wide saucepan is perfect. The oil is ready when it's slightly smoking and a drop of batter sizzles vigorously.

Gently dust the shiitake mushrooms with the remaining flour. This will help the batter to cling to the shrooms.

Dip the shrooms into the batter, covering them all over, and put them straight into the hot oil. Don't be too precious here; quickly works best. The closer your batter bowl is to the pan, the less batter you'll dribble everywhere. Fry in batches (don't overcrowd the pan) for 1–2 minutes, then remove using a slotted spoon and drain very well on paper towels.

Continue frying until you've used all the shiitakes. The warm oven is handy for keeping the tempura crispy, so have a baking tray with a wire rack (to allow the excess oil to drain) handy when frying. This takes a little of the pressure off to get everything done in double-quick time. Tempura MUST be crispy.

Serve hot, with watercress or spinach leaves and small bowls of the wasabi mayo on the side. If you have any leftover batter, consider frying any other fruits and vegetables that are in the vicinity. Tempura is a batter bonanza for all produce!

Extras

- Tempura is so versatile. Mix the batter with chopped onions and some corn, spoon into hot oil, fry for a minute or so and you have yourself a fritter.

- Tempura parsnips are incredible and can be made in the same way as the shiitakes – just add one more minute to the cooking time.

Chestnut & Enoki Mushroom Gyoza with Teriyaki Dipping Sauce

MAKES 20 DUMPLINGS

Enoki mushrooms are Asian in origin, but are widely available here nowadays. Egg-free dumpling wrappers can be found in Asian food shops – they normally come in quite big packages, so I freeze them in small batches to use later. If your dumpling wrapper looks yellow, it's probably got egg in it. Egg-free wrappers are normally quite pale. The dumplings are a little tricky to make, but once you get your groove on, they become easier and pack a heavyweight flavor punch. I pan-steam mine, but they can be fried if you like – the results are, as you'd imagine, crispy, golden and delicious. Pan-steaming these dumplings means you get a nice soft top and a crispy base, like proper Japanese *gyoza* (*jiaozi* in China – these types of dumplings are sometimes called "pot-stickers"). These gyoza freeze wonderfully. I usually make a double batch and keep half to be cooked at a later date.

Gluten-free option: you can find GF dumpling wrappers made with rice.

THE BITS

10 roasted chestnuts (see method on next page), peeled and finely chopped

2 cloves of garlic, peeled and finely grated

1½ inches (4cm) fresh ginger, peeled and finely grated

½ a yellow bell pepper, finely diced

2 scallions, finely sliced

½ an eggplant, finely diced

2 teaspoons toasted sesame oil

2 tablespoons vegetable oil

3 ounces (80g) enoki mushrooms, roughly chopped, woody stems discarded

1½ tablespoons tamari

20 egg-free wonton wrappers

⅓–⅔ cup (100–150ml) water

chili oil to taste

1 x teriyaki sauce (see page 305) or see an alternate dipping sauce at the end of this recipe

(continued) →

DO IT

First make your teriyaki sauce.

If your chestnuts are not already roasted, make a small incision in the domed end of each one and place on a baking tray. Preheat the oven to 350°F (180°C) and roast for 20 minutes, turning them over once. They should be lovely and sweet and tender inside by then (and not exploding!). I normally do a whole bunch at once and save the rest to use in another recipe.

Put the garlic, ginger, yellow pepper, scallions, eggplant and sesame oil into a food processor and pulse a few times, until well broken up and coarse.

Warm 1 tablespoon of vegetable oil in a frying pan on medium heat. Add the eggplant mixture and cook for 5–7 minutes, then add the mushrooms, chestnuts and tamari. Cook for another 5 minutes, until any liquid has evaporated.

Lay out your wonton wrappers. Lightly moisten the upper half of the wrapper with a light brushing of water. Spoon 1½ teaspoons of the filling into the center of the wrapper and fold the bottom half up to meet the top half. Press the center down, then gently press the edges down to seal. Don't overfill the dumplings or they'll explode! You may exhibit your origami skills here – I like to fold them like mini empanadas – or you can just press the edges lightly between your index finger and thumb, making a classic-looking dumpling that stands up.

Brush a large frying pan with 1 tablespoon of vegetable oil and place on medium-high heat. When it is getting hot and slightly smoking, add the dumplings and sizzle for a minute to get them lightly golden. Add the water, cover tightly with a lid and leave to steam away. The dumplings are done when all the water has evaporated and one side is golden brown – 1–2 minutes will suffice. Add more water to the pan if it evaporates very quickly, and keep an eye on it. Take the lid off and add the remaining oil, then cook for another minute, until the bases are dark brown and crisp and the tops are steamed. The dumplings may stick to the pan a little, which is fine – remove them gently with a thin spatula.

Serve straight from the pan, with chili oil and/or teriyaki sauce, or combine 3 tablespoons of tamari, 3 tablespoons of rice wine vinegar and 2 teaspoons of brown rice syrup to make a simple Japanese dipping sauce. Dig in!

Lentil & Quinoa Falafel with Tahini Lemon Sauce

MAKES 20–24

This is a brilliant vegan barbecue idea. The tahini sauce adds wonderful richness and a heightened sense of a Lebanese street corner. Once you get the falafel mix together you can manipulate it into whatever shape you like: quarter-pounders normally go down very well on the barbecue, or you can go for the usual, smaller falafel shape. The lentils and quinoa are best cooked in advance, cooled and mixed together. You can keep them in the fridge until needed. These are also wonderful with the green tomato, ginger & orange chutney (on page 307).

Gluten-free option: use gram (chickpea) flour instead of the breadcrumbs, and GF wraps.

THE BITS

1 cup (175g) dried brown or green lentils

1 cup (175g) uncooked quinoa

1 small onion

3 cloves of garlic, peeled

1-inch (2.5cm) cube of ginger

1 teaspoon cumin seeds

2 teaspoons coriander seeds

1 tablespoon olive oil

½ teaspoon ground turmeric

¼ teaspoon ground allspice

¼ teaspoon red pepper flakes or ¼ teaspoon chili powder

1 teaspoon sea salt

3½ ounces (100g) silken tofu

¾ cup (80g) very fine breadcrumbs or a scant ½ cup (50g) gram (chickpea) flour

½ teaspoon baking soda

3 tablespoons toasted sunflower seeds

½ tablespoon sesame seeds

a handful of fresh parsley, finely chopped

2 tablespoons raisins, finely chopped

zest of ½ a lemon

For dusting

¼ cup (25g) gram (chickpea) flour

½ tablespoon sesame seeds

For the tahini lemon sauce

⅓ cup (100g) tahini (gluten-free, if needed)

zest and juice of ½ a lemon

2 ounces (50g) silken tofu

1 large clove of garlic, peeled and crushed

¼ teaspoon ground cumin

a large pinch of sea salt

⅓ cup (75ml) water

To serve

4–6 whole wheat wraps

2 tomatoes, finely chopped

3 scallions, finely sliced

¼ tablespoon toasted sesame seeds

½ a handful of fresh parsley, chopped

crisp salad leaves

1 teaspoon sumac (optional)

DO IT

To cook the lentils, put them into a pot and cover with water. Pick out any funny-looking bits that come to the top. Drain, then cover completely with fresh water. Bring to a boil, then lower the heat to a slow simmer and cook for 30–35 minutes, until tender. Drain well and leave to cool.

(continued) →

Put the quinoa into the same pan and cover with ¾ inch (2cm) of water. Bring to a light boil, then cover and leave to simmer for 15–20 minutes (according to package instructions). Fluff up with a fork, then leave to cool. Mix with the lentils and set aside.

Put the onion, garlic and ginger into a food processor and blend to a thick paste.

Toast the cumin and coriander seeds in a large heavy-bottomed frying pan for a minute, until fragrant, then grind with a pestle and mortar. Put 1 tablespoon of olive oil into the same frying pan and warm on medium heat. Drop in the onion paste and fry for 5 minutes, stirring regularly, until it turns slightly golden. Add the spices and salt and warm through for about 2 minutes, until fragrant. Now stir in the silken tofu and leave to cool.

Place the breadcrumbs/gram flour and baking soda in a food processor with the onion mixture and two-thirds of the lentils and quinoa, and blend until smooth. Transfer to a large bowl and add the seeds, parsley, raisins, lemon zest and the rest of the lentils and quinoa. Combine well with a wooden spoon and place in the fridge for 30 minutes.

Preheat the oven to 350°F (180°C).

Using your hands (wet them a little; it's a lot easier), shape the mixture into falafel shapes (think golf ball but slightly larger). Scatter the gram flour and sesame seeds for dusting on a plate and toss the falafels in this mixture, giving them a good coating. Place them on a large, well-oiled baking tray, turning them over to coat them in oil. Bake in the oven for 25–30 minutes, turning them once.

To make the tahini lemon sauce, place all the ingredients except the water in a food processor and blitz together, adding the water gradually. You should have a thin and rich sauce, easily pourable.

Serve the falafels on warm whole wheat wraps, with crisp salad leaves and chopped tomato and scallions, drizzled with the tahini and lemon sauce (with more in a small bowl for dipping purposes) and with a sprinkle of sesame seeds and chopped parsley. If you have some sumac handy, sprinkle it on top as well.

Raw Lumpia with Dipping Sauce

MAKES 12 SPRING ROLLS

Lumpia are a type of spring roll popular in Manila. They are usually served with a brown, Asian-style dipping sauce, but I also like Pinakurat, a fermented coconut vinegar (if you can get it), and malt vinegar is fine, too. Lumpia are normally very simple – carrots, bean sprouts and cabbage – but I have gone a little wild and added some of my favorite ingredients. I've also made them raw, because although the fried version is delicious, it has a habit of being quite greasy. These spring rolls are light and very easy to prepare. They should be nice fat spring rolls, two per person.

THE BITS

12 rice spring roll wrappers

1 x Asian-style dipping sauce (see page 306)

For the filling

½ a small sweet potato, peeled and coarsely grated

2 big handfuls of bean sprouts

½ a yellow bell pepper, sliced into fine matchsticks

6 leaves of Chinese (napa) cabbage or bok choy, finely shredded

7 ounces (200g) firm tofu, pressed (see page 18) and crumbled

3 scallions, finely sliced

3 tablespoons grated coconut or desiccated coconut

2 cloves of garlic, peeled and crushed

1½ inches (4cm) fresh ginger, finely grated

1 large red chili, deseeded, very finely diced

a handful of cashews, finely chopped

juice and zest of ½ a lime

¼ teaspoon Chinese five-spice powder

a handful of finely chopped fresh cilantro

½ teaspoon sea salt

To serve

⅓ cup (75ml) coconut vinegar (Pinakurat; optional), tamari or sweet chili sauce

DO IT

First make the dipping sauce. It's best made a little in advance, to allow for flavor mingling.

Put all the filling ingredients into a large bowl and combine well.

Soak your rice wrappers in warm water, following the package instructions. Lay out the wrappers on a slightly damp chopping board and place 3 tablespoons of filling on each, closer to one edge than the other. Wrap 'em up into long spring rolls by folding both ends over the filling, then turning the roll over once and then again. This should make a tight, slightly translucent spring roll. You'll get the hang of this – it's a great life skill. Once a spring roller, always a spring roller!

You can serve them whole, or slice them diagonally down the middle, so you can see all the glorious innards. Serve with bowls of the dipping sauce and coconut vinegar, if you have it.

Masarap (tasty)!

Olive, Artichoke & Pine Nut Pissaladière

FOR 4

This is a lovely thin-style pizza from Provence. I don't like a lot of soft dough when I munch a pizza – it has to be crispy and light. There are normally a few anchovies on top, but I think the olives, sweet peppers and artichokes in this recipe more than make up for the lack of fishiness. My mate Mike (the meatiest geezer alive) makes the best *pissaladière* I have ever tasted. I am sure he'd be happy with this plant-inspired version. This dish works best with high-quality black olives and jarred, well-rinsed artichokes (unless you have time to prepare fresh ones).

THE BITS

3–4 tablespoons olive oil

3 large onions, peeled and chopped

2 cloves of garlic, peeled and crushed

½ teaspoon unrefined light brown sugar (see page 20)

1 tablespoon balsamic vinegar

2 red bell peppers, deseeded and cut into long, thick strips

4 tablespoons black olives, pitted and cut in half lengthwise

2 tablespoons fresh thyme leaves 7 ounces (200g) artichoke hearts, thinly sliced

sea salt and freshly ground black pepper

For the dough

1 teaspoon dried yeast

¾ cup (175ml) water

1¾ cup (250g) unbleached bread flour

½ teaspoon salt

2 tablespoons olive oil

For the garnish

4 tablespoons pine nut Parmesan (see page 313)

DO IT

To make the dough, dissolve the yeast in 1 tablespoon of the water. Sift the flour and salt into a large bowl. Make a well in the center, pour in the yeast and the rest of the water, along with the olive oil, and mix together with your hands to make a tacky dough. Knead on a lightly floured surface for 5–6 minutes, or until the dough is nice and elastic. Lightly oil the dough with your hands and pop it into a bowl. Cover it with a damp kitchen towel and leave in a warm place for about an hour, until doubled in size.

Now heat 1 tablespoon of olive oil in a heavy-bottomed frying pan and add the onions. Cook for 45 minutes on low heat, stirring regularly, until the onions are caramelized and very golden. Add a splash of water and lower the heat slightly if the onions are sticking. Add the garlic, turn up the heat, and cook for 3 minutes more, then add the sugar and balsamic vinegar. Stir and cook for another 10 minutes. By this time you should have something resembling a sweet and slightly sticky onion marmalade. Perfect. Heat 2 teaspoons of olive oil in a small frying pan and sauté your red peppers. Cook for 8–10 minutes, until they are caramelized all over. Preheat the oven to 400°F (200°C).

Give your dough a quick knead, then roll it out very thinly on a lightly floured piece of parchment paper into a roughly 10 x 14-inch (25 x 30cm) rectangle. Remember, it will rise a little in the oven. Using the parchment paper, lift the base onto a baking tray and spread on a layer of onions, then sprinkle with the olives and thyme and add a good covering of artichokes and peppers. Drizzle lightly with olive oil and a sprinkle of sea salt and pepper. Brush the crust with olive oil and pop into the oven for 20–25 minutes, until the base is crisp and golden brown. Sprinkle with the pine nut Parmesan and serve.

Seitan & Sweet Potato Kebabs with Mango Barbecue Sauce

FOR 6 LARGE KEBABS

Full of tang and sweetness, these kebabs are the perfect skewer to whip out when you have friends and family coming over who are not part of the tofu brigade. Try to buy seitan in big chunks for these kebabs – it tastes like meat (which will confuse everybody!).

THE BITS

8½ ounces (240g) seitan, well drained, cut into 2-inch (5cm) chunks

2 tablespoons tamari

2 sweet potatoes, scrubbed and cut into 1-inch (2.5cm) cubes

1 tablespoon vegetable oil

1 yellow bell pepper, cut into 2-inch (5cm) chunks

1 green bell pepper, cut into 2-inch (5cm) chunks

1 plantain, cut into 2-inch (5cm) chunks

1 red onion, cut into quarters, then halved

6 large red chilies (if you like chilies!)

3 tablespoons olive oil

sea salt and freshly ground black pepper

1 x mango barbecue sauce (see page 301)

For the garnish

6 handfuls of watercress or spinach

DO IT

You will need six long wooden or metal skewers. If you are using wooden ones, soak them in water for 1 hour beforehand (this stops them from burning).

Either preheat the oven to 350°F (180°C) or start heating your barbecue grill. You can also use a grill pan on the stove. Put the seitan into a bowl (squeezing out any excess liquid) and add the tamari. Mix together and leave to marinate for 30 minutes in the fridge. Toss the sweet potatoes in a little vegetable oil and roast in the oven for 20 minutes to soften them slightly before barbecuing.

Have all your ingredients handy. You don't have to be exact, just get a good spread of seitan and vegetables on each kebab, completing each one with a nice fat chili. Place on a large tray or platter, brush well with olive oil and sprinkle with salt and pepper.

Make the mango barbecue sauce. Leave 6 tablespoons of the sauce in the food processor and blend until smooth. This will be your marinade for the kebabs. The rest will be your sauce.

The key here is to not burn the kebabs on the barbecue (it's a lot easier to control the temperature in an oven). The heat must be constant, but not blazing. Wait until the flames have died down and there is a white glow to the embers – about 30 minutes. Spread them out a little to form a good base of heat, then place your oiled kebabs on the grill.

Barbecue the kebabs for 10 minutes, turning them regularly but not overdoing it. Once they are well colored, begin to brush on your marinade and continue turning and basting for 10 minutes. If using a grill pan, set it on medium and turn the kebabs every few minutes. They should take 15–20 minutes – baste them regularly towards the end of cooking. You can also oven-roast the veggies.

Serve the kebabs on some watercress, drizzled with the mango sauce.

Seitan & sweet potato kebabs with mango barbecue sauce, page 165

Lazy Lahmacun

FOR 4

I tend to save bread-making for special occasions, and this lazy *lahmacun* is a "quickie," designed for almost instant satisfaction. Lahmacun is a thin Turkish pizza, normally served topped with ground meat and cooked in a wood-fire oven. You can make your own base for the lahmacun, or you can buy some great whole wheat pita or flatbreads. The flatter and thinner the better – you could even try cutting a normal pita in half. Nothing in the vegetable world comes closer to the texture and rich flavors of meat than roasted eggplant. When combined with roasted red pepper, toasted pine nuts and fresh herbs, this quickly becomes an epic pizza. It makes a great small or big plate – you can cut it into wedges to serve as an appetizer, or roll it around some salad for a meal. Cashew hummus (see page 144) is a perfect accompaniment.

THE BITS

1 large eggplant

1 red bell pepper

3 tablespoons olive oil

1 small onion

5 cloves of garlic, peeled and crushed

5½ ounces (150g) mushrooms, sliced

1 teaspoon ground coriander

a large pinch of ground cinnamon

½ teaspoon ground cumin

⅓ teaspoon chili powder

½ teaspoon sea salt

½ teaspoon black freshly ground pepper

1 teaspoon dried basil

2 tomatoes, grated

½ a handful of fresh flat-leaf parsley, chopped

4 whole wheat flatbreads

juice of ½ a lemon

For the topping

1 x lemon tofu feta (optional; see page 101)

5 tablespoons cashews, roughly chopped

DO IT

Preheat the oven to 400°F (200°C). Pierce the eggplant many times with a fork, then put it on a baking tray with the red pepper and rub them both with olive oil. Bake in the oven – check after 15 minutes, then turn them over with a spatula and bake for 15 minutes more. Take out the pepper and leave the eggplant in for another 10 minutes. They should both be soft and well colored. Deseed the pepper, trim the eggplant, and roughly chop them both.

Warm 1 tablespoon of oil in a frying pan over medium-high heat. Add the onions and fry for 6–8 minutes, then add the garlic, mushrooms, spices, salt and pepper, and continue cooking for 3–4 minutes. Add a splash more oil if needed. Now add the red pepper and eggplant, with the basil and tomatoes, and warm through on a low simmer for 6–7 minutes more. Stir in the parsley, cover and keep warm.

Bring the oven back to 400°F (200°C), lay out your flatbreads on baking trays and brush them with olive oil (especially the edges). Spread the vegetable mixture thinly over the bread – 4 tablespoons per lahmacun is normally good. Top with cashews and tofu feta (if you're using it) and pop into the oven for 12–15 minutes.

Serve drizzled with a little more olive oil and even a little squeeze of lemon juice.

Big Plates

Big plates = big appetites. Here we have some hearty vegan fare, capable of quenching even the most ferocious hunger.

I hear many non-vegans comment on the lack of richness in vegan food, something that I find surprising. With the addition of nuts and tofu, rich sauces and dishes can be devilishly satisfying, with the added benefit of being easily digestible. No after-dinner sloth is a real bonus for plant munchers!

I regularly cook with carnivores in mind – it's a wonderful challenge to please a meat-eater. Certainly this book has been written with them in mind. It's all part of my quest! I'm always thrilled to see a few more people down at the health food shop raiding the tempeh shelves and discovering the wonders of nutritional yeast flakes, realizing the vast potential of the humble bean in its multifarious forms and textures. "I would eat more vegetarian food if it tasted like this!" is one of the highest compliments you could ever pay a vegan cook.

As a vegan, I feel a little sorry for friends and family when they come to visit and even worse when I visit them, especially on special occasions like birthdays or Christmas. When I told them I was writing a cookbook, most said the same thing: "Thank God, we'll know what to cook for you next time!" I was surprised at their exasperation, but I understand all too well how much pressure can build around food and in the kitchen, particularly when you're cooking for the people you love. You want to give them the best.

I hope this book will be helpful when you are on the receiving end of a vegan visit. Firstly, please don't panic; I assure you, we come in peace. I speak for all vegans when I say that we have very low expectations when "eating out" (unfortunately).

The truth is, vegans are more than happy to nosh on a plate of tepid beans, maybe with a carrot thrown in there. Anything else is always a real bonus. The pressure is off – we know how complicated we are (you should try being us!).

Here I present some Big Plates, fit for special occasions and festive dinners, when the lovely vegan in your life is at the table. There are generally quite a few steps to preparation, but the methods are all simple and the delicious results are more than worth the extra effort.

Oven-Baked Squash Gnocchi with Fennel, Sun-Dried Tomatoes & Spinach Pistou

FOR 4–6

Making gnocchi with colored vegetables makes brilliant sense. Any starchy root works well: parsnip, sweet potato, purple potatoes, cassava, pumpkin . . . But the vivid orange of squash really electrifies the plate (and the palate). With its vibrant oranges, reds and greens, this dish is a feast for the eyes as well as the belly!

Pistou is actually just a Provençal variation on pesto, without the hard cheese and pine nuts. It's lighter than pesto and allows the herbs more room to express themselves, although I've thrown in a few hazelnuts for richness. This pistou is even better made the day before. Used in moderation, it brings herbal joy to soups, stews and, of course, pasta.

Gluten-free option: use gram (chickpea) flour or potato flour instead of wheat flour.

THE BITS

1 large winter squash, about 3¼ pounds (1.5kg) (starchy varieties are best, such as butternut), peeled and roughly chopped

olive oil, for roasting

a little sea salt

1 large fennel bulb, thinly sliced lengthwise

8½ ounces (240g) firm tofu, pressed (see page 18)

2¼ cups (300g) unbleached all-purpose flour, sifted

1 teaspoon sea salt

½ teaspoon white pepper

1½ teaspoons dried sage

2 big handfuls of sun-dried tomatoes, roughly chopped

1 x spinach pistou (see page 309)

For the topping

2 tablespoons roughly chopped roasted hazelnuts

DO IT

First make the spinach pistou (if you can, make it the day before).

Preheat the oven to 400°F (200°C).

Place the squash on an oiled baking tray. Rub a little oil and salt over it and bake for 30 minutes, turning the pieces gently over once. You're not looking for loads of color here, just lovely soft, golden squash. Toss the fennel in olive oil, place on a separate baking tray and scatter with a pinch of sea salt. Bake for 30 minutes, turning once, until it's golden, crisp and sweet. When the squash is ready, put it into a processor with the tofu and blend until smooth. Place it in a large bowl and stir in the flour, salt, pepper and sage until a soft dough forms. Leave to cool down and firm up – it will be a lot easier to handle.

Using two teaspoons, make gnocchi shapes (lovely little flat oval dumplings) with the squash mixture and place on an oiled baking sheet, leaving about 2 inches (5cm) of space for each gnocchi to grow. Brush the gnocchi with a little more oil and bake for 20–25 minutes, until crisp and slightly golden.

Serve the gnocchi warm, on nice big plates, drizzled liberally with the pistou. Scatter the crispy fennel and sun-dried tomatoes on top with a little more pistou, and finish with some chopped roasted hazelnuts.

Black Kale, Leek & Pumpkin Farrotto with Pan-Roasted Maple Endive & Pecans

FOR 4–6

"Farrotto" is basically risotto without the rice, using spelt (or farro) instead, which is far more nutritious than your average white risotto rice. It's low in gluten and has a magnificent nutty flavor that mingles nicely with the sweetness of the maple and roasted pumpkin in this dish. Black kale, aka lacinato kale or cavolo nero, is one of the most nutritious and delicious leaves known to earthlings! I use it in everything, even smoothies and juices (see pages 63–6). I love its contrast with pumpkin here. You need big herb flavors when playing with spelt, and sage and rosemary are well up to the challenge. The pecans are an added luxury – not necessary, but with the maple syrup they add another killer combo to this dish.

Gluten-free option: use normal risotto rice or brown rice instead of farro, altering cooking time accordingly.

THE BITS

4 tablespoons olive oil

14-ounce (400g) sugar/pie pumpkin, peeled and cut into 1-inch (3cm) dice

10 ounces (275g) leeks, cleaned and finely sliced

4 cloves of garlic, peeled and crushed

4 sprigs of fresh thyme, leaves only

6 fresh sage leaves, finely chopped

2 teaspoons finely chopped fresh rosemary leaves

1½ cups (300g) uncooked farro

½ cup (125ml) white wine (vegan)

6⅓ cups (1.5 liters) vegetable stock

7 ounces (200g) black kale, woody stalks removed, finely sliced into fine ribbons

1 teaspoon sea salt

1 teaspoon freshly ground black pepper

For the pan-roasted maple endive

4 large endive heads, halved lengthwise

2 tablespoons maple syrup

1 tablespoon olive oil

a handful of pecans, very roughly chopped

juice and zest of ½ a lemon

⅔ cup (150ml) vegetable stock

a pinch of sea salt

For the garnish

a few sprigs of fresh thyme

DO IT

Warm 1 tablespoon of olive oil in a frying pan, then panfry the pumpkin on high heat until it is nicely caramelized (around 5–7 minutes). You're looking for golden, slightly charred outsides and firm innards here – the pumpkin will cook through in the farrotto later. Cover and set aside.

In a large saucepan, warm 1 tablespoon of olive oil and begin to soften the leeks. Add the garlic and after 3 minutes pop the herbs in. Cook for 2 minutes, then add the farro, stir, and cook on a medium heat for a couple of minutes.

Now add the wine and bring to a boil, stirring frequently. Cook until the wine has been almost completely absorbed, then add 2 ladlefuls of stock and stir. Allow all the stock to be absorbed and then proceed to add more, stirring regularly, one ladleful at a time.

Now's a good time to get your endive started. Pick off any bruised or discolored outer leaves and brush the face of the endive pieces with a little of the maple syrup. In a large frying pan, warm ½ tablespoon of olive oil on medium-high heat and add the endive face down. Cook for 5–7 minutes. Once the endive has some good caramelization, flip it over, add the rest of the ingredients and cover. Lower the heat and simmer for 20–25 minutes, until the endive is nice and soft.

Once soft, take the endive pieces out of the cooking liquid and cut them again (so they are now in quarters). Set aside and keep warm. The cooking liquid should be thick, but if not, continue cooking it with the lid off until it's nice and sticky.

After roughly 30 minutes of cooking the far-rotto, add the pumpkin and kale. Continue until the farro is soft and chewy, which will take a while – maybe 40–50 minutes in total (roughly twice the length of time of a risotto). Make sure there is a decent amount of liquid left in the farrotto . . . there is nothing worse than dry spelt! When it's ready, stir in 2 table-spoons of olive oil, check the seasoning, pop a lid on and remove from the heat.

Ladle the farrotto into warmed shallow bowls and top with pieces of endive, making sure everybody gets some of the pecans. Spoon over a little of the thick cooking sauce, garnish with a few sprigs of thyme, and serve.

Asparagus & Cashew Cream Tart with Fig & Apple Compote

FOR 4–6

Asparagus always tells me that summer is around the corner. The brief asparagus season is a joy each year, and at our house in Spain it grows wild and free in the dried-up river beds. Multilayered, multicolored and brimming over with flavor, this tart is perfect for a warm evening with a glass of something dry and crisp. Although it sounds quite complex, this meal takes little preparation and cooking. It's one of those dishes that looks impressive without much effort. You can use sunflower seeds instead of the cashews, or half of each for an economical option. And if asparagus is out of season, try roasted zucchini or broccoli instead. A crisp green salad is a great accompaniment.

THE BITS

1 pound (500g) thin asparagus spears (if you have thick ones, cut them in half lengthwise)

2 teaspoons olive oil

sea salt and freshly ground black pepper

10½ ounces (300g) spinach leaves

1 pound (500g) puff pastry (from the freezer – stress-free is best)

a handful of pinenuts (optional)

1 x fig & apple compote (see page 308)

For the cashew cream

1 cup (150g) cashews, soaked in water for 2 hours

1 tablespoon cornstarch

⅔ cup (150ml) unsweetened almond milk

½ teaspoon lemon juice

1 tablespoon nutritional yeast flakes

¼ teaspoon salt

1½ teaspoons Dijon mustard

DO IT

First make the compote, then preheat the oven to 400°F (200°C).

Bring a pot of water to a boil and trim your asparagus spears (just snap the woody ends off). Dunk the spears in the water and blanch quickly, then remove and immerse in cold water. Pat them dry, toss with a little olive oil and a pinch of sea salt and set aside.

Now blanch your spinach in the same pot, cooking for 1 minute, and drain well. Place it in the center of a kitchen towel or muslin and gather in the edges, twisting and squeezing out as much excess liquid as you can (or press firmly in a colander).

With a rolling pin, roll the pastry out on a cold surface, until quite thin, about 2.5mm thick. Make a shape that roughly fits a typical-size baking tray (about 13 x 18 inches). Push the pastry snugly into each corner and trim off any straggly edges (or leave them for a disheveled look). Score a 1cm border around the edge, using a sharp knife, and prick the base of the pastry with a fork. Place in the fridge for 20 minutes.

Place the soaked cashews in a food processor and blend until creamy – you should have something resembling thin peanut butter. You will need to scrape the sides of the food processor a few times. Add the rest of the ingredients, drizzling in the milk. Blend until a smooth sauce is formed, adding a little more water if needed, but remember – too thin and it will spill over the edge.

Pop the pastry into the oven and blind bake for 12 minutes, then turn the tray 90 degrees and bake for another 12 minutes, until almost cooked. Check the base – it should be dark golden. Press the base down along the borders using a metal spatula, making an indention in the center for your filling.

Gently spread your cashew cream over the pastry to meet the borders. Break the spinach up and sprinkle a good layer on top. Now place your asparagus spears on top in neat rows widthwise. Sprinkle with sea salt and black pepper (and pine nuts if you like). Lightly brush the borders with olive oil. Put back into the oven for roughly 10–12 minutes on the top shelf, until the pastry borders are a nice deep golden color.

Serve the tart in big squares, with a spoonful of compote on the side.

Eggplant & Tomato Nut Roast with Macadamia Mustard Sauce

FOR 6

This is *the* nut roast, a heavenly, light slice of nuttiness, and the creamy macadamia mustard sauce is the big fat cherry on top of the cake. You use a lot of nuts here, but it's a real treat dish, a Sunday special. You can use any combination of nuts; just steer clear of peanuts, as their flavor can dominate. High-quality canola oil is a wonderful ingredient and adds a lovely butteriness to the dish, but vegetable oil is perfectly acceptable. A pile of roasted or steamed veggies rounds things off nicely (the winter roots braised in porter on page 122 would be perfect).

THE BITS

2 eggplants

canola oil

2 teaspoons cumin seeds

2 teaspoons coriander seeds

1 large onion

4 cloves of garlic

½ teaspoon ground cinnamon

4 ripe tomatoes, roughly chopped

a handful of sun-dried tomatoes, finely chopped (including any oil)

½ teaspoon salt

¼ teaspoon freshly ground black pepper

1 teaspoon dried mint

1 teaspoon dried thyme

2 handfuls each of walnuts, cashews, sunflower seeds, pumpkin seeds, hazelnuts, all soaked for 4 hours, plus a handful of unsoaked sunflower seeds for the pan

2 tablespoons golden raisins, soaked for 2 hours

a handful of almond meal

a big handful of gram (chickpea) flour or 2 handfuls of breadcrumbs (more if needed)

1 teaspoon sea salt

1 teaspoon freshly ground black pepper

2 large handfuls of fresh parsley, finely chopped

1 x macadamia mustard sauce (see page 302)

For the garnish

2 tablespoons finely chopped fresh parsley

DO IT

Preheat the oven to 400°F (200°C). Rub the whole eggplants with oil and place on a baking tray. Bake them for 40–45 minutes, turning them at least once, until very tender. Cover and set aside. When cooled, scoop out the soft insides and roughly chop. Discard the skins. Lower the oven temperature to 300°F (150°C).

Roast the cumin and coriander seeds in a small skillet for 1 minute, until they pop and are slightly brown. Grind together with a pestle and mortar or clean coffee grinder. Peel the onion and garlic and blend together in a food processor. Warm ½ a tablespoon of oil in a large frying pan on medium heat, add the blended onion and garlic, and cook for 4 minutes, stirring often. Add the cumin, coriander and cinnamon and cook for 1 minute. Add the eggplant, chopped tomatoes, sun-dried tomatoes, salt and pepper, followed by the dried herbs, and cook on a high simmer for 12–15 minutes, until the tomatoes have broken down and a thickish sauce has formed. Check the seasoning.

(continued) →

Blitz the nuts and raisins in a food processor until a rough crumb is formed. Put into a large bowl and mix in the rest of the ingredients, adding the warm tomato mixture last. With your trusty wooden spoon or your hands, combine well. It should be slightly dry, but definitely sticky to the touch. You should be able to form small balls with the mix. Add more flour or breadcrumbs if too wet.

Sprinkle a layer of sunflower seeds in the bottom of an oiled 8½ x 4½-inch (1 pound/450g) loaf pan and pack in the nutty mixture. Bake for 35–40 minutes, until the top begins to brown and crisp. Check with a skewer – the middle should be piping hot. Remove from the oven and allow to rest in the pan for about 5 minutes before turning out onto a wire rack.

While the nut roast is in the oven, make the macadamia mustard sauce.

Place the loaf on a warm serving platter and slice into hearty slabs. Serve with the macadamia mustard sauce, and sprinkle some fresh parsley over the top.

Persian Fava Bean, Seitan & Green Herb Stew

FOR 4-6

This is a version of *ghormeh sabzi*, the national dish of Iran, and the Iraqis and Azerbaijanis are quite partial to it, too. Iranian food is both distinct and diverse, and it has influenced all the countries around it, stretching as far as India and the Mediterranean. The name of the dish means "herb stew," and we use LOTS of herbs. Don't scrimp on them here; they're what makes this dish sing. Seitan can be picked up in select supermarkets or your local health food store, or you can make it at home (see page 18). Dried limes are a popular ingredient in Iranian cooking and are found in the "world food" aisles. You can use preserved lemons as a backup. Traditionally, red kidney beans are the way to go, but I tried it with fava beans once and have never looked back. Iranians would use fresh fenugreek leaves, but they can be hard to come by so I have opted for dried instead (also called methi leaves, used frequently in Indian cooking).

THE BITS

2 medium white onions, peeled and cut into thick wedges

3 tablespoons olive oil

⅓ cup (50g) gram (chickpea) flour, or unbleached all-purpose flour

sea salt and freshly ground black pepper

10½ ounces (300g) seitan, or pressed firm tofu, cut into 1-inch (3cm) cubes

1 teaspoon ground turmeric

1 tablespoon dried fenugreek (methi) leaves

5 sprigs of fresh thyme, leaves only

1½ cinnamon sticks, or 1 teaspoon ground cinnamon

2 bay leaves

2 dried Iranian limes, well pricked

3 strips of lemon rind

3 medium carrots, quartered lengthwise and cut into ¾-inch (2cm) dice

2 celery stalks, halved lengthwise and cut into 1cm pieces

a handful of small radishes, trimmed and halved

generous ¾ cup (200ml) white wine (vegan)

2 tablespoons tomato paste

4 portobello mushrooms (or any other meaty mushroom), cut into 2-inch (5cm) chunks

2 cups (250g) dried fava beans, soaked overnight and cooked (reserve the cooking liquid)

1¼ cups (300ml) mushroom stock or bean cooking liquid

2 big handfuls of fresh parsley (reserve a little for garnish)

a big handful of fresh dill (reserve a little for garnish)

6 big handfuls of spinach, finely chopped

To serve

a handful of pomegranate seeds

steamed white rice

DO IT

In a large sauté pan (one that has a lid), cook the onions in 1 tablespoon of olive oil for 10 minutes, until caramelized and soft. Scrape any stuck onions off the bottom of the pan. Set the onions aside in a large bowl.

Put the gram flour into a flat bowl and stir in a teaspoon of salt and a generous grinding of pepper. Drain the seitan well and add to the bowl. Toss together with your hands to give it a decent coating, shaking off any excess. The natural moisture of the seitan will make the flour stick.

Return the pan to medium-high heat, pour in a tablespoon of olive oil, and fry the seitan until slightly charred. Add it to the bowl with th onions and cover. Depending on the size of your pan, you may need to do this in batches. Scrape the bottom of the pan if the seitan is sticking.

Return the onions and seitan to the pan on medium heat, along with the turmeric, fenugreek, thyme, cinnamon, bay leaves, dried limes and lemon rind. Cook for a minute, then add the carrots, celery and radishes. Pour in the wine and add the tomato paste. Stir and cook on high heat for around 2–3 minutes, until the sauce reduces and thickens.

Add the mushrooms, fava beans and the mushroom stock or bean cooking liquid and bring to a boil. Cover and simmer for 20–25 minutes on a low heat.

Remove the lid and check that the carrots are nice and soft. Stir in the fresh herbs and spinach, pop the lid back on and take the pan off the heat. Leave to sit for 5 minutes, to let the flavors mingle and the spinach wilt a little. The sauce should be nice and thick, not runny. Check for seasoning – if you've used bean cooking liquid, it may need a hit of saltiness. Stir in 1 tablespoon of olive oil just before serving to add a lovely shine.

Spoon the ghormeh sabzi over some steamed white rice and top with a scattering of the reserved fresh herbs and the pomegranate seeds. Warm flatbread is also a treat with this dish.

Tofu Fillets in a Spicy Cornmeal Crust with Golden Beet & Blood Orange Salsa

FOR 4

I had my first taste of tofu in a Thai street – a blob of crispy, creamy gorgeousness that I could not believe wasn't some form of cream cheese. Since then, I have been a complete tofu convert and love its versatility. Use a firm tofu here – the firmer the better for frying. When pressed well it absorbs lots of the marinade and this means bags of flavor. It's even better marinated overnight.

THE BITS

1 pound (500g) firm tofu, pressed (see page 18), then cut into 1cm steaks

⅔ cup (80g) polenta/coarse cornmeal

½ teaspoon chili powder

½ teaspoon ground turmeric

½ teaspoon sea salt

4 tablespoons sunflower oil

For the marinade

3 tomatoes

juice of 1 lime

zest of ½ a lime

a handful of fresh cilantro leaves

½ a handful of mint leaves

1 jalapeño chili (or any hot chili), finely chopped

2 cloves of garlic, peeled and finely chopped

1-inch (3cm) piece of fresh ginger, peeled and finely chopped

½ teaspoon ground cumin

½ teaspoon salt

For the golden beet & blood orange salsa

1 large golden or regular beet, peeled and finely diced

1 green apple, cored and finely diced

1 blood orange or 1 small red grapefruit, peeled, de-pithed and finely chopped

1 small cucumber, peeled, deseeded and finely diced

a handful of roasted peanuts, roughly chopped

½ a handful of fresh mint leaves, roughly chopped

a pinch of sea salt

juice of ½ a lemon

DO IT

Begin by pressing the tofu to remove excess moisture, making sure to leave it for a full hour.

Place all the marinade ingredients in a blender and blitz together; it should be nice and thick. Put the tofu fillets into a large container with a lid and cover well with the marinade. Cover and pop into the fridge for at least an hour. Toss the salsa ingredients together in a bowl, then squeeze the lemon juice on top.

On a large plate, combine the cornmeal, spices and salt. Remove the tofu fillets from the marinade and shake off the liquid (reserve the marinade). Lay the fillets on the cornmeal and flip them to cover all sides – top, bottom and the thinner edges. When you are happy that all sides have a decent coating of cornmeal, pop them onto another plate.

Heat the oil in a medium frying pan on a high heat and shallow-fry your tofu pieces in batches until they turn a wonderful reddish-gold color – 1 or 2 minutes per side should do. Put them on a large plate covered with paper towels, and keep warm. Be careful not to dislodge the crust when handling. Serve the warm tofu fillets with the salsa and marinade in small serving bowls on the side.

Maple & Orange-Glazed Tempeh with Bok Choy & Soba Noodles

FOR 2

Foods like tempeh, tofu and seitan have been eaten in the East for many, many years. Tempeh is not for the faint-hearted vegan as it is semi-fermented and ever so slightly meaty in texture.

Gluten-free option: use 100 percent buckwheat noodles and GF miso, and no seitan.

THE BITS

7 ounces (200g) tempeh, seitan or pressed firm tofu

1–2 tablespoons vegetable oil

9 ounces (250g) bok choy, leaves halved lengthwise

For the maple & orange glaze

1 teaspoon toasted sesame oil

¾ inch (2cm) fresh ginger, peeled and finely grated

1 clove of garlic, peeled and crushed

½ red chili, deseeded and finely diced

3 tablespoons tamari

2½ tablespoons maple syrup

zest and juice of ½ an orange

1 tablespoon rice wine vinegar

For the miso noodle broth

5 ounces (135g) soba noodles

1 tablespoon tamari

1 star anise

3–4 tablespoons brown miso

For the topping

a handful of fresh cilantro, finely chopped

2 scallions, sliced thinly at an angle

DO IT

Drain the tempeh in a sieve and dry well, pressing out excess liquid. To make the marinade, warm the sesame oil in a small pan and add the ginger and garlic. Cook for a minute, then add the rest of the ingredients. Bring slowly to a boil, then gently simmer for 5 minutes. Add the tempeh and cover. Set aside to marinate for 30 minutes to an hour.

Drain your tempeh, keeping the lovely marinade. Heat 1 tablespoon of vegetable oil in a large frying pan on medium-high heat, and when hot add the tempeh. Fry for 2–3 minutes, adding the marinade gradually until the glaze becomes sticky – this should take around 10 minutes on a steady simmer. Set aside, cover and keep warm. Rinse out the pan for later.

To cook the noodles, fill a large pot half full of water and bring to a boil. Cook your noodles according to the instructions on the package. Drain in a colander, reserving about 2 cups (500ml) of the noodle water, then keep the noodles warm in a bowl, stirring in a little oil to prevent them from sticking together.

Pour the reserved noodle cooking water back into the pan, put it back on the heat and add the tamari and star anise. Put the miso into a small bowl and mix in a couple of tablespoons of the warm water until a runny paste is formed. Add this paste to the pan and keep covered, simmering the broth on a low heat. The flavor should be strong – add more tamari and miso if needed.

Heat ½ tablespoon of oil in your frying pan and add the bok choy. Cook for 2 minutes on a high heat, then add 3 tablespoons of the miso broth and continue cooking for 1 minute more. Bring the simmering broth to a slow boil. Divide your noodles between warm bowls, top with bok choy and ladle over some of the broth. Stack on a decent pile of tempeh, topped with some sliced scallions and a scattering of fresh cilantro.

Parsnip & Walnut Rumbledethumps with Baked Beans

FOR 4

Scotland is a place where I misspent many of my formative years, and this is proper Scottish fare. This dish is a real rib-hugger – just the thought of it makes my hunger evaporate. Home-made baked beans are best; I don't care what it says on the can. Give them a try – they're not quite as sweet as the famous canned variety, but few things are. However, this is a quick dinner, so you are definitely forgiven if you reach for the can opener on occasion. I normally cook double the quantity of the patties and beans, as they freeze wonderfully.

Gluten-free option: forget about the flour dusting – they're very tasty without!

THE BITS

2 large potatoes, scrubbed and cut into small chunks

2 carrots, scrubbed and cut into small chunks

3 parsnips, scrubbed and cut into small chunks

1–2 teaspoons sea salt

a large pinch of white pepper

scant ½ cup (100ml) soy milk

3 tablespoons canola oil

2 red onions, finely chopped

5½ ounces (150g) brussels sprouts, trimmed and finely sliced

1 teaspoon dried sage

1 teaspoon dried thyme

3 tablespoon whole wheat flour, for dusting

½ teaspoon sea salt

For the baked beans

1 tablespoon sunflower or canola oil

1 onion, finely diced

2 cloves of garlic, peeled and crushed

1 apple, peeled, cored and finely diced

2 tablespoons tomato paste

4 large tomatoes, roughly chopped

2 teaspoons mustard powder

a large pinch of allspice

2 tablespoons molasses or brown rice syrup (not blackstrap molasses)

1 teaspoon sea salt

¼ cup (50ml) water

1 tablespoon sherry vinegar

2 bay leaves

1 cup (175g) dried navy beans, soaked and cooked

For the mustard & walnut topping

3 tablespoons whole grain mustard

2 handfuls of toasted walnuts, finely chopped

½ tablespoon high-quality canola oil

½ a handful of fresh parsley, finely chopped

DO IT

Put the potatoes, carrots and parsnips into a large pot of cold water, add a little salt, bring to a boil and simmer until very tender – 20 minutes should do. Drain well and allow the vegetables to steam dry for 2–3 minutes. Put them all into a large bowl and mash with more salt, the pepper and the soy milk, adding the milk gradually until you get a good consistency that isn't too wet. Cover and set aside. Check for seasoning – mashes love salt!

Heat 1 tablespoon of canola oil in a frying pan on medium-low and add the onions. Cook gently for 15 minutes, until sweet and golden, then add the brussels sprouts and dried herbs and continue cooking for 3–4 minutes. Once this mixture is nice and soft, stir it into the mash. Check the seasoning.

Form the mash mixture into four large cakes. Mix together the flour and salt, and dust the cakes on both sides. Pop into the fridge for 1 hour.

To make the beans, heat the sunflower oil in a large heavy-bottomed pan and cook the onions, stirring for 10 minutes until nicely caramelized. Well-cooked onions provide the base for fuller flavor. Add the garlic and cook for 2 minutes more, then add the apples, tomato paste, tomatoes, mustard powder, allspice, molasses, salt, water, sherry vinegar and bay leaves. Bring to a boil, then cover the pan and cook for 30 minutes on low heat, checking on it and stirring occasionally.

Give the mixture a good stir to break down the apples, onions, etc., into a thick sauce, then mix in the cooked beans and cover. Cook for 20 minutes more on low heat. You should be left with a nice thick sauce. If this is not the case, cook further with the lid off.

Heat the remaining 2 tablespoons of canola oil in a large frying pan and fry each rumbledethump for 5 minutes per side, until golden and crisp. Mix the topping ingredients in a bowl, spoon on top of the rumbledethumps and serve warm with the homemade beans.

Layered Filo Pie with Roasted Cauliflower Mash & Carrot Purée

FOR 2 INDIVIDUAL PIES (2–4 PORTIONS)

The layered technique for this pie can be used with any combination of ingredients your mind can conjure up – the filo pastry works as the perfect light crust for a whole host of puréed perfection. However, try not to use so many flavors that it makes your taste buds malfunction (which means you taste very little and the individual ingredients merge into one). You will need some small deep individual pie dishes here, the springform type. I can eat a whole one of these pies, but most people only manage half. I have cooked them in deep bowls, but it is harder to get them out in one piece and you don't get to see all the lovely layers. Potato can be used instead of cauliflower, but I like the lightness that the cauliflower brings. Best served with steamed greens of your choice.

THE BITS

5 cloves of garlic, unpeeled

1 onion, roughly chopped

1 small cauliflower, roughly chopped

1½ teaspoons sea salt

2 tablespoons olive oil

⅓ cup (75ml) almond milk or soy milk

1 teaspoon lemon zest

2 tablespoons chopped parsley

3 large carrots, scrubbed and chopped

¼ teaspoon freshly ground nutmeg

2 teaspoons nutritional yeast flakes

6 sheets of filo pastry

2 tablespoons olive oil

For the topping

1 large red bell pepper, deseeded and finely diced

2 cloves of garlic, peeled and crushed

1 teaspoon fennel seeds

2 handfuls of black olives, pitted and roughly chopped

2 tablespoons nonpareil capers, well drained (if large, roughly chopped)

2 teaspoons lemon juice

½ teaspoon freshly ground black pepper

4 tablespoons roasted almonds, roughly chopped

a large pinch of sea salt (if needed)

1 tablespoon olive oil

(continued) →

DO IT

Preheat the oven to 425°F (220°C). Put the garlic, onion and cauliflower onto a baking tray, sprinkle with 1 teaspoon of sea salt and toss in 1 teaspoon of olive oil. Bake in the oven for 15 minutes, then check that the garlic is soft and remove it. Turn the onion and cauliflower over and put them back into the oven for 10–15 minutes more. All should be nicely cooked and slightly caramelized. Once they have cooled slightly, push the garlic out of the skins and put them into a blender with the onions, cauliflower, almond milk, lemon zest and parsley. Blitz until creamy, then check the seasoning, cover and set aside.

Toss the carrots in 1 teaspoon of olive oil and pop on a baking tray, cover with parchment paper or foil and bake in the oven for 30–35 minutes, until soft. Place in the blender with the nutmeg and yeast flakes and pulse a few times, leaving some chunks. Cover and set aside.

On a lightly floured surface, lay out a sheet of filo pastry, making sure to handle it gently. Brush well with olive oil, lay on another sheet, brush with oil once more, layer and brush. That's three sheets of filo per pie. Lay the filo over a small (8 inches [20cm] wide, 4 inches [10cm] deep) circular pie dish, press and ease it in gently with your fingers, right down into the corners. Repeat the process with the other pie dish. Reduce the oven to 400°F (200°C).

Your fillings should be cooled, but still warm. Using a spoon, place a layer of carrot purée in each pie, again pressing it into the edges to form a nice distinct layer. Top with your cauliflower mash until it is 1cm below the rim of the pie dish. Trim the square edges of the filo, but leave a good 1½-inch (4cm) overlap. The idea is that it gathers around the pie and looks vaguely like a flower with filo petals. Brush the pies gently with olive oil and place in the oven. Bake on the middle shelf for 15 minutes, checking that the filo is not cooking too quickly. Cover with foil if this happens.

Heat 1 tablespoon of olive oil in a frying pan. Add the peppers and sauté for 6–8 minutes, until beginning to caramelize. Add the garlic and fennel seeds, stir and sauté for 2 minutes, then pop in the olives, capers, lemon juice, pepper and almonds. Check if it is salty enough (the capers normally do the trick). Cover and warm through on a low heat for 10 minutes. Set aside.

Serve the warm pies with a layer of the peppers and almonds as a topping. Pat yourself on the back and enjoy the fruits of your artistry.

Chipotle Chocolate & Beet Beans with Spicy Baked Polenta & Avocado & Cilantro Salsa

FOR 6–8

The Mexicans have been using chocolate in savory food for ages. The first time I tried *mole poblano* (a rich dark sauce made with chocolate, chili, bananas and peanuts, among other things), my whole approach to food shifted, relaxed and heaved a sigh of relief. Chipotle chilies or paste are relatively easy to locate – try the "world food" section of your local supermarket. If they still elude you, try smoked paprika to get that wonderful and essential smoky flavor. I recommend deseeding fresh chilies if they are really incendiary – but otherwise, leave the seeds in.

THE BITS

1 tablespoon sunflower oil

2 large beets, peeled and cut into ¾-inch (2cm) cubes

2 red bell peppers, chopped into random ¾-inch (2cm) chunks

1 tablespoon balsamic vinegar

2 onions, finely chopped

4 cloves of garlic, peeled and crushed

2 celery stalks, finely chopped

16 mushrooms (chestnut or similar), cleaned, stems trimmed and halved

2–3 large chipotle chilies, finely chopped, or 1 extra-fresh red chili plus 2 teaspoons smoked paprika

1–2 red chilies (to taste), deseeded and finely diced

2 teaspoons dried oregano

2 tablespoons tomato paste

1 teaspoon ground allspice

2 teaspoons ground cumin

1¼ cups (225g) dried black beans, soaked and cooked

1⅔ cups (400ml) vegetable stock (or bean cooking liquid)

3 ounces (75g) very dark vegan chocolate, finely chopped

1–2 teaspoons sea salt

For the baked chili polenta

2 ears of corn (or 1 can – roughly 7 ounces [200g] drained weight)

2 tablespoons olive oil

2 cloves of garlic, peeled and crushed

1½ cups (200g) polenta/coarse cornmeal

3¼ cups (750ml) very hot water

1 tablespoon nutritional yeast flakes (optional but tasty)

1 teaspoon dried oregano

1 large red chili, finely diced, or ½ teaspoon red pepper flakes

1 teaspoon salt

½ teaspoon baking soda

For the avocado & cilantro salsa

1 avocado, peeled, pitted and cut into small chunks

a handful of fresh cilantro, roughly sliced

juice and zest of ½ a lime

a pinch of sea salt

DO IT

In a large heavy-bottomed frying pan, add ½ tablespoon of oil and slowly fry the beets for 5 minutes, tossing them and stirring regularly. Add the peppers, turn the heat up and panfry for 5 minutes. Now add the balsamic vinegar and give it a minute to evaporate slightly, then add 2 tablespoons of water, cover, and allow to steam for 10 minutes on the lowest heat.

In a large pan, warm ½ tablespoon of oil on medium heat and sauté the onions for 5 minutes. Add the garlic, celery, mushrooms, chilies, oregano, tomato paste and spices and cook for 5 minutes more. Ladle in the cooked beans and enough stock (or better still, bean liquid) to make a nice thick sauce. Allow it to come to a gentle boil. Add the beets and peppers, spoon in any cooking juices, then cover and simmer slowly for 15–20 minutes.

Now add the chocolate and allow it to melt, then place an immersion blender in the stew and pulse a couple of times, creating a creamy texture in the sauce. Check the seasoning.

To cook the polenta, first boil the water. Remove the corn from the cobs by holding them vertically and sawing a sharp knife downwards – the kernels should leap off. It takes a little practice, so watch your fingers!

Preheat the oven to 375°F (190°C). Oil a baking dish (9 x 11 inches [23 x 30cm] sounds about right) and line the base with parchment paper.

Heat the olive oil in a heavy-bottomed pan and sauté the sweet corn for 2 minutes, until starting to caramelize. Add the garlic, stir for a minute, then pour in the cornmeal and heat for another minute, combining everything. Now add a quarter of the hot water, stirring and flattening out any lumps as you go.

With the heat on medium-low, keep giving it some elbow grease with your spatula, adding the water gradually, a quarter at a time, checking that the cornmeal doesn't stick to the bottom of the pan. Continue for 6–8 minutes – it will come together and absorb the water. Stir in the nutritional yeast flakes, oregano, chili, salt and baking soda. Have a taste – the polenta should be soft. If there are still lumps, get the immersion blender out again and whiz it up.

Spoon the polenta into the prepared baking dish and flatten the surface with a spatula. It should be about 1 inch (2.5cm) thick all over. Bake in the oven for 30–35 minutes, until a dark golden crust is formed. Leave to rest in the dish for 5 minutes, then, using a flat spatula (two work best), loosen the edges of the polenta and ease it out onto a wire rack. Let it cool for 5–10 minutes – it will firm up nicely on the rack. Slide it onto a chopping board and cut into squares or triangles or whatever other cool shapes you like (you could use a pastry/cookie cutter, star shape, etc.).

This seems like a lot of work, but I can think of few better ways of enjoying polenta. It is well worth the effort – crispy around the edges and soft inside.

Mix the salsa ingredients together in a bowl.

Ladle the stew over the polenta and serve the avocado and lime salsa on the side.

Spicy baked polenta, page 190

Avocado & cilantro salsa, page 190

Chipotle chocolate &
beef beans, page 190

Pappardelle with Artichoke & Almond Sauce, Purple Kale & White Asparagus

FOR 4

This dish is a delight! So many shades of green, all bursting with flavor and nutrition. Artichokes make a surprisingly creamy purée. Throw a few almonds into the mix and you're well on your way to deliciousness. In Spain, I buy fresh artichokes for pennies – pounds of the things are piled around our small kitchen and it can be difficult to know what to do with them. However, I recommend using high-quality jarred artichokes here. In this dish I tend to use white asparagus, but in autumn and winter I'd try to seek out some salsify. It's a rich root vegetable, perfect with this tangy sauce.

Gluten-free option: use GF pasta.

THE BITS

14 ounces (400g) purple kale, stalks removed, thickly chopped

8–10 white asparagus spears

2 teaspoons olive oil

⅓ cup (75ml) nice white wine (vegan)

sea salt and freshly ground black pepper

14 ounces (400g) pappardelle (or similar egg-free pasta)

For the artichoke & almond sauce

5 tablespoons olive oil

a handful of almonds, soaked for 2 hours, skins removed if you have time

2 cloves of garlic, peeled and crushed

4 big handfuls of watercress leaves

14 ounces (390g) artichoke hearts

juice of ½ a lemon

For the topping

a small handful of toasted almonds, finely chopped

a big handful of fresh parsley, chopped

a handful of watercress

DO IT

To make the sauce, heat 1 tablespoon of oil in a frying pan and add the almonds. Sauté for 1 minute, then add the garlic and continue cooking for 2 minutes more. Add the watercress leaves, cover the pan, remove from the heat and allow to cool.

Place the contents of the frying pan in a food processor with the artichokes, lemon juice and 4 tablespoons of olive oil, and blend to a smooth purée. The sauce should be thick and shiny. Add water to thin it out if necessary.

Heat 2 teaspoons of olive oil in a large heavy-bottomed frying pan on medium and add the asparagus. Panfry for 6–8 minutes, until nicely caramelized. Add a glug of white wine, and when the liquid has evaporated, season and cover. Leave to sit.

Bring a big pan of salted water to a boil and cook your pasta for roughly 8 minutes, until al dente. Add the kale halfway through the cooking time. Drain well, keeping aside a little of the pasta water. Add the drained pasta and kale to the artichoke sauce and toss together, adding some of the pasta water if it is looking a bit dry.

Spoon into warm shallow bowls and top with criss-crosses of asparagus and a sprinkling of toasted almonds and parsley. Garnish with the watercress and season with sea salt and black pepper.

Curries

I remember the first time I went to a curry house. I was seven and we all ordered chicken chow mein and soggy boiled rice, fries and mushy peas. It was the late eighties and we hadn't got the hang of Indian food yet. Much has changed since then! I cringe at the thought of the incredible food we missed out on, and I've been making up for the oversight ever since.

I've been through India a number of times, from peak to plain: I've hiked the Himalayas, I've woken up on a beach in Kerala, I've meditated for weeks in monasteries and eaten like a happy Buddha, I've lived with remote tribal communities and helped milk yaks (which put me off milk forever). I've even cooked fresh pasta in the back of a jeep during an avalanche (the pasta was slightly overcooked, but we survived!).

I am captivated by the bright lights and wonders of the ancient carousel of Indian culture and history, the ubiquitous spice markets, the fiery masala chai first thing in the morning. Curry (a very Western term) encapsulates so much of the diversity and magic of this fascinating land. Traveling through India is a constant adventure and teaches so much about life, the universe and everything!

Indian cuisine changes, sometimes drastically, from region to region, all heavily influenced by trade and conquerors, sometimes dating back thousands of years. The word "curry" has no meaning in India; each dish has its own unique moniker and generally a long tradition, with stringent rules of preparation. I tend to adapt these rules and come up with something a little different, and my Indian friends typically like the results!

Curry is my favorite thing to cook; I love playing with spices and colors. Indian cuisine is so massive and diverse you need never cook the same dish twice. Dishes range from the simple tasty morsels offered by street vendors up to the lavish wedding banquets that last for days, where fine ghee is poured over food from silver teapots and the days of the maharajahs are reenacted via mountainous biryanis. India is an awe-inspiring land, with a culinary tradition to match.

Indian cooking can also be really healthy. Buying a few key spices – ground turmeric, cumin, coriander, paprika, maybe asafetida – is a good idea (see pages 23–9). Spices are always better freshly ground, so buy them in small batches and use often. When to add the spices to a dish depends on the dish and the spice. There is no right or wrong way; just don't burn them. If you are a spice connoisseur, there is no substitute for roasting your own spices (primarily cumin and coriander) and using others whole (cinnamon sticks, star anise, cloves). At your local Indian food store you may also pick up fresh turmeric, a magical ingredient.

Even better, go to Delhi, jump in an auto-rickshaw and do a restaurant crawl. Invade the sweet-shops for snacks, the *dhabas* for *thalis* and the finer restaurants for a whiff of the opulence of Mughal times. The only way to fully experience food is in the appropriate setting, the land from which it hails. Every plate and forkful is an expression of a culture; we learn so much about people by what they eat.

Most of the dishes here are highly untraditional. I have tampered with many – I have Indian friends whose eyes almost pop out when I go through the ingredients, muttering something along the lines of "Insane!" or "Mother would not be happy." Still, cooking is about playing, expressing and, most of all, enjoying.

Whenever possible, I like to veer away from cans and jars and keep things natural, even sauces. I know it is much easier to use canned tomatoes, but a freshly made sauce cannot be beaten and hardly takes any more time or effort. Buying good tomatoes makes all the difference – if the tomatoes are tasteless off the vine, they'll be tasteless in the bowl. Adding a large pinch of sugar and salt can bring the flavor out a little, but really, if you want to be in the good sauce gang, tasty toms are a must!

Om Namah Shivaya!

Turnip & Spinach Kashmiri Curry with Beet Raita

FOR 4

Kashmir! The name alone conjures up some epic, desolate, sublime corner of our world. Kashmir is famous for its turnip farming and you can see why, if you've ever tried one from there – they are in a league of their own. The secret to cooking turnips in Kashmir is to salt them, which draws any bitterness out, before roasting them until beautifully golden. Rutabagas are a good substitute if you can't get turnips, though they do take a little more cooking. Best enjoyed with a heap of your preferred rice.

THE BITS

1½ pounds (750g) turnips, scrubbed and cut into 2-inch (5cm) wedges

sea salt

3 tablespoons vegetable oil

1¼ pounds (600g) spinach leaves (the bigger the leaf, the better), sliced into ¾-inch (2cm) ribbons

2 teaspoons cumin seeds

2 teaspoons coriander seeds

5 tablespoons unsweetened soy yogurt

1 onion, sliced

1 inch (2.5cm) fresh ginger, grated

3 cloves of garlic, peeled and crushed

1 tablespoon fenugreek (methi) leaves

½ teaspoon ground fenugreek

1–2 teaspoons chili powder

juice of ½ a lemon

1 x beet raita (see page 306)

DO IT

Place the turnips in a colander, sprinkle over 1 tablespoon of salt and mix it all around with your hands. Place the colander over a bowl or the sink and leave for 30 minutes. Meanwhile, warm a pan on medium heat and add a slight splash of oil and half your spinach. Stir and the spinach will begin to wilt. Pop a lid on and lower the heat. Leave to cook for a few minutes, then drain well.

In a small skillet, toast the cumin and coriander seeds for about 1 minute, until they start to pop, then grind with a pestle and mortar. Mix the soy yogurt into the cooked spinach. Place in a food processor and blend to a bright green sauce.

Rinse the turnips in cold water and dry with a clean kitchen towel. Heat half the oil in a large heavy-bottomed frying pan and fry the turnips on a high heat until golden, about 8–10 minutes. Remove, cover and set aside. Add the rest of the oil to the frying pan and begin to cook your onions. Cook on high heat for 6 minutes, until they begin to caramelize. Add your ginger, garlic and fenugreek leaves and sauté for 2 minutes, then add the ground fenugreek, cumin, coriander and chili powder. Cook for another 2 minutes and let the spices warm, mingle and infuse.

Add the turnips to the pan and stir in the green sauce with 3 tablespoons of water and the rest of your spinach. Heat uncovered for 5 minutes – the sauce will thicken and the turnips will be nice and soft. Remove from the heat and cover. Make the beet raita.

After a couple of minutes resting, the curry will be perfect! Thin the sauce with a little water if needed, then stir in the lemon juice and add salt to taste. Serve with a hearty dollop of the vivid purple raita.

Spiced Chana Masala with Brown Chickpeas, Tamarind & Kale

FOR 4

Straight from the Punjab, the green land of many rivers in northwest India. This is a very fecund area, where *chana* (chickpeas) thrive. Punjabi food is full-flavored and sometimes quite rich. Here's a simple and hearty curry for those times when you want maximum flavor for minimum effort. Brown chickpeas have a more robust texture, are slightly smaller and contain tons more fiber than your average chickpea. You can use normal chickpeas, but they pale in comparison. Best served with lots of whole wheat chapatis (or brown rice chapatis, see page 217), or piles of steaming basmati rice.

THE BITS

6 large kale leaves (any variety is fine), de-stemmed and finely sliced

1¼ cups (240g) dried brown chickpeas, soaked and cooked

generous ¾ cups (200ml) chickpea cooking broth, or vegetable stock

For the masala

2 tablespoons vegetable oil

1 teaspoon cumin seeds

2 bay leaves

1 small cinnamon stick (or 1½ teaspoons ground cinnamon)

6 cloves

1 large onion, finely diced

2 carrots, scrubbed and roughly grated

3 cloves of garlic, peeled

1½ inches (4cm) of fresh ginger, peeled

1 hot red chili, finely sliced

2 teaspoons garam masala

4 dates, soaked in water for 2 hours, then finely diced

a handful of cashews, soaked in water for 2 hours

6 ripe tomatoes, diced

2 teaspoons tamarind paste

¾ teaspoon sea salt (or to taste)

¾ teaspoon freshly ground black pepper (or to taste)

For the garnish

2 tablespoons roasted cashews, roughly chopped

½ a handful of fresh cilantro leaves, roughly chopped

DO IT

Heat the oil in a large frying pan on medium heat. Add the cumin seeds, bay leaves, cinnamon stick and cloves and fry for 30 seconds until they begin to pop, then add the onions and carrots, stirring well. Cook for 6–8 minutes, until the onions go soft and brown.

Put the garlic, ginger and chili into a food processor and blend until smooth, adding ¼ cup (50ml) water to make a loose paste. Pour into the pan, and stir and cook for a minute. When you can really smell that garlic roasting, add the garam masala. Cook for 2 minutes, stirring frequently and making sure the spices don't stick (add 1 tablespoon of water if this happens).

Drain your dates and cashews, add them along with the tomatoes and tamarind paste to the food processor (no need to clean it out this time), and blend together until smooth (you can do this in advance). Add this tomato sauce to the pan and stir, then set the heat to a decent simmer and cook slowly for 15 minutes. Add the kale and simmer for another 5 minutes. Add the chickpeas and thin out the sauce with the chickpea cooking stock (if needed – the sauce should be thick and concentrated). Season (be heavy-handed with the black pepper). Stir and warm through for 5 minutes, then sprinkle with the chopped cashews and cilantro.

Pakistani Pumpkin & Beet Bhuna with Banana & Lime Raita

FOR 6

Pakistani food has always seemed really intense and earthy to me when compared to that of its neighbor, India. This style of *bhuna* (a curry with a thick sauce made using fried spices) is really easy – just spread it all out on a tray and roast until gorgeous and golden. The sauce should be shimmering and rich, the spices well toasted. This bhuna is a dry-style curry, so don't expect loads of liquid here; that's where the raita comes in. The masala can be made the night before, which intensifies the flavors. Beet leaves are a magical ingredient with huge amounts of nutrients. If they look a little past their prime, or if you cannot source beets with leaves on, use ruby chard or large spinach leaves instead. Serve this with fluffy rice.

THE BITS

2 large beets, scrubbed and cut into 2-inch (5cm) wedges, plus the leaves, roughly chopped, and stems, finely chopped

3 tablespoons canola or vegetable oil

1½ teaspoons cumin seeds

1 teaspoon black mustard seeds

1 small sugar/pie pumpkin, scrubbed, deseeded and cut into 2-inch (5cm) wedges

5 banana shallots or 1 large onion, cut into wedges roughly the same size as the beets

½ teaspoon sea salt

½ teaspoon freshly cracked black pepper

10 large cloves of garlic, peeled

For the masala

½ tablespoon vegetable oil

1 large onion, finely sliced

4 cloves of garlic, peeled and crushed

1 inch (2.5cm) fresh ginger, peeled and chopped

½ teaspoon chili powder

¼ teaspoon ground cardamom (or 4 cardamom pods, crushed)

½ teaspoon ground turmeric

⅓ teaspoon ground cinnamon

6 large tomatoes, chopped

1 tablespoon tomato paste

scant ½ cup (100ml) water

2 teaspoons garam masala

½ teaspoon sea salt

For the banana & lime raita

1⅔ cups (400ml) unsweetened soy yogurt

2 just-ripe bananas, peeled, halved lengthwise and cut into 1cm chunks

a handful of fresh cilantro, finely chopped

juice of ½ a lime

1 teaspoon lime zest

½ teaspoon salt

For the garnish

1 tablespoon vegetable oil

1 large onion, finely sliced

1 yellow bell pepper, finely sliced

a handful of fresh cilantro leaves

DO IT

Preheat the oven to 400°F (200°C). To make the masala, heat the oil in a large frying pan, add the onion and sauté for 3 minutes. Mash the garlic and ginger with a pestle and mortar or a food processor and add to the onions, cook for 3 minutes, then add the chili, cardamom, turmeric and cinnamon and warm through for a minute, stirring frequently.

(continued) →

Now add the tomatoes, tomato paste and water to the pan and cook on a steady simmer with a lid on for 20 minutes. Stir in the garam masala and the chopped beet leaves and season with salt. Set aside and allow to cool. Pour into a food processor and blend until smooth (or blitz with an immersion blender).

In a large ceramic baking dish, toss the chopped beets in oil. Cover and bake for 25 minutes. Add the cumin and mustard seeds, along with the pumpkin, shallots, salt and pepper. Toss together well, making sure there is space between the veggies. If not, use a second baking tray. Put back into the oven and roast for 30–35 minutes, turning everything over halfway through cooking. When you turn them, add the garlic cloves and beet stems. The veggies should be nicely caramelized and softened by now, but a mile away from mushy. Check the beets – they can be a little stubborn.

To make the banana and lime raita, mix all the ingredients together in a bowl. To make the garnish, put a heavy-bottomed frying pan on high heat, add the oil, and when hot, throw in the onions and peppers and stir-fry for 5–6 minutes, until everything is sweet and a little charred around the edges. Season with a pinch of salt. Keep warm.

Drop the oven temp to 350°F (180°C). Pour the masala over the roasting veggies and combine well (being careful not to break up the pumpkin). Warm through in the oven for 10 minutes. The sauce should be getting nice and concentrated by now, which is what we're looking for.

Sprinkle the bhuna with the warm onions and peppers, top with fresh cilantro and place center stage on the table. Big spoonfuls of the raita are a must.

Roasted Almond & Kohlrabi Koftas with Tomato & Ginger Masala

MAKES 14 KOFTAS

Koftas are like saucy croquettes combining India's finest flavors. Wonderfully crisp on the outside and gooey in the middle, they're normally fried, but I have gone for a baked treatment for healthier results. Koftas are typically cooked in a rich masala, but I like their crisp nature, so I just spoon on the sauce at the end, to help retain their crunch. Koftas can be made with most combinations of vegetables – they are a great technique to have in your vegan repertoire and are a traditionally gluten-free option, using gram (chickpea) flour to bind the ingredients together. Ground coriander always adds a lovely nutty flavor and has the added benefit of acting as a thickener. Add as many almonds as you like here, the more the merrier! The potatoes are best cooked well in advance and refrigerated. The drier your potatoes, the firmer your koftas. Cauliflower "rice" (see page 128) would be an ideal accompaniment, along with a mound of fresh green leaves.

THE BITS

1½ pounds (750g) potatoes, peeled and cut into small cubes

1 teaspoon sea salt

3 tablespoons sunflower oil

2 red onions, finely sliced

1 large carrot, scrubbed and coarsely grated

1 large kohlrabi, peeled and coarsely grated

2 red chilies, deseeded, very finely diced, or 1 teaspoon red pepper flakes

2 teaspoons coriander seeds

2 teaspoons cumin seeds

1 teaspoon ground turmeric

½ teaspoon ground cardamom

½ teaspoon ground cinnamon

1/8 teaspoon asafetida

2 handfuls of fresh cilantro (stems and leaves), finely chopped

2 big handfuls of roasted almonds, roughly chopped

3 tablespoons gram (chickpea) flour

3 heaped tablespoons cornstarch, for dusting the kofta

For the tomato and ginger masala

6 cardamom pods or ½ teaspoon ground cardamom

1 large pinch of sea salt

3 cloves of garlic, peeled and grated

2 inches (5cm) fresh ginger, peeled and grated

1 tablespoon vegetable oil

1 teaspoon cumin seeds

1 large onion, peeled and grated

1 large pinch of asafetida

1 teaspoon fennel seeds

1 red chili, finely sliced, or ½ teaspoon red pepper flakes

½ teaspoon ground coriander

5 large tomatoes, roughly chopped

scant 1 cup (225ml) water

1 tablespoon gram (chickpea) flour or almond meal

1 teaspoon unrefined brown sugar (depending on the sweetness of your tomatoes; see page 20)

½ tablespoon lemon juice

olive oil

For the garnish

a handful of fresh cilantro leaves, chopped

(continued) →

Put the potatoes into a large pan and cover them with cold water. Add ½ teaspoon of sea salt and bring to a boil, then reduce the heat and simmer for 35 minutes, until tender. Press a knife tip into a potato – when they are ready it should pass through it with ease. Drain the potatoes and allow to cool slightly. When warm but not hot, mash until smooth. (In an Indian kitchen you'd grate them, but this takes ages!)

To make the tomato and ginger masala, first mash the cardamom pods with a pestle and mortar and pick out the cardamom husks, leaving the black seeds in the mortar. Add the salt, garlic and ginger and mash some more, to form a nice paste.

Heat the oil in a frying pan on medium-high heat. Add the cumin seeds and sauté for 30 seconds, until fragrant, then add your grated onion. Fry for 3 minutes, then add the ginger mix. Sprinkle in the asafetida, fennel seeds, chili and ground coriander and fry for 1 minute more, stirring constantly. Now add the tomatoes, water, gram flour and sugar. Simmer with a lid on for 10 minutes, then remove from the heat and check the seasoning.

Leave the sauce to cool slightly, then pour into a food processor (or use an immersion blender) and pulse until smooth. It keeps for a day in the fridge and can even be served cold or used as a tasty dip. Whether serving warm or cold, add the lemon juice and a splash of olive oil just before serving.

To make the koftas, heat 1 tablespoon of oil in a frying pan on medium-low heat. Add the onions and cook for 10 minutes, getting them well caramelized. Lower the heat if they are becoming charred. Add the carrot and cook for 3 minutes more (turn the heat up), then add the kohlrabi, chilies, spices and ½ teaspoon of salt. Continue to cook for 7 minutes, stirring regularly. We'd like the veggies to caramelize slightly, removing some of their water content.

Preheat the oven to 350°F (180°C).

Put the potatoes into a large bowl and add the kohlrabi mix, fresh cilantro, toasted almonds and gram flour. Blend it all together with a trusty spoon (or use your hands) until everything is very well incorporated. Check the seasoning (you may need a tad more salt).

Pour 2 tablespoons of oil onto a large baking tray and put the corn flour on a large plate. Using your hands, form the kofta mixture into ten fat sausage shapes (roughly 2 tablespoons of the mixture per kofta). Roll each kofta lightly in the corn flour, giving them a good dusting all over, then knock off any excess and place them on the oiled baking tray, rolling over once to coat them in oil. Bake for 20 minutes, then turn them all over and bake for another 15 minutes. The koftas should be golden and crispy.

Serve the koftas on warm plates with a few spoons of the tomato and ginger masala and a sprinkling of fresh cilantro.

Green Pea, Rose & Cauliflower Pulao with Coconut & Mint Chutney

SERVES 6–8

This is a light and fragrant rice dish, with the added wonders of coconut milk, saffron and a splash of rose water to bring luxury and a real sense of authenticity to a dish I've enjoyed countless times in India. *Pulao* comes in many forms – a type of South Asian pilaf, its name basically translates as "a ball of rice." This particular recipe adds an extra level of loveliness to humble rice. Adding a little rose water can bring a totally new and slightly floral dimension to vegan cooking. Too much rose water can kill a dish, though, and make it taste like a cheap boudoir, so err on the side of caution when using. The chana dal used in the chutney is a type of split chickpea popular in Indian cuisine, and is also known as Bengal gram dal.

THE BITS

2 cups (400g) uncooked high-quality basmati rice

2 tablespoons coconut oil (or vegetable oil)

a big handful of cashews (halved lengthwise is best, like nutty half-moons)

½ a handful of curry leaves

1½ teaspoons cumin seeds

1½ teaspoons fennel seeds

3 onions, finely sliced

1½ inches (4cm) fresh ginger, peeled and grated

4 cloves of garlic, peeled and crushed

1 cinnamon stick, broken in half

10 green cardamom pods, cracked

1 x 14-ounce (400ml) can of coconut milk

1½ teaspoons saffron, soaked in 1 tablespoon warm water (optional)

a handful of golden raisins

½ a small cauliflower, roughly chopped into small florets, using the stem as well

1 teaspoon sea salt

2 big handfuls of fresh green peas (frozen will also work)

1–2 tablespoons rose water (to taste)

For the garnish

½ a handful of toasted cashews, halved lengthwise

a handful of fresh cilantro, chopped

For the coconut & mint chutney

½ inch (1.5cm) fresh ginger, peeled and grated

1–2 small green chilies (to taste)

1 large clove of garlic, peeled and grated

½ a fresh coconut, grated (or 1⅓ cups [120g] desiccated coconut, soaked for 2 hours)

1 tablespoon lemon juice

2 handfuls of fresh mint leaves, finely sliced

¼ cup (50g) chana dal or ¼ cup (25g) gram (chickpea) flour

a large pinch of sea salt

½ cup (125ml) fresh water

DO IT

Wash your rice, covering it with fresh water and swooshing the rice around with your hand, then pouring the dirty water away. Rice has normally come a long way and it can get a little grubby. Repeat this until the water is running clear-ish. Drain again, then soak the rice in fresh water for 30 minutes. Drain well again.

Heat the coconut oil in a large frying pan on medium heat and when hot, toast the cashews, curry leaves, cumin seeds and fennel seeds for 30 seconds. Throw in your onions and ginger and cook, stirring well, until golden – 10–12 minutes will do nicely. Remove 3 tablespoons of the onion mixture and set aside for the garnish.

Now add the garlic, cinnamon sticks and cardamom pods and panfry for 2 minutes – things will be getting really aromatic right about now.

Pour in the drained rice and stir well. Monitor the heat of your pan and take it off the heat if it's going crazy and starting to burn the rice. Set aside 2 tablespoons of the coconut milk and add the rest the pan with the saffron, golden raisins, cauliflower and salt. Then pour in enough water to cover the rice by 1cm. Stir and bring to a gentle boil. Cover tightly with a well-fitting lid and cook for 25 minutes on the lowest setting possible (without peeking!).

To make the coconut and mint chutney, put the ginger, chili and garlic in a mortar or a food processor and blend together. Add the coconut, lemon juice, mint and the dal or gram flour and blend further, adding water gradually to make a thick paste. Add salt to taste. That's it! This chutney will thicken if kept in the fridge, so stir in a little more water if necessary to get a nice, creamy consistency.

Fluff up the pulao with a fork, add the peas, then cover and allow to cook for 5 minutes longer, adding a touch more water if needed. The pulao should be more moist than normal boiled rice, with a little sauce. Just before serving, stir in the rose water to taste, remembering that a little goes a long way. Mix in the reserved coconut milk for a final saucy flourish.

I like to serve rice dishes like this in one big pyramid on a large serving platter or plate. Garnish with the reserved caramelized onions and a scattering of cashews and fresh cilantro. Serve the chutney on the side in small bowls, or drizzled around the base of the pulao for maximum "eye candy" effect.

Keralan Coconut & Vegetable Curry with Pineapple & Watermelon Salad

FOR 4

This dish is called *avial* and comes from tropical Kerala, in southwestern India. I've taken the liberty of adding some "English vegetables" to the mix (this is what the older Keralans still call things like carrots and green beans), along with fistfuls of the lifeblood of this lovely part of the world: coconut. In Kerala they use a large vegetable called "drumstick," which resembles an elongated okra and adds a lovely subtle flavor. When I'm cooking over there I normally pick them straight from the tree. They're a real star ingredient when you have them. The general rule with curry leaves is the fresher, the better. You should be able to find them at Indian groceries. When pineapples and watermelons are out of season, try making the salad with fruit combinations like apple and peach, or pear and orange. Serve with your preferred rice.

THE BITS

2–3 fresh green chilies (to taste)

2 big handfuls of freshly grated or desiccated coconut

2 teaspoons cumin seeds

scant 1 cup (220ml) coconut milk or unsweetened soy yogurt

2 large carrots, scrubbed

2 large potatoes, scrubbed

1 large zucchini

6 fat asparagus spears

2 green plantains, peeled

generous ¾ cup (200ml) water

1 heaped teaspoon ground turmeric

½ teaspoon sea salt

a big handful of snow or sugar snap peas, or green beans

2 tablespoons coconut oil

2 teaspoons mustard seeds

3 tablespoons curry leaves

For the pineapple & watermelon salad

½ of a small pineapple

⅓ of a small watermelon (don't bother deseeding)

1 large cucumber

1 small handful of fresh cilantro, roughly chopped

a pinch of sea salt

a large pinch of chaat masala mix or black salt (optional)

DO IT

With a pestle and mortar or a food processor, blend together the chilies, coconut and cumin seeds (if you're using desiccated coconut, add 2 tablespoons of the coconut milk to make a thick paste). This is best done in advance and can be left overnight in the fridge to develop a zing.

Cut the carrots, potatoes, zucchini, asparagus and plantains into 1-inch (2.5cm) pieces. Heat the water in a large pot and add the turmeric, salt, carrots and potatoes. Bring to a steady boil, then lower the heat to a simmer and pop a lid on. Cook for 10 minutes, then add the zucchini and plantains and cook for 10 minutes more, still with the lid on.

Add the coconut paste to the curry with the coconut milk or yogurt and gently stir to combine. Cook uncovered for 8–10 minutes on a gentle simmer. Check that the carrots and potatoes are tender, then add the asparagus and peas or beans and remove the pot from the heat. Cover and set aside for a few minutes.

To make the salad, peel the pineapple, watermelon and cucumber and cut into 1cm chunks. Put into a bowl with the rest of the salad ingredients and mix.

In a small frying pan, warm the coconut oil and roast the mustard seeds and curry leaves for 1 minute. Remove from the heat (you can leave them to sit a while – this intensifies the flavors). Stir the seasoned oil into the avial and serve with rice and a small bowl of the pineapple and watermelon salad on the side.

Tiger Mountain Beans with Red Pepper Masala, Peanut & Cilantro Salad & Sesame Pancakes

FOR 4

I live on Tiger Mountain in North Wales, so called because of the vivid orange and black stripes that can sometimes be seen during autumn sunsets. This simple everyday curry is a staple at that time of year and combines two of my favorite things, curry and beans. It makes a wonderful base for all kinds of additions, my favorite being smoked tofu. I can be quite heavy-handed with my spices, but have realized that subtlety is key, and a gently spiced dish can have as much effect as something highly spiced. This tomato and pepper masala sauce is softly spiced and the perfect accompaniment to the hearty kidney beans. The sesame pancakes are delicious, but the dish is equally wonderful served with simply cooked rice.

Gluten-free option: opt for GF flatbreads instead of the pancakes.

THE BITS

4 teaspoons coriander seeds

4 teaspoons cumin seeds

1 tablespoon vegetable oil

1 large carrot, cut into ¾-inch (2cm) chunks

1 celery stalk, cut into ¾-inch (2cm) chunks

1 eggplant, cut into ¾-inch (2cm) chunks

2 bay leaves

½ teaspoon ground cardamom or 6 cardamom pods, mashed and husks removed

¼ teaspoon ground cinnamon

½ teaspoon chili powder

generous 1 cup (200g) dried red kidney beans, soaked and cooked

about ⅓ cup (75ml) bean cooking liquid or water (as needed)

1½ teaspoons ajwain seeds or dried thyme

1 teaspoon sea salt

¼ teaspoon freshly cracked black pepper

2 handfuls of green beans, cut into 2-inch (5cm) pieces, or snow or sugar snap peas

1 teaspoon jaggery (or unrefined brown sugar; see page 20)

7 ounces (200g) smoked tofu or pressed firm tofu, cut into 1cm cubes (optional, but awesome)

For the red pepper masala

2 red bell peppers

a little vegetable oil

3 cloves of garlic, peeled

1½ inches (4cm) fresh ginger

1 large onion

5 large tomatoes

For the peanut & cilantro salad

2 handfuls of raw unsalted peanuts

2 tablespoons vegetable oil

a pinch of sea salt

1–2 red chilies (to taste), deseeded and finely diced

½ a red onion or 3 scallions, as finely diced as possible

1 tablespoon lemon juice

a big handful of fresh cilantro leaves, roughly chopped

1 x sesame & sweet corn pancakes (see page 125), omitting the sweet corn and made immediately before serving

To serve

soy yogurt (optional)

DO IT

Preheat the oven to 400°F (200°C). Rub the red peppers with a little oil and roast them in the oven for 30 minutes, or chop them up and cook them in a lightly oiled pan for 10 minutes on medium heat. Either way, make 'em sweet and lovely.

Warm a large heavy-bottomed frying pan (something like a traditional karhai), add the coriander and cumin seeds and toast them gently for 1–2 minutes, keeping them moving all the time. They will be fragrant and popping. Grind them with a pestle and mortar. Take out roughly 1½ teaspoons of the toasted spices and set aside, leaving the rest in the mortar.

Using the same pan, dry roast the peanuts for your salad. Put them into the pan on medium heat and stir until they are turning golden and slightly charred. Add half the peanuts and the salt to the spices in the mortar and pour in 2 tablespoons of oil (you could also use a food processor here), then crush the peanuts until a chunky crumb is formed. Add the rest of the nuts and do the same again. Put the peanuts into a bowl and mix with the chilies, onions, lemon juice and fresh cilantro. Set aside.

Roughly chop all the ingredients for the red pepper masala, then turn on a food processor and, with the motor running, add the bits in this order: garlic, ginger, onion, peppers. Make a thick, smooth purée, remove from the processor and set aside. Now add the tomatoes to the processor and blend until smooth. Set aside.

To make the Tiger Mountain beans, heat 1 tablespoon of oil in your frying pan on medium heat and add the carrots, celery and eggplant. Cook for 6 minutes, add the reserved 1½ teaspoons of toasted spices, the bay leaves, cardamom, cinnamon and chili powder, stir for a minute and then pour in the red pepper mix. Cook on a high simmer for 5 minutes, stirring well, until the masala is getting nice and sweet!

Add the cooked kidney beans, with about ⅓ cup (75ml) of their lovely cooking juices, the blitzed tomatoes, thyme or ajwain seeds, salt and pepper and cook for 5 minutes more. Add the green beans or peas, jaggery and smoked tofu, then pop a lid on the pan and continue to cook for 2 minutes, warming things through. Remove from the heat and keep warm. I like there to be a good amount of sauce with my Tiger Beans – add more kidney bean stock if needed. Check the seasoning.

Make your sesame pancakes at the last minute and keep them warm, wrapped in a kitchen towel.

Serve the Tiger Mountain beans with the peanut and coriander salad on the side, and with piles of sesame pancakes nearby. Adding some soy yogurt to the plate would not hurt at all, and you may even like to turn it all into a wrap!

Travels in India.

Clay-Baked Potatoes & Parsnips with Roasted Garlic & Date Masala

FOR 4–6

Baking in clay is an ancient tradition and it is still popular in my Spanish neck of the woods, Murcia. It gives an intangible addition to the flavor of the food, but if you don't have a clay dish, just use a large casserole instead. This is a sweet and warming cold-weather curry, using the wonderful roots that get us through those bleak, chilly nights tempered by warm fires and mugs of spicy chai (see page 69). The combination of dates and almonds is probably as old as cooking in clay pots. The dried chilies used here are the large, flat Indian variety, not the very spicy squat ones. They add a little piquant and smoky spice to the dish. Serve with a nice Indian pickle (such as lime or garlic) and towers of whole wheat chapatis. A little saucy dal would be awesome, too. It's an Indian feast!

THE BITS

½ a small butternut squash

4 large waxy potatoes

4 parsnips

2 carrots

2 onions, skins on, halved (red ones look cooler)

10 cloves of garlic, unpeeled

4 large tomatoes, halved

3 tablespoons vegetable oil

sea salt

6 big dates, soaked for 2 hours in 4 tablespoons water, pitted

a large handful of almond meal

1½ inches (4cm) fresh ginger, roughly chopped

¼ teaspoon ground allspice

⅔ cup (150ml) water

zest and juice of ½ a lime

vegetable oil, for drizzling

½ teaspoon ground turmeric

1 teaspoon cumin seeds

½ teaspoon black mustard seeds

5 red chilies

a large pinch of freshly cracked black pepper

For the garnish

a handful of toasted sliced almonds

a handful of fresh cilantro leaves, finely chopped

DO IT

If you have a couple of large clay dishes, submerge them in water for at least an hour. Alternatively, grab a few baking trays or casserole dishes, or a combination. You'll need three in total.

Preheat the oven to 350°F (180°C). Deseed the squash, scrub the potatoes, parsnips and carrots, then cut them all into large similar-size wedges. Place the parsnips and squash on one dish and the potatoes and carrots on another and set aside.

Toss the onions, garlic and tomatoes in the oil and place on the remaining baking dish. Sprinkle with sea salt and place in the oven for 30–35 minutes, until the onions are well caramelized and the tomatoes have some color. Turn the onion and garlic after 10 minutes using a metal spatula. The smaller garlic cloves may be ready to remove from the oven at this point.

Put the dates, almond meal and ginger into a food processor and blitz to a smooth paste. Add the roasted onion and garlic (pop them out of their skins), plus the tomatoes, allspice and water and pulse again until a nice thick sauce is formed. Pour into a pan and bring to a steady boil, cooking on a low simmer for 20 minutes. Stir in the lime zest and juice, check the seasoning, put a lid on the pan and keep warm.

Drizzle all the vegetables with oil and sprinkle with the turmeric, cumin seeds and mustard seeds, along with the red chilies, a sprinkling of black pepper and 1 teaspoon of sea salt. Mix it all together using your hands.

Pop the dishes into the oven with the potatoes at the top. Bake for 25 minutes, turning everything over at least once. The parsnips will stick, so keep your eye on them. Remove the squash and leave the potatoes in for another 10 minutes (if needed). When the potatoes and carrots are soft, remove and turn the oven off.

Gently scrape the roast veggies into one dish and pour the almond and date sauce on top. Combine gently with a spatula or wooden spoon (not a metal spoon). Cover and leave to mingle for 5 minutes in the still warm oven. Serve sprinkled with toasted sliced almonds and fresh cilantro.

Matar Dal with Watercress, Braised Red Cabbage Sabji & Brown Rice Chapati

FOR 4

When you sit down to a bowl of dal, you are not alone – about a billion other people are probably doing the exact same thing. Dal can be second only to rice in the global food-loving stakes, and for me is the ultimate comfort food. It's the lifeblood of India and, with a warm chapati, is one of my favorite foods. Matar dal is made with green split peas, which add a great color and a nice richness and texture. This dal is much thicker than most that you are served in India, but you can add water to make it more soup-like. This dish is amazing with a spoonful of sweet mango pickle (to make your own, see mango chutney on page 307).

THE BITS

For the matar dal with watercress

generous 1 cup (225g) dried green split peas

4¼ cups (1 liter) water

1 inch (2.5cm) fresh ginger, peeled and grated or crushed

8 cardamom pods, crushed with the ginger

4 dried red chilies, cut into ¾-inch (2cm) pieces

½ teaspoon ground cumin

1 teaspoon ground coriander

¼ teaspoon asafetida

2 tablespoons curry leaves

3 handfuls of watercress, washed well, or spring greens/kale, very finely sliced

sea salt and freshly ground black pepper

For the red cabbage sabji

1 tablespoon coconut or vegetable oil

½ a red cabbage, finely sliced, tough stalk removed

juice of ½ an orange

1 teaspoon orange zest

2 star anise

2 teaspoons cumin seeds

½ a handful of curry leaves

1 inch (2.5cm) fresh ginger, peeled and grated

4 cloves of garlic, peeled and grated

1 teaspoon garam masala

For the brown rice chapatis (makes 8–10)

1¾ cups (350g) brown rice, cooked

scant 2 cups (450ml) water

¼ teaspoon salt

¼ cup (40g) whole wheat flour

For the garnish

3 tablespoons grated carrot

1 tablespoon toasted sesame seeds

(continued) →

DO IT

Rinse the split peas, put them into fresh water and leave to sit for 10 minutes, picking out anything dodgy that floats to the surface. Drain, then put the split peas into a large heavy-bottomed saucepan with the water and bring to a boil. Drop in the ginger, cardamom pods, chilies, spices and curry leaves. Bring to a rolling boil, then lower the heat and simmer for 50 minutes to 1 hour, skimming off any white froth. Stir the dal regularly, ensuring that it doesn't stick to the bottom of the pan. Add the watercress and simmer for another 5 minutes (10 minutes if using kale or spring greens). When the peas are cooked you should be left with a thick dal, the consistency of heavy cream. Season well and cover, removing from the heat.

To make the red cabbage sabji, heat ½ tablespoon of oil in a large frying pan on medium-high heat and add the red cabbage. Cook for 5 minutes, stirring regularly, until the cabbage is beginning to get some nice color. Add the orange juice, zest and star anise, cover the pan, drop the heat to the lowest setting and allow to steam for 5 minutes. Set the cabbage aside and keep warm with a lid on.

Add another ½ tablespoon of oil to the pan and warm on a medium-high heat. Pop in the cumin seeds and curry leaves and sizzle for a minute. Quickly add the ginger and garlic and cook for another minute, then put the cabbage back into the pan with the garam masala and sauté for 2 minutes more. Stir continuously to prevent the spices from sticking, adding small drizzles of water if needed. Cook until the cabbage is tender and has that beautiful, toasty, braised look about it.

To make the chapatis, put the rice, water, salt and flour into a food processor and blitz until smooth. On a well-floured surface, work the dough, sprinkling flour regularly to stop it from sticking. It will come together a bit, but nothing like a normal bread dough. Don't worry; it will work itself out in the pan. Roll the dough into a ball and stick in the fridge for 30 minutes.

Heat a large heavy-bottomed frying pan (or *tawa* if you are the real-deal chapati aficionado) on medium-high heat. Grab a squash-ball-size amount of dough and gently roll out into a circle with a rolling pin on a floured surface. Sprinkle well with flour and don't mind too much about it sticking. Sometimes just pressing it out with your fingers and the heel of your hand is easier than rolling. Using a metal spatula, pop the dough circle into the warm pan and sprinkle the top side with a little more flour. Cook for 2 minutes, then flip over and cook the second side for 1 minute. While this is going on, get your next chapati ready. Keep the cooked chapatis warm, wrapped in a clean kitchen towel. I normally make two or three chapatis per person.

Serve the braised red cabbage in a shallow, wide bowl with the matar dal piled centrally on top. You might like to finish with a sprinkle of grated carrot to add even more color to the bowl, and some lovely toasted sesame seeds. Don't forget the chapatis, which are warm and primed for action.

Burgers & More

Just when you thought you'd ventured to the far shores of the great burger sphere, in comes the vegan crew with a whole host of new and wild combos to try. I am sure normal burgers are very tasty, but they'll struggle to compete with this colorful bunch for nutrition and sumptuous flavors.

Veggie burgers can be hopelessly hit-and-miss. They need to be packed with flavor and have the right texture, otherwise you're left with a crumbling pile of bean matter or a dense and sloppy patty.

Vegan burgers open so many doors in your culinary repertoire, offering an almost infinite palette of ingredients to play with and merge into delicious discs. The question is, how much can you handle in one bun? How far can we push this format until we reach the stage of a three-course burger?

Vegan food in general requires a little thought and dedication, otherwise you end up living on chips and bananas. I won't claim that these burgers and bangers are as easy to prepare as their meaty counterparts, but that's not the point! I know you all love cooking, so spending time in the kitchen is a pleasure, right? Elbow-deep in vivid green *bhaji* mix or grappling with vibrant vegan chorizos, I can see you there, smiling and enjoying every minute well spent.

Here I give you burgers and bangers that are dressed to impress, with over-the-top trimmings and then some. Glorified sandwiches that demand complete taste bud attention and will no doubt prompt finger-licking happiness in vegans and non-vegans alike.

Portobello Pecan Burgers with Roasted Pumpkin Wedges

MAKES 6–8 MAMMOTH BURGERS

Here we have a burger that is rich, with a deep flavor from the mushrooms, cumin and miso. It is packed with heavy umami flavors, with the seaweed, pecans and miso working their potent charms. Sun-blushed, or semi-dried, tomatoes ooze fragrant tomato all over this burger. This burger mix will keep very well in the fridge, 5 days easy. Try making it into "meatballs," with a tomato sauce and pasta.

Gluten-free option: just cook 2 tablespoons (25g) more rice and omit the breadcrumbs, and use GF miso.

THE BITS

4 tablespoons olive oil

¾ pound (350g) portobello mushrooms, cut into cubes

1 eggplant, chopped into ¾-inch (2cm) pieces

a large pinch of sea salt and freshly ground black pepper

3 tablespoons fresh oregano leaves or 1 teaspoon dried oregano

1 onion, sliced

2 celery stalks, finely diced

4 cloves of garlic, peeled and crushed

¾ ounce (20g) dried nori (seaweed), cut into very fine ribbons

1 cup (175g) dried flageolet beans, soaked overnight, then cooked with ½ teaspoon baking soda and cooled, or 3 cups canned, drained

1¼ cups (120g) toasted pecans

½ cup (100g) red or brown rice, cooked and cooled

2 heaped tablespoons brown miso

1 teaspoon baking soda

1 cup (100g) fine whole wheat breadcrumbs

For the pumpkin wedges

1½ pounds (750g) sugar/pie pumpkin, scrubbed, deseeded and cut into 2-inch (5cm) wedges

2 tablespoons vegetable oil

a large pinch of sea salt

1 x tarragon aioli (see page 305)

To serve

8 seeded whole wheat rolls, halved (for gluten-free aternative, use your favorite GF bread)

a big handful sun-blushed (semi-dried) tomatoes

buttery lettuce leaves (something like oak-leaf)

DO IT

To make the pumpkin wedges, preheat the oven to 350°F (180°C). Put the pumpkin on a baking tray, toss with the oil and salt, and roast for 30 minutes, turning over once. The pumpkin should be tender and nicely colored.

Heat 3 tablespoons of oil in a large heavy-bottomed frying pan on medium-low and add the mushrooms and eggplant. Cook for 10 minutes, then add the salt and pepper. Cook for another 5 minutes, until the eggplant is soft. Stir in the oregano leaves and set aside in a bowl.

In the same pan, heat 1 tablespoon of oil on medium-high and cook the onion and celery for 5 minutes. Add the garlic and seaweed and cook for another 2 minutes, then remove from the heat and combine with the eggplants and mushrooms.

In a food processor, combine half of the beans, pecans, eggplant mixture and rice with the miso, sifting in the baking soda. Blitz to a thick paste. Add the breadcrumbs and the rest of the beans, pecans, rice and eggplant mixture. Pulse until a chunky mix forms, coarse in texture but finely chopped. Check the seasoning – the miso is quite salty. Transfer to a bowl, combining it all well with your hands. Form into six to eight fat burgers. Put them into the fridge for 30 minutes to firm up. Meanwhile, make the tarragon aioli.

Pop an ovenproof frying pan on medium-high heat and lightly oil it. Cook each burger for 5 minutes per side, until beautifully light brown. If they lose shape and are unruly in the pan, press them down using the back of a metal spatula. Veggie burgers are sensitive and need to be handled with care.

Put all the burgers into a warm oven, 300°F (150°C), for 10 minutes to finish cooking.

Cut your bread rolls in half and put them into the warm oven for 5 minutes. On the base of each warm roll, scatter sun-blushed tomatoes (with a little of their oil) and top with a lettuce leaf, the burger and a good smattering of tarragon aioli. Serve with the warm pumpkin wedges.

Portobello pecan burgers
with roasted pumpkin
wedges, page 222

Beet Quarter-Pounders with Pineapple, Butter Bean Purée & Chickpea Fries

MAKES 6–8, DEPENDING HOW CHUNKY YOU LIKE YOUR BURGERS!

This style of "beet" burger is one of my all-time favorite things. You can play around with the accompaniments, but the burger itself is a legend in vegan circles far and wide. You can give the burgers a crunchy coating by patting them with cornmeal (the purple with the yellow looks very cool indeed), although I've left them naked here so we can see the charred outside and lovely pink middle.

Try to get your breadcrumbs really dry for this – toast them slightly in the oven beforehand and they will be even better at binding everything together. Brown rice is a brilliant substitute for buckwheat. The butter bean purée is best made in advance, even the day before, if you can. Homemade ketchup (see page 304) is a welcome addition to the party.

Gluten-free option: use GF breadcrumbs or finely crushed GF crackers, as well as GF bread.

THE BITS

½ tablespoon vegetable oil

1 small onion, peeled and grated

3 cloves of garlic, peeled and grated

1⅓ cups (225g) buckwheat groats, cooked and cooled, not too mushy

⅔ cup (115g) brown or green lentils, cooked and cooled, drained well

9 ounces (260g) beets, grated

¼ cup (30g) fine whole wheat breadcrumbs

1½ teaspoons ground cumin

1 teaspoon ground coriander

1½ teaspoons English mustard

4 tablespoons cashew butter (or almond butter)

½ teaspoon salt

¼ teaspoon freshly ground black pepper

vegetable oil, for frying

For the butter bean purée

1 cup (175g) dried butter beans, soaked overnight

½ teaspoon baking soda

1 large clove of garlic, peeled and crushed

juice of ½ a lemon

a handful of fresh parsley, finely chopped

a large pinch of sea salt and freshly ground black pepper

⅓ cup (75ml) olive oil

For the chickpea fries

2 cups (250g) gram (chickpea) flour

2 tablespoons nutritional yeast flakes

3 ⅓ cups (800ml) water

1½ tablespoons olive oil

a large pinch of sea salt

vegetable oil, for frying

To serve

6–8 big whole wheat bread rolls, halved

1 small red onion, finely sliced

Little Gem lettuce leaves

6–8 rounds of fresh pineapple, very thinly sliced

(continued) →

DO IT

To make the butter bean purée, drain the soaked butter beans and put them into a pot with plenty of fresh water to cover them. Add the baking soda and bring to a boil, then cook on a fast simmer for 45 minutes, until the beans are very tender. Drain them and cool slightly. Put them into a food processor with the other ingredients, drizzling in the oil as the blades are running. Check the seasoning, allow to cool completely, then pop into the fridge.

Heat ½ tablespoon of vegetable oil in a small frying pan and cook the onion for 5 minutes. Add the garlic and cook for another 2 minutes. You're just sweetening them a little.

In a food processor, pulse the buckwheat and lentils with the grated beets and the cooked onion and garlic. Blitz until the mixture comes together, but still has a slightly rough texture. Transfer it to a mixing bowl and add the rest of the ingredients, apart from the frying oil. Use your hands to mix it all very well. Everything should be completely incorporated. Place the mixture in the fridge for 30 minutes to chill and firm up.

To make the chickpea fries, sift the gram flour into a heavy-bottomed saucepan and add the yeast flakes, water, olive oil and salt. Cook over medium-low heat until it becomes a thick paste, stirring constantly. This usually takes about 10 minutes. When the mixture starts to pull away from the sides, remove from the heat and quickly spread the paste out onto a shallow baking tray or deep plate. Allow to cool, then place in the fridge for 1 hour until completely cold.

Cut the chickpea mixture into sticks (however you like your fries). Heat 1 inch (3cm) of vegetable oil in a heavy-bottomed saucepan and fry them in batches for a couple of minutes per side, or until they they are golden and crisp. Remove with a slotted spoon and drain on paper towels. Sprinkle with sea salt and keep them warm in a low-temperature oven. If you prefer a healthier option, you can bake the fries in a preheated oven on a well-oiled baking tray for 20 minutes at 400°F (200°C), turning them halfway through.

Heat a large frying pan (thick-bottomed, preferably) on medium-high. Now form the chilled burger mixture into fat quarter-pounder shapes. To get well-shaped burgers, use a large ring or other shaped cutter (stars and animals work great for kids).

Pour a very thin layer of oil into the pan and cook the burgers for about 10–12 minutes, flipping them occasionally and pressing down gently with a spatula. Drizzle in a little more oil as needed. The burgers should be charred at the edges and heated through – they should look medium rare!

Stack your pounders! Spoon some butter bean purée onto each bread roll, followed by a red onion slice and a lettuce leaf, then your burger, topped with two thin slices of pineapple and the top of the roll. Serve right away, with piles of chickpea fries.

Spinach Bhaji Burgers with Mango Chutney, Mint Raita & Peanut Masala Fries

MAKES 8 BIG BURGER BHAJIS

Vividly green, crispy bhajis and tangy, sweet chutney . . . creamy, cooling raita and crunchy masala fries! This is the best of Indian street food wrapped up in a bun, inspired by a delicious Mumbai street snack called *pav bhaji*. If you can, use unripe green mangoes, normally found in Caribbean and Asian food stores. Failing that, use as unripe a mango as you can find. Green tomatoes and pineapples will also work perfectly in a chutney like this. If your mango is a little sweet, add a touch of white wine vinegar to the chutney to get that glorious balance of sweet and sour. These burgers are definitely best served fresh from the oven, nice and crispy.

Gluten-free option: replace the all-purpose flour with gram (chickpea) flour.

THE BITS

1 teaspoon vegetable or peanut oil

9 ounces (250g) spinach leaves

4½ ounces (125g) silken tofu

3 large cloves of garlic, peeled and crushed

1¾ cups (200g) gram (chickpea) flour

⅓ cup (50g) unbleached all-purpose flour

1 teaspoon baking soda

1 teaspoon ground turmeric

1 teaspoon freshly ground cumin

½ –1 teaspoon chili powder (to taste)

1½ teaspoons dried mint

⅔ cup (150ml) water

10½ ounces (300g) cauliflower, chopped into small florets

2 large red onions, finely sliced

1 teaspoon sea salt

vegetable oil, for shallow-frying

1 x mango chutney (see page 307)

1 x mint raita (see page 306)

For the peanut masala fries

vegetable or peanut oil, for deep-frying

1¼ pounds (600g) potatoes, peeled and cut into your favorite fry shape

½ teaspoon ground turmeric

½ teaspoon chili powder

a large pinch of sea salt

1½ teaspoons unrefined brown sugar (see page 20)

½ teaspoon dried mango (amchoor) powder

1½ teaspoon cumin seeds

a big handful of raw peanuts (unsalted)

1 tablespoon sesame seeds

To serve

8 soft bread rolls, halved (for a gluten-free alternative, use your favorite GF bread)

1 small red onion, finely sliced

1 large tomato, thinly sliced

a handful of fresh cilantro leaves

DO IT

Make the mango chutney and the mint raita.

To make the bhajis, heat 1 teaspoon of vegetable oil in a pan on medium-low, then add the spinach and wilt down until any liquid has evaporated. Place in a food processor with the silken tofu and garlic, and blend together until smooth.

(continued) →

Put the flours, baking soda, spices and mint into a bowl. Make a well in the center and add the spinach mix, then gradually add the water until a thick batter is formed. Stir in the cauliflower pieces and the onions and season with salt. Make sure everything is well mixed.

Warm 1cm of oil in a large frying pan (we're shallow-frying these bhajis) on medium heat (drop a little of the mix into the oil and watch it sizzle – now you're ready). Spoon 2 heaped tablespoons of mix per bhaji (nice big 'uns) into the pan, frying three or four bhajis at a time. Press down into a burger shape, and loosen the bases after a minute using a metal spatula. This will stop them from sticking. Splash a little oil over the bhajis to help them cook evenly, like you do when frying an egg. Fry until both sides are golden brown and the bhajis are cooked through – this will take 10–15 minutes.

Remove the bhajis using the metal spatula and drain well on paper towels. Fry the rest, adding more oil as needed. When they are all done, put them into the oven for 10 minutes at 300°F (150°C) to finish cooking. Check that the centers of the burgers are piping hot before serving.

To make the peanut masala fries, take a separate large saucepan, cover the base with 1 inch (2.5cm) of oil and place over medium-high heat. It is hot enough when you can stick a fry into the oil and it sizzles frantically.

Pat the potatoes dry and lower them into the oil in small batches. Fry for 6 minutes, jiggling them in the pan to make sure they're not sticking together. When they are turning golden and becoming tender, sprinkle the turmeric, red chili powder, salt, sugar, dried mango powder and cumin seeds into the pan. Turn up the heat and continue to fry for 4–5 minutes, until the fries are nice and crisp. Remove from the pan using a slotted spoon and drain well on paper towels.

While the potatoes are frying, heat a small frying pan on medium. Add the peanuts and toast for 2–3 minutes. Keep them moving, otherwise one side will burn. Add the sesame seeds and warm for a minute more. Sprinkle the nuts and seeds over the drained fries and mix well.

Spread a bun base with the raita and top with the onion, tomato and cilantro leaves. Pop the spinach bhaji on top and spoon on some mango chuntey, then place the bun lid on the top. Serve with hot peanut masala fries, small bowls of extra chutney and raita, and a Ravi Shankar raga flowing in the background.

Smoked Tofu Sausage Sandwiches with Red Onion Marmalade & Kale Chips

MAKES 8 CHUNKY SAUSAGES (2 PER SANDWICH)

If I'm left in the kitchen for long enough, this is the kind of thing that happens. This is a souped-up banger fit for vegan royalty. Smoked tofu is delicious, but if you can't get it, use firm tofu and add ½ teaspoon of smoked paprika to the mix. Making vegan sausages is not quite as easy as opening a package and sticking them in a pan, but your efforts will be so worth it.

THE BITS

3 tablespoons canola oil

1 large leek, finely chopped

1 green apple, cored, peeled and finely chopped

3 tablespoons fresh thyme leaves or 1½ teaspoons dried thyme

10 ounces (275g) smoked tofu, or pressed firm tofu (+ ½ teaspoon paprika), mashed with a fork

2 tablespoons apple juice concentrate

1 cup (125g) toasted hazelnuts

7 ounces (200g) silken tofu

3 cups (200g) fresh white breadcrumbs or panko

½ a handful of fresh parsley, finely chopped

4 teaspoons Dijon mustard

sea salt and freshly ground black pepper

4 large soft buns

For the coating

⅓ cup (40g) unbleached all-purpose flour

⅓ cup (475ml) unsweetened soy milk

¾ cup (90g) dry breadcrumbs or panko

3 tablespoons vegetable oil, for baking

For the kale chips

10½ ounces (300g) kale leaves, de-stemmed and roughly torn into 2-inch (5cm) pieces

2 tablespoons vegetable oil

1 tablespoon nutritional yeast flakes (optional)

a large pinch of sea salt and freshly ground black pepper

1 x red onion marmalade (see page 308)

DO IT

In a heavy-bottomed frying pan, warm the oil on medium heat. Add the leeks and apple and cook until soft and golden – about 10 minutes. Add the thyme, smoked tofu and apple juice concentrate, then set aside to cool.

In a food processor, pulse the hazelnuts until a rough crumb is formed. Add the silken tofu and blend to a thick paste.

In a large mixing bowl, combine the breadcrumbs, hazelnut mixture, leek mixture, parsley, and mustard and season well with salt and pepper. Mix until all is well incorporated. The mixture should have the texture of a classic stuffing.

With damp hands, shape the mixture into your average sausage shape. Dip the sausages in flour to lightly coat them, knock off any excess, then splash them into the milk. Roll them in the dry breadcrumbs, pressing down very gently, getting a good coating. Place the sausages on a plate, cover and leave in the fridge for 30 minutes to firm up.

Preheat the oven to 350°F (180°C). Place the sausages on a well-oiled baking tray, drizzling them with a touch more oil (using a pastry brush here may help). Bake for 20–25 minutes, turning twice to cook evenly.

To make the kale chips, wash and completely dry the kale leaves (any moisture at all will make them soggy and they won't crisp up). Put the oil, yeast flakes (if using), pepper and salt into a large bowl. Toss the kale in the oil and salt, giving it a good, shiny coating. Place the kale on a baking tray, or two trays if it's getting crowded. Bake for 10–15 minutes, checking regularly after 10 minutes, and turning them over. Slightly overcooking the kale leaves will make them burnt and bitter, while slightly underdoing it makes them soft and un-crispy. When they're ready, sprinkle with more yeast flakes.

Serve the sausages in a bun, with a healthy spoonful of the red onion marmalade and a nice pile of kale chips.

Chickpea, Butternut & Apricot Burgers with Red Onion, Orange & Black Olive Salad

MAKES 6–8 BULKY BURGERS

Like flat, elaborate falafels, these burgers transport us to somewhere towards the center of the globe. The spice mix baharat is from the Middle East – it is so versatile, and whenever my cooking strays to that part of the world, baharat is never far behind. These burgers are not designed to be very thick and they cook quickly. Served in warm flatbreads with some creamy avocado cheese, they are a crunchy, fruity special treat. To make a real meal of these, try serving them with mujadarra (see page 126) and a lovely tangy green tomato chutney (page 307). The onion really makes this salad. Some parts of the world have such mild, sweet red onions, but they can be hard to find here. If the onion is bitter, the salad just isn't quite the same, so get the sweetest onions you can.

Gluten-free option: use GF pita breads.

THE BITS

1 teaspoon cumin seeds

2 teaspoons coriander seeds

1 tablespoon vegetable oil

9 ounces (250g) butternut squash, finely diced

1 cup (200g) dried chickpeas, soaked overnight

3 scallions, finely sliced

2 cloves of garlic, peeled and crushed

½ a handful of finely chopped fresh cilantro

¼ teaspoon cayenne pepper

½ teaspoon ground cardamom

½ teaspoon ground turmeric

(or 2 teaspoons baharat spice mix instead of all the spices)

a handful of dried apricots, finely diced

¾ teaspoon baking powder

½ teaspoon salt

2 tablespoons tahini (gluten-free, if needed)

2 tablespoons gram (chickpea) flour

3 tablespoons water

vegetable oil, for shallow-frying

3 tablespoons gram (chickpea) flour, for dusting

For the avocado cheese

2 ripe avocados

5 ounces (150g) firm tofu

2 tablespoons lemon juice

a pinch of sea salt and freshly ground black pepper

½ tablespoon nutritional yeast flakes (optional)

For the red onion, orange & black olive salad

1 teaspoon cumin seeds, toasted

4 medium oranges, peeled and sliced, bitter pith removed

1 large red onion, finely sliced

4 dates, finely sliced

½ a handful of pitted black olives, finely sliced

a pinch of sea salt and freshly ground black pepper

2 tablespoons lemon juice

3 tablespoons olive oil

To serve

4 whole wheat pita breads

a handful of pomegranate seeds (optional)

DO IT

In a large frying pan, toast the cumin and coriander seeds on medium heat for 1 minute, moving them all the time in the pan. When popping and fragrant, pour into a mortar and grind. Heat 1 tablespoon of oil in the same pan on medium, and add the butternut squash. Stir and cook for 15 minutes, until tender and cooked through.

(continued) →

Rinse and drain the soaked chickpeas and blitz in a food processor with the scallions, garlic, half the squash and the cilantro. The mix should hold itself together, but not be mushy. Add the rest of the squash, the spices, apricots, baking powder, salt, tahini, gram flour and water and mix together by hand. Cover the mixture and leave in the fridge for an hour or until ready to use.

To make the salad, toast the cumin seeds in a small skillet for 1 minute. Arrange all the salad bits in a flat bowl and leave the flavors to mingle for half an hour.

To make the avocado cheese, place all the ingredients in a shallow bowl and mash together with a fork. The avocados must be ripe, otherwise you will not be able to mash them up. (Try placing unripe avocados in a bowl with some bananas for a day or so. This normally does the trick.)

Heat 1cm of oil in a deep frying pan until a small piece of the burger mixture sizzles when dropped in.

With damp hands, press 2 heaped tablespoons of the mixture into the palm of your hand and make a slender burger-shaped patty, roughly 4 inches (10cm) in diameter. Place the gram flour on a plate and give each burger a light dusting, then drop them into the hot oil and fry for 2–3 minutes on each side, until golden. Drain on paper towels, flipping them to absorb excess oil.

Warm your pitas in the oven or on the grill (don't toast them) – they should still be nice and soft. Make a slit in each pita and form a pocket. Stuff the pocket with some of the salad, the chickpea burgers and the avocado cheese. You can even sprinkle on pomegranate seeds if you want.

Puy Lentil & Walnut Burgers with Roasted Fennel & Jerusalem Artichoke Frites

MAKES 6-8 BURGERS

The nuttiness of Puy lentils makes them a perfect burger base. This is the kind of burger that's ideal for the colder months. Parsnip purée is one of my favorite wintertime treats, so simple and with a glorious sweet flavor. I've called it clotted cream because it reminds me of very heavy Cornish cream. Flaxseeds are outrageously good for us and are also very high in fiber. When soaked they form something like a seedy gel, which not only adds loads of nutrition, but also binds things together. These burgers need careful handling in the pan, but caramelize beautifully.

Gluten-free option: use GF oats and burger buns

THE BITS

¾ cup (150g) dried Puy (petite French green) lentils

2 bay leaves

1 tablespoon vegetable oil

1 medium leek, finely sliced

4 cloves of garlic, peeled and crushed

8 fresh sage leaves, sliced into fine ribbons, or 1½ teaspoons dried sage

1 tablespoon fresh thyme leaves or ⅓ teaspoon dried thyme

2 teaspoons tamari

2 cups (200g) walnuts

8 ounces (225g) firm tofu, pressed (see page 18)

4 tablespoons flaxseeds (preferably ground), soaked in 4 tablespoons water for 1 hour

generous ¾ cup (85g) uncooked rolled oats

¼ teaspoon freshly ground black pepper

1 cup (240ml) vegetable stock

vegetable oil, for frying

For the roasted fennel & Jerusalem artichoke frites

1 pound (500g) Jerusalem artichokes, scrubbed and cut into long thin "frites"

1 large bulb of fennel, cut into ¾-inch (2cm) slices lengthwise

2 tablespoons olive oil

a large pinch of sea salt and freshly ground black pepper

For the parsnip clotted cream

2 large parsnips, peeled and diced

generous 2 cups (500ml) almond milk or oat milk

a pinch of grated nutmeg

a pinch of sea salt

To serve

6–8 of your favorite burger buns, halved

2 handfuls of watercress

DO IT

Place the lentils and bay leaves in a large pot and add 3¼ cups (750ml) of water. Bring to a boil, then reduce the heat and simmer for 25–30 minutes, until the lentils are tender. Drain well in a colander, removing the bay leaves. Set aside to cool in the colander, tossing the lentils regularly to remove excess liquid.

To make the parsnip cream, simply put the parsnips, milk, nutmeg and salt into a small heavy-bottomed saucepan. Bring slowly to just below boiling, then simmer on a very low heat for 1 hour, stirring regularly, until the parsnips are very tender. The liquid should reduce by about half. Parsnips burn easily when cooked like this, so keep an eye on them and lower the heat if necessary. Rushing this will not end well – you can turn a seductive white purée into a beige blob quite easily! Pour into a food processor and blend into a thick cream. Check the seasoning and set aside.

Meanwhile, make the roasted fennel and Jerusalem artichoke frites. Preheat the oven to 375°F (190°C). Toss the veggies in the oil and seasoning. Place them separately on lightly oiled baking trays and roast for 40 minutes, turning them twice. When they are all nicely colored and tender, remove from the oven and keep warm.

Now to the serious business of burger making. Heat the oil in a frying pan on medium, add the leeks, and cook for 6 minutes. Add the garlic, sage, thyme and tamari and cook for another 2 minutes. Pop the walnuts into a food processor and blitz to a rough crumb. Add the tofu, flaxseeds, cooked lentils, oats, pepper and the leek mixture, and pulse together until a coarse paste is formed, adding the vegetable stock as needed. Remember that the oats will absorb a lot of liquid, so make it quite a sticky, loose mixture – it will firm up in the fridge. Place in the refrigerator for 30 minutes.

Form the mixture into thick burgers. Warm a large frying pan on medium heat and lightly oil it. Brown the burgers on both sides, then cook them for 15 minutes, until heated through. They will firm up nicely in the pan, but be careful with your flipping!

Warm the parsnip cream in a small pan and spread a generous amount over each of your halved buns. Place a burger on top and crown with a couple of roasted fennel slices. Scatter on a little watercress and top with the bun lid. Toss the crispy artichoke frites in a little sea salt and serve on the side.

Chargrilled Chorizo Pinchos with Pistachio & Cilantro Pesto

MAKES 9 FAT CHORIZOS

The tapas bars of San Sebastián are some of the best food emporiums anywhere in the world, and that's where you'll find the greatest *pinchos*. Going on a pub crawl in San Sebastián is gourmet heaven, and in the morning you can have a nice stroll along the beach and let the fresh sea air get to work on your appetite for breakfast (see tostada con tomate, page 56).

Pinchos are normally a one or two bite affair, but I've made these chorizos into something slightly more substantial, venturing into main course territory as opposed to a canapé. They can also be cut in half lengthwise and grilled.

Panini-style bread is ideal for these pinchos, as it offers a good flat base for stacking, but you can use ciabatta or any nice flatbread. The pinchos can also be embellished with chunks of roasted peppers, to make the stack even higher.

Gluten-free option: use GF breadcrumbs and paninis to replace the wheaty stuff.

THE BITS

a handful of sun-dried tomatoes (in oil)

2 tablespoons olive oil

1 large onion, grated

10½ ounces (300g) tempeh, broken up with your fingers into a rough crumble

1 red chili, finely diced, or ½ teaspoon chili powder

3 large cloves of garlic, peeled and crushed

1½ teaspoons dried oregano

2 teaspoons smoked paprika

1 tablespoon sweet paprika

2 tablespoons sherry vinegar

5 ounces (150g) silken tofu

1⅔ cups (100g) fresh whole wheat breadcrumbs

½ teaspoon sea salt

½ teaspoon freshly ground black pepper

extra olive oil, for brushing

1 x pistachio & cilantro pesto (see page 309)

To serve

2 paninis, halved

3 handfuls of fresh arugula leaves

½ a handful of green olives, pitted

wooden skewers, cut in half

DO IT

Blend the sun-dried tomatoes in the food processor until smooth. Heat the oil in a frying pan on medium and sauté the onion until soft and slightly golden — at least 10 minutes. Add the tempeh, chili, garlic, oregano and spices and cook for 2 minutes. Now stir in the sun-dried tomato purée and vinegar and heat through. Add the silken tofu and let it warm through.

Place the breadcrumbs, salt and pepper in a food processor and blitz together with the tempeh mixture until nice and smooth. The mixture should be firm, and should stick together when pressed between your finger and thumb. Add more breadcrumbs if needed. Pop into the fridge to cool for 30 minutes while you make the pesto.

Using your hands (rub a little oil into them), form the mixture into nine fat and dumpy chorizos (if you have time, pop them into the fridge for a while to become even firmer). Warm a large grill pan on medium heat. Brush generously with oil and cook each chorizo for 5 minutes each side. Don't mess with them too much, just gently flip them once. We'd like some cool-looking char-lines. For traditional-looking pinchos, cut the chorizo in half lengthwise and grill for slightly less time. Once the chorizos are crisp and warmed through, set aside and keep warm in a low-temperature oven.

Cut the paninis in half and brush them with olive oil on both sides. Toast on the grill pan for a couple of minutes, pressing them down firmly and often. Once toasted, cut each piece of bread into thirds. Any leftover bread can always be sneakily dipped into the pesto (when no one is looking).

Top each piece of warm bread with a scattering of arugula leaves, then spoon on the pistachio pesto and place the chorizos on top, keeping things neatly in place with skewers. Pop an olive on the end of each skewer and serve on a large platter. Dive in with reckless abandon and smiles!

Chestnut, Millet & Sage Sausages

FOR 15 SMALL SAUSAGES

Chestnuts can be used in a variety of dishes, both savory and sweet. They come to life when paired with the robust and earthy sage, and will in sing harmony with most herbs. I like to use them in sausages and burgers because they are quite starchy and help with the binding process, which can be a major failing in many vegan sausage and burger recipes. Most vegan sausages/burgers are best cooked straight from the freezer – they hold their shape better that way. The key is to be gentle with them in the pan, and don't mess with them unnecessarily. They just need a precise flip on occasion and they will be perfectly happy. These are great on some warm toast. And normally I'll add a few green leaves to the plate. Sausage sandwich, anyone?

THE BITS

⅓ cup (75g) millet

2 cups (250g) cooked chestnuts

10½ ounces (300g) firm tofu, pressed (see page 18), and mashed with a fork

3 tablespoons nutritional yeast flakes

a handful of toasted sunflower seeds

1 onion, grated

3 cloves of garlic, peeled and minced

2 tablespoons very finely chopped fresh sage

2 tablespoons very finely chopped fresh rosemary

1 red chili, deseeded and finely diced

a large pinch of ground allspice

2 tablespoons lemon juice

1¼ cups (150g) very fine whole wheat or gluten-free breadcrumbs

1 tablespoon tamari or ¼ teaspoon sea salt

vegetable oil

1 x raw ketchup (see page 304)

DO IT

To cook the millet, put it into a small pan and cover with ¾ inch (2cm) of cold water. Bring to a boil, then pop a lid on, reduce the temperature to low and leave to cook for 20 minutes. Fluff up with a fork – the millet should be soft and tender but quite sticky. This is perfectly normal. Allow to cool.

In a food processor, blitz your chestnuts to fine crumbs. Add half the tofu and pulse a few times until smooth. In a large bowl, mix the chestnuts and tofu with the rest of the ingredients, except the vegetable oil. The mixture should be firm enough to form into sausages, and slightly tacky to the touch. Check the seasoning and add more tamari or salt if needed.

Using dampened hands, form your sausages, making them look like small bratwurst. You should get about fifteen sausages, or you may prefer to make fewer longer ones instead. Place them on a plate and cover lightly with plastic wrap, then pop into the fridge and chill them for 30 minutes (you can also freeze them at this point).

Put ½ tablespoon of oil into a large frying pan on a medium heat and fry your sausages for 5 minutes, turning them regularly to get a good color all over.

Serve with a big dollop of raw ketchup.

Asparagus Club Sandwiches with Rainbow Chard & Pine Nut Cream

MAKES 2 SANDWICHES (ENOUGH FOR 4 TO SHARE)

The Trump Tower of sandwich construction, the Empire State Building of munch, the Shard of . . . you get the idea. This one is quite tall. Incredibly green and healthy, with a touch of chard technicolor among the layers, it's a light and quick sandwich to whip up and stack. Three tiers of tofu and panfried asparagus goodness here, with a smooth pine nut cream. Delicious served with homemade vegetable chips (see page 135). And try it with tomato, ginger and orange chutney (see page 307). The trick here is to try to slice your bread as thinly as possible.

THE BITS

11½ ounces (325g) firm tofu, pressed (see page 18), or tempeh, cut widthwise into 3 x ¾-inch (8 x 2cm) slices

1 tablespoon unbleached all-purpose flour

sea salt and freshly cracked black pepper

2 tablespoons olive oil

6 scallions, trimmed and halved lengthwise

6 asparagus spears, halved lengthwise

1 teaspoon fennel seeds

2 cloves of garlic, peeled and crushed

6 large leaves of rainbow chard, cut into ¾-inch (2cm) ribbons

¼ cup (50ml) dry vermouth or dry sherry

a handful of basil leaves

For the pine nut cream

¾ cup (100g) toasted pine nuts (hazelnuts would also be delicious)

4½ ounces (125g) silken tofu

1 small clove of garlic, peeled and crushed

½ tablespoon lemon juice

a large pinch of sea salt and freshly ground black pepper

To serve

6 thin slices of sourdough bread

olive oil, for brushing

1 large ripe tomato, thinly sliced

DO IT

To make the pine nut cream, put the pine nuts into a food processor with the rest of the ingredients and blitz until smooth and creamy. Check the seasoning and set aside.

Pat the pressed tofu dry. Season the flour with sea salt and cracked pepper and place on a plate. Dust the tofu slices with the seasoned flour – they have to be very dry to crisp up nicely.

Heat 1½ tablespoons of oil in a large heavy-bottomed frying pan on medium heat. Add the scallions and sear for 5 minutes, until tender. Remove and keep warm, then add the tofu slices in the center of the pan, arranging the asparagus around the edges. Fry the tofu and asparagus until nicely golden – this will only take 2 minutes on each side for both. The asparagus may need turning more than the tofu, but see how they get on. Remove everything from the pan and keep warm.

Add ½ tablespoon of oil to the same pan on medium heat and add the fennel seeds and garlic. Heat through for a minute, then drop in the chard. Stir and sauté for 3 minutes. Drizzle in the vermouth and let it steam for a moment, then add the basil leaves, season, and cover tightly with a lid. Turn the heat down to low and allow to steam for 5 minutes.

Brush your sourdough bread with olive oil and lightly toast on both sides. Time to build your triple-decker! Grab two pieces of toasted bread, spread them with a thick layer of the pine nut cream, then top each one with a couple of slices of tomato and two pieces each of tofu, asparagus and scallion. Top with a second slice of bread and repeat for the next layer, but this time spoon some of the chard and basil on top instead of the asparagus and onion. Press down firmly, then cut the sandwiches in half.

Tempeh Chorizo & Chickpea Wraps with Orange, Avocado & Cilantro Salsa

FOR 4

Chargrilled chorizo was one of the hardest things to give up when I first became a vegetarian. We used to eat it in little clay tapas bowls down at our local tavern in Spain. They cooked it in sherry and it was quite spectacular. So when I'd made my mind up that meat was no longer a part of my world, I set about creating a reasonable substitute for chorizo.

This is like the loose-style raw chorizo, easy to put together when making a quick lunch-time wrap. You'll get all the familiar spices of chorizo, with a nice caramelized touch from the onions and tempeh. Sometimes I use cream sherry instead of sherry vinegar, to remind me of my former favorite tapas. If you are in quick-lunch territory, you can use store-bought wraps. The cashew hummus on page 144 goes really well with this.

Gluten-free option: use GF wraps instead of the chickpea wraps.

THE BITS

For the tempeh chorizo
1 tablespoon vegetable oil

12 ounces (350g) tempeh, well drained and crushed with a fork

1 teaspoon cumin seeds

1 bay leaf

½ an onion, grated

1 teaspoon smoked paprika

1 teaspoon sweet paprika

½ teaspoon ground coriander

½ teaspoon dried oregano

½ teaspoon dried thyme

a large pinch of ground cloves

a large pinch of ground cinnamon

¼ teaspoon chili powder

½ teaspoon sea salt

⅓ teaspoon freshly cracked black pepper

2 cloves of garlic, peeled and crushed

1½ tablespoons sherry vinegar

1 cup (250ml) vegetable stock

For the chickpea wraps (makes 4 big ones)
generous ⅓ cup (60g) whole wheat flour

½ cup (60g) gram (chickpea) flour

½ teaspoon baking soda

½ tablespoon vegetable oil

1 teaspoon tamari

scant ½ cup (100ml) soy milk or almond milk

scant ½ cup (100ml) water

3–4 tablespoons vegetable oil, for frying

For the orange, avocado & cilantro salsa
1 orange

2 scallions, trimmed and finely sliced

1 ripe avocado, peeled, pitted and finely diced

1 red chili, deseeded and finely diced

½ a handful of cherry tomatoes, quartered

½ a handful of fresh cilantro leaves, roughly chopped

a large pinch of sea salt

To serve
1 small head of oak-leaf lettuce, or any soft lettuce

½ a beet, scrubbed and grated (optional)

DO IT

To make the salsa, peel the orange, then run a knife along the inner edge of each segment, trimming the pith off, and the rest of the skin should easily slip off with a little careful tugging. Pith is bitter and not welcome at this party. Finely dice the segments with a sharp knife. Combine in a bowl with the rest of the salsa ingredients and set aside.

To make the tempeh chorizo, heat the oil in a large frying pan on high heat and panfry the tempeh, cumin seeds, bay leaf and onion for 3 minutes. Add the rest of the herbs and the spices, salt and pepper along with the crushed garlic. Continue cooking for 5 minutes, then add the sherry vinegar and stock. Cook on a fast simmer for 5 minutes, until all the liquid has been absorbed by the tempeh. Put the chorizo into a warmed bowl and cover.

To make the chickpea wraps, sift the flours and baking soda into a large mixing bowl. In a separate smaller bowl whisk together the oil, tamari, milk and water until well combined. Mix the dry ingredients into the wet ingredients until a thin batter is formed. Cover the mixture and place in the fridge for 20 minutes to chill.

Wipe your frying pan with paper towels and then lightly oil the bottom and set it over medium-high heat. Spoon roughly 3 tablespoons of the mixture at a time onto the hot pan and spread it out in circular motions, using the back of the spoon. We're looking for thin wraps. Cook until one side is golden brown, about 2 minutes. Flip over and fry the other side for slightly less time. Wrap the finished ones in a clean kitchen towel to keep them warm.

Now get your wraps together. Place a wrap on a plate, layer a couple of lettuce leaves in the center, and sprinkle with a line of grated beet. Spoon 3 tablespoons of the chorizo on top and then 2 tablespoons of salsa. Flip one edge over the filling and tuck it under with both hands, then roll it over gradually with both hands until tightly wrapped.

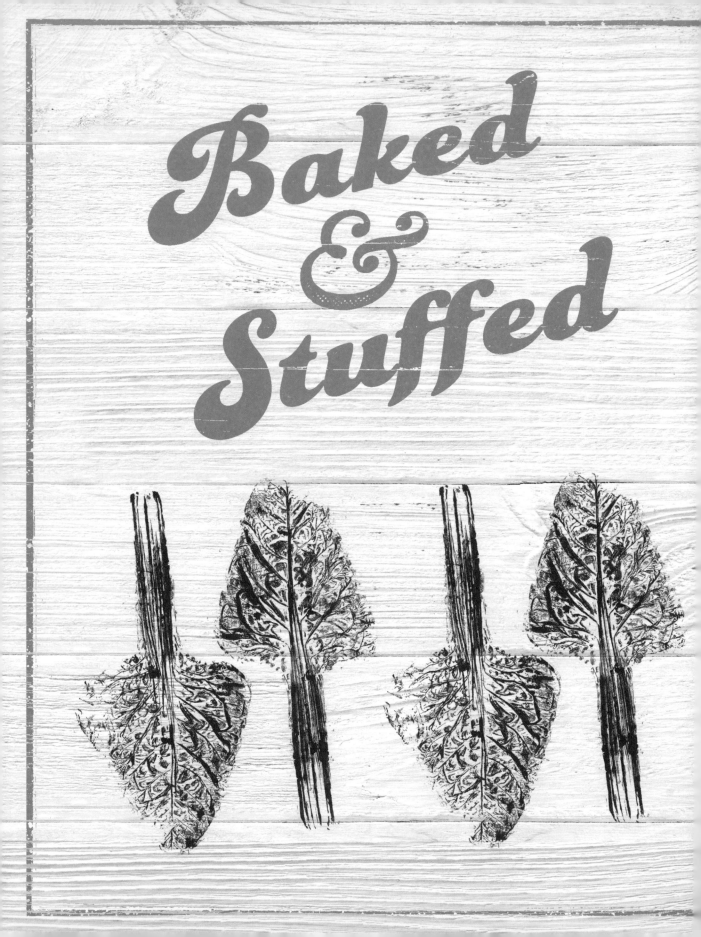

Baked & Stuffed

These bombastic baked dishes will sing from your oven and fill the house with wafts of something very tasty; they dance in the imagination and leave us all well-satisfied and ready for a nice sit-down.

The term "casserole" conjures up an image of a pasta something-or-other, lathered with cheap Cheddar, the fat pooling on top (or is that just me?). But they don't have to be a greasy slab of slop; they can add a slice of color and an incredible melding of flavors, compressed and carefully layered. The humble baked dish is suddenly transformed into a space for magnificent experiments in food.

Most of these casseroles are quickly put together and not too vexing. Some, however, are more complex – we'll just call these special-occasion dishes. Well worth the effort, I may add. Good food is rarely convenience food.

"Stuffed" has almost as bad a rap as "casserole" in food vocabulary, but in many cultures stuffing things is the height of culinary excellence. The stuffing here is done with tons of love and delicacy.

Here I hope to revive both of these misrepresented cooking techniques and give them all the green goodness of a full-on vegan makeover. Expect colorful and nutritious results that dance a jig all over your taste buds.

Stuffed Round Zucchini with Artichokes, Sun-Dried Tomatoes & Tofu Ricotta

MAKES 8

I work in an idyllic little retreat center called Trigonos, where I often serve stuffed zucchini like these. The center has its own organic vegetable garden and I am spoiled for choice when it comes to glorious produce. Round zucchini are generally small and dumpy fellows, perfect for stuffing. If you can't get them, long zucchini work just as well – you just need to be a bit more careful when filling them. Yellow (or golden) zucchini are fabulous and add an eye-catching element to this dish. High-quality jarred artichokes don't always need rinsing. Artichokes normally come already cut into quarters, so here you'll need twelve pieces for the filling.

THE BITS

8 round zucchini

3 tablespoons fruity olive oil

1 onion, finely diced

1 carrot, finely diced

1 teaspoon dried mint

3 tablespoons sun-dried tomatoes, finely diced, plus a little of their oil

3 artichoke hearts, cut into quarters (canned ones are fine, but rinse them well)

juice and zest of ½ a lemon

1 tablespoon fresh thyme leaves or 1 teaspoon dried thyme

2 tablespoons fresh oregano leaves or 1½ teaspoon dried oregano

a handful of toasted almonds or pistachios, roughly chopped

¼ teaspoon sea salt

freshly cracked black pepper

For the tofu ricotta

10½ ounces (300g) firm tofu, pressed (see page 18) and roughly chopped

2 tablespoons lemon juice

1 tablespoon nutritional yeast flakes

a large pinch of sea salt

a handful of cashews, soaked for 2 hours (optional, for added creaminess)

For the garnish

2 handfuls of radishes, scrubbed and halved lengthwise

8 cloves of garlic, unpeeled

3 handfuls of arugula leaves

extra virgin olive oil

a handful of toasted almond or pistachios, finely chopped

DO IT

Preheat the oven to 350°F (180°C).

Trim your radishes and tidy them up, leaving the stems on if they look in good condition. Cut the base off the zucchini, just enough to make them stand up tall and steady. If you are using normal zucchini, cut them in half lengthwise, leaving the stem attached.

Brush a baking tray with 2 teaspoons of olive oil. Arrange your zucchini, radishes and garlic on the tray and bake for 20 minutes, turning the the radishes and garlic once. The zucchini should still be firm and not squishy at all, otherwise they'll just fall apart when you try to handle them. The garlic should be soft and the radishes roasted – pop them back into the oven for 5 minutes longer if necessary. Set the zucchini aside, uncovered, to cool. Cover the radishes and garlic and keep warm.

(continued) →

When the zucchini have cooled, lop the tops off, making little green hats (with the stems attached). Use a teaspoon or melon baller to scoop out the innards and seeds. Use your hands to squeeze out any excess water from the innards, then roughly chop.

Heat 2 tablespoons of olive oil in a frying pan on medium heat. Add the onions and carrot and sauté for 6–8 minutes, until the carrot is softened. Add your zucchini innards, dried mint, sun-dried tomatoes and artichokes and cook for another 4 minutes. Add the lemon juice and zest, along with the fresh herbs and almonds, and season with sea salt and pepper. Cover and set aside.

To make the tofu ricotta, put all the ingredients into a food processor and blend until thick and creamy. If using the cashews, add them first and blend well, then add the other ingredients.

Spoon your artichoke mixture into the hollowed-out zucchini. Pack it down lightly with the base of your spoon, leaving a shallow indentation for the tofu ricotta to sit in. Mound some of the ricotta into the zucchini and bake on a lightly oiled oven tray for 10 minutes, until warmed through. Remove from the oven and pop their little hats back on (preferably at a jaunty angle!).

On a large serving plate, arrange the zucchini with plenty of space between them. Scatter the arugula leaves in between, sprinkle the roasted radishes and garlic around, and top with a drizzle of olive oil, a scattering of nuts and a pinch of sea salt.

Mexican "Pastor" Pie

FOR 4-6

I love Mexico and have spent many happy times there. *Pastor* means "shepherd" *en español*, so you can see what I've done here – I've adapted many of the brilliant flavors of Mexico and whacked them into a vibrant and healthy version of the old-school shepherd's pie. This has more color, more flavor and more nutrition than the original. The sweet potato changes things totally, in hue as well as in health. Firm tofu is a good substitute for the seitan if you can't find it. I rarely use factory-made flavorings in my cooking, but sweet chili sauce is an exception. For the fresh chilies, use good strong jalapeños if you can. There should be a little fiery Mexican twang to the sauce. This is great with lots of green leaves and avocado with a nice citrus dressing.

THE BITS

For the mash

1¼ pounds (600g) sweet potatoes, peeled and roughly diced

14 ounces (400g) baking potatoes, peeled and roughly diced

5 scallions, finely sliced, green bits, too

1–2 teaspoons salt

generous ¾ cup (200ml) unsweetened soy milk or almond milk

For the filling

1 tablespoon vegetable oil

1 teaspoon cumin seeds

1 onion, finely diced

1 celery stalk, finely diced

8 kale leaves, de-stemmed and sliced into 2-inch (5cm) strips

2 ears of corn, kernels removed

2 chilies (jalapeño are best), finely diced

3 teaspoons chipotle chili paste or 1½ teaspoons smoked paprika

1 teaspoon ground coriander

2 teaspoons dried oregano

¼ teaspoon ground cinnamon

1 large zucchini, cut into ¾-inch (2cm) cubes

6 tomatoes, roughly chopped

2 tablespoons tomato paste

1 cup (175g) dried red kidney beans or adzuki beans, soaked in water and cooked

7 ounces (200g) seitan or pressed firm tofu, cut into ¾-inch (2cm) cubes (optional but very good)

2 tablespoons sweet chili sauce

½ teaspoon sea salt

¼ teaspoon freshly cracked black pepper

For the topping

2 teaspoons vegetable oil

2 red bell peppers, thinly sliced

a pinch of sea salt

½ a handful of fresh cilantro leaves

DO IT

Put all the potatoes into a large pan and cover completely with salted water. Bring to a boil, then reduce the heat and simmer for 35 minutes, until they are tender and a knife tip can be pressed into them without resistance. Drain well and leave to cool in the colander. (Keep the cooking water – it makes magnificent stock.)

To make the filling, heat the oil in a large heavy-bottomed frying pan on medium. Sprinkle in the cumin seeds, followed by the onions and celery. Cook, stirring frequently for 5 minutes, until soft. Add the kale, corn, chilies and all the herbs and spices. Warm through, stirring often, for 3 minutes.

(continued) →

Add the zucchini, tomatoes and tomato paste, along with the cooked beans (plus about 1¼ cups [300ml] of their cooking juices), seitan and sweet chili sauce. Simmer for 10 minutes, then remove from the heat. Season with salt and pepper, cover the pan and set aside.

Mash your potatoes, giving them a good pummelling. Stir in the scallions, salt and milk (as needed). We're looking for a lovely smooth orange mash, not runny.

Preheat the oven to 400°F (200°C).

Ladle your filling into the base of a large warmed baking dish. Cover with your mash, spreading it to meet every edge of the dish. Drizzle with a little oil and run a fork over the top, creating cool-looking spiral patterns in the mashed potatoes. Place the dish on a large baking tray (to catch any overspill) and stick in the oven for 35 minutes.

Clean out the frying pan, put it back on high heat and add 2 teaspoons of oil. Add the peppers and cook for 10 minutes, stirring often until well caramelized and superbly sweet. Add a pinch of salt.

After 35 minutes, the mash should be slightly toasted and golden brown and the filling will probably be bubbling over a bit. This is perfect. Remove from the oven, leave the pie to sit for 10 minutes, then scatter the red peppers and fresh cilantro on top. Serve with big spoons and even bigger appetites. ¡Viva "El Pastor!"

Rainbow Chard
with Rutabaga, Dill & Dijon Mash

FOR 4–6

A gorgeously straightforward casserole that takes your average weeknight fare into the realm of a weekend treat, with little added effort and a few savvy vegan twists. You don't have to use rainbow chard – it just looks so cool on the plate, turning a mashed dinner into a kaleidoscopic feast. Swiss chard, ruby chard…whatever you can get your hands on is fine. Kale or bigger-leaved varieties of spinach would be lovely, too. Try to buy unrefined, high-quality oil to add to the mash, as it makes a big difference.

THE BITS

For the mash

1 small rutabaga, peeled and diced

5 large potatoes, scrubbed and diced

2 tablespoons canola oil

½ tablespoon Dijon mustard

2 tablespoons nonpareil capers, well rinsed

1–2 teaspoons sea salt

scant ½ cup (100ml) almond milk (or other milk of your choice)

a handful of fresh dill, roughly chopped

For the chard

1 tablespoon vegetable oil

4 large shallots, cut into wedges, or 1 large onion

3 cloves of garlic, peeled and minced

4 sprigs of fresh thyme, leaves only

a large pinch of sea salt

½ cup (125ml) white wine (vegan)

1 tablespoon tomato paste

1 pound (500g) rainbow chard, base of roots trimmed, leaves cut into 2-inch (5cm) ribbons

3 big handfuls of cherry tomatoes

freshly cracked black pepper to taste

For the garnish

a handful of toasted hazelnuts, roughly chopped (optional)

DO IT

Put your rutabaga and potatoes into a large pot of cold salted water and bring to a boil, then reduce the heat and simmer for 35 minutes. When tender, drain well, put into a large bowl with the rest of the mash ingredients and mash until smooth. Check the seasoning, then cover and keep warm.

Preheat the oven to 400°F (200°C).

Heat 1 tablespoon of vegetable oil in a large frying pan on medium-high and sauté your shallots for 3 minutes, until slightly browned. Add the garlic, thyme, salt and pepper and fry for 2 minutes. Add the white wine and tomato paste, followed by the chard, then cover the pan and cook for 3 minutes. Now lower the heat to the lowest setting, drop in the cherry tomatoes, and check the seasoning. Pop the lid back on and turn off the heat.

Spread the chard and tomato mixture in a large warmed oven dish and spoon the mash on top, making sure the chard is covered, although the mash doesn't need to touch the sides of the dish. Drizzle with a little more oil.

Place in the oven and bake for 20 minutes, until the mash is crispy on top. Remove from the oven and top with a smattering of toasted hazelnuts, if you're feeling decadent.

Beet, Millet & Raisin-Stuffed Ruby Chard Bundles with Brazil Nut & Rosemary Cream

MAKES ROUGHLY 16 BUNDLES

Wrapping things in leaves is old hat – the Greeks perfected it with vine leaves and rice (aka dolmades). We need to try something new, so I've reached out to the veggie patch for these bright leaves and roots. I love the color of ruby chard; it reminds me of pinot noir. Any type of chard can be used, but it may ruin your finely crafted color scheme. If there are any leaves on your beet, you can either sauté them and use them as a side dish, or chop them up and mix them in with the rest of the filling. Any leftover filling can be kept in the fridge, to be mixed later with a few leafy greens and served as a mighty tasty salad. Brazil nut butter may be tricky to find, but you can make your own using Brazil nuts, a pinch of salt and a blender. Just blitz until creamy and smooth.

THE BITS

¾ cup (160g) millet

1 sprig of rosemary

1 bay leaf

2 bundles of ruby chard (roughly 16 decent-sized leaves), left whole, with the stems cut off and finely diced

½ tablespoon olive oil

1 large beet, scrubbed and finely diced

1 large carrot, scrubbed and finely diced

2 tablespoons balsamic vinegar

1 onion, finely diced

1 celery stalk, finely diced

4 cloves of garlic, peeled and crushed

a handful of toasted pumpkin seeds

½ a handful of raisins, roughly chopped

a handful of fresh parsley, finely chopped, plus extra for garnish

½ teaspoon sea salt

a large pinch of freshly ground black pepper

For the Brazil nut & rosemary cream

3 tablespoons Brazil nut butter

5 ounces (150g) silken tofu

1 teaspoon fresh rosemary, very finely chopped

1 clove of garlic, peeled and crushed

1 tablespoon lemon juice

a large pinch of sea salt

⅔ cup (150ml) almond milk or soy milk

1 tablespoon olive oil

DO IT

Warm a pan on medium heat and add the millet. Dry toast these little yellow seeds, continuously stirring them for 6 minutes. They should turn slightly darker in color. Cover the millet with ½ inch (1.5cm) of water, drop in the rosemary sprig and bay leaf, and bring to a rolling boil. Place a lid on the pan and lower the heat to the minimum setting. Leave to cook for 35 minutes without lifting the lid. You should have perfectly fluffy millet. Use a fork to fluff it up further. Cover and set aside.

Bring a pan of water to a boil and set a steamer on top. Steam the chard leaves for 5 minutes, until tender and pliable, but not cooked through. Spread out on a large plate and allow to cool uncovered.

(continued) →

Heat ½ tablespoon of oil in a large frying pan on medium-high. Add the beet and carrots and panfry for 10 minutes, then add the balsamic vinegar and 2 tablespoons of water. Cook until all the liquid has evaporated, then add the onions, celery and chard stems and cook for another 5 minutes. Add the garlic, pumpkin seeds and raisins (plus any beet leaves or small chard leaves can also be thrown in here) and cook for another 5 minutes. Add the cooked millet (removing the rosemary sprigs and bay leaf) and chopped parsley, season well with salt and pepper, stir and leave to cool slightly. (Note: if the millet is sticky, this is perfectly normal – just break up the larger clumps using your fingers.)

To make the Brazil nut and rosemary cream, put the Brazil nut butter, tofu, rosemary, garlic, lemon juice and salt into a food processor. Blend to a paste, gradually adding the milk until the texture resembles thick cream. Warm in a small saucepan, without boiling, for 20 minutes. Just before serving, stir in the oil. This gives a nice sheen to the cream. While your sauce simmers, start constructing the chard bundles.

Preheat the oven to 350°F (180°C). Place a chard leaf on your work surface, with the widest end nearest you, and spoon in roughly 2–3 tablespoons of the millet filling (depending on the size of your leaves). Roll the leaf away from you once, then tuck in the outside edges and roll again, tucking the ends in again. Keep going until you have a nice, neat parcel. Repeat with the other leaves.

Place the parcels on a large lightly oiled baking tray, well spaced out, and brush them with a tad more oil. Sprinkle them with 3 tablespoons of water (to stop them from browning and becoming bitter) and bake for 12–15 minutes, until they are warmed through.

Check the consistency of your simmering sauce and add more milk if needed. Adjust the seasoning if needed. Ladle some sauce into the centers of your plates and arrange two parcels per person in the middle of each. You should have enough sauce left over to pour into a bowl and allow people to help themselves. They'll definitely be looking for more!

You can garnish with chopped parsley, or even some sprouts or finely chopped Brazil nuts, although I think they look great just the way they are.

Cauliflower Cashew Cheese
with Purple Sprouting Broccoli

FOR 6–8

This is a very healthy, nutrition-packed version of a British childhood favorite, cauliflower cheese. I pulled out all the vegan stops here to replicate a creamy cheese sauce, and it works – your mouth enjoys the rich "cheesiness" of the dish, but your belly is light as a feather and your heart loves you. The cashew cheese sauce can be made well in advance and keeps nicely in the fridge – use it as you would any other cheesy sauce. It also makes a fabulous dip, especially when spiced up with some chipotle paste or sprinkled with pickled jalapeños. The almonds and sprouting broccoli create a fancy topping, but you can always be a purist and leave them out.

THE BITS

3 tablespoons olive oil

2 red onions, sliced

1 large cauliflower, cut into small florets, including most of the upper stem, finely chopped

1 pound (500g) purple sprouting broccoli, tough lower stems chopped off, larger stems halved lengthwise

a large pinch of sea salt

1 x creamy cashew cheese sauce (see page 303)

For the topping

½ a handful of toasted sliced almonds

2 tablespoons nutritional yeast flakes

DO IT

Heat 2 tablespoons of olive oil in a frying pan on medium and gently fry the onions until caramelized, about 10 minutes. Set aside and keep warm. Make the creamy cashew cheese sauce.

Put your cauliflower into a large pot of salted boiling water and cook for 8 minutes, until just tender (it will cook more later in the sauce). Don't mess with the cauliflower too much, otherwise it will break up. We want nice fat florets, undiminished by metal spoon antics. Using a slotted spoon, gently remove the cauliflower and place in a colander over a sink. Reserve the cooking water.

Preheat the oven to 400°F (200°C).

Blanch your broccoli in the cauliflower water for 3–4 minutes, until tender. (Save this water – it's soup/stew gold in liquid form.) Add the cauliflower and onions to the simmering sauce and gently combine them with a wooden spoon or a spatula. You may need to thin the sauce out with a little more milk.

Toss your broccoli with 1 tablespoon of olive oil and a pinch of sea salt. Arrange the broccoli stems in the center of a large ovenproof dish, in one neat, green line. Surround with a stacked border of cauliflower cashew cheese. Bake until the broccoli is slightly charred and the cauliflower cheese is golden and bubbling.

The entire plate now gets a good scattering of almonds and cheesy yeast flakes. Serve with smiles – no further embellishments required.

Roasted Chestnut & Fennel Casserole with Oregano Crumble

FOR 4

I've adapted this from a recipe of my old pal Dan's – a brilliant dabbler in all things vegan. I have also tried this dish with rhubarb instead of fennel and it works beautifully. No chestnuts? Use walnuts. To make it gluten-free, just swap the breadcrumbs for your favorite gluten-free loaf or crackers.

THE BITS

7 ounces (200g) roasted chestnuts (see method below)

1 tablespoon canola oil

2 carrots, quartered lengthwise and cut into 1cm chunks

2 leeks, cut the same size as the carrots

2 bay leaves

1 large bulb of fennel, fronds trimmed, cut the same size as the other veggies

4 cloves of garlic, peeled, crushed

5 fresh sage leaves, finely sliced, or ¾ teaspoon dried sage

2 sprigs of fresh rosemary or 1 teaspoon dried rosemary

4 tablespoons fresh oregano or 1 teaspoon dried oregano

½ cup (125ml) white wine (vegan)

⅔ cup (150ml) vegetable stock, or bean cooking liquid

1 tablespoon cornstarch

1 red chili, deseeded and finely diced

4 ripe tomatoes, cut into eighths

1 tablespoon tamari

1 cup (175g) dried borlotti/ cranberry or rosecoco beans, soaked and cooked, or 3 cups canned beans, drained

a large pinch of sea salt

¼ teaspoon freshly cracked black pepper

For the oregano crumble

1 cup (125g) whole wheat breadcrumbs (nice and dry)

a large pinch of sea salt

2 tablespoons canola oil

For the mash

2¼ pounds (1kg) baking potatoes, scrubbed and cut into chunks

1 tablespoon canola oil

⅓ cup (75ml) unsweetened soy milk

1–2 teaspoons sea salt (to taste)

DO IT

Preheat the oven to 400°F (200°C).

Using a razor-sharp knife, cut a small slit in the skin of each chestnut. Place them on a baking tray and bake for 25 minutes, turning them over once during cooking.

Meanwhile, put your potatoes into a large pan of salted water. Bring to a boil, then reduce the heat and simmer for 30 minutes. Drain them in a colander and leave to cool for 10 minutes, then mash them in a large bowl with the canola oil and milk, and salt to taste.

While the potatoes are cooking, warm 1 tablespoon of canola oil in a large shallow casserole dish (stove-friendly) on medium heat and sauté the carrots and leeks for 3 minutes. Add the bay leaves, fennel, garlic, sage, rosemary and half the oregano and cook, stirring, for 2 minutes. Glug in the white wine and allow it to bubble for a minute, then add the vegetable stock or bean liquid. Mix cornstarch with 2 tablespoons of water into a thick, lump-free paste and add to the dish. Toss in the chili, tomatoes and tamari, bring to a boil and stir. Wearing a sturdy pair of oven mitts (the dish is going to be slightly volcanic), pop a well-fitting lid on the pan and place it in the oven for about 40 minutes.

The chestnuts are done when the skins open and become slightly blackened, and the insides are soft, sweet and delicious. Allow to cool for 10 minutes, then peel away the outer skin and the pithy inner skin and cut into quarters. Finely dice about a quarter of the chestnuts for the crumble, then cut the rest in half and set aside. Put the diced chestnuts into a bowl with your breadcrumbs, salt and oil. Combine well.

Check the casserole after 40 minutes to see if the carrots are done. Remove from the oven and stir in your beans and chestnuts. Check the seasoning and remove the rosemary sprigs and bay leaves. Give the casserole a decent scattering of the breadcrumb mix and put it back into the oven without the lid for 12–15 minutes, or until it's bubbling and the top has turned a wonderful shade of deep golden brown. Sprinkle with the rest of the oregano and serve with heaps of the mash.

Potato, Eggplant & Basil Gratin with Crispy Onions

FOR 4–6

This is a variation on one of my mother's classic gratins. When you cut into them, they were full of cheese, onion and soft potatoes. Enough to make any hungry teenager weak at the knee. I've dropped the cheese, taken the onions up a level and made them delightfully crispy, and added some Mediterranean touches in the guise of basil and eggplant.

Salting eggplants is not always essential, though I have to say that it does make them more pliable and flexible when layering in this dish. Also, Mum swears by this practice and I couldn't even contemplate going against her advice!

The colder months are the time when comfort food really comes into play. At home we have a massive roaring fire, our only heat source come Arctic times, and we eat in front of it every night, normally curled up around a casserole like this one. It's real hard-core sustenance, not for waistline watchers.

THE BITS

2 large eggplants, stems removed, sliced thinly lengthwise

2 tablespoons plus ½ teaspoon sea salt

4 tablespoons olive oil

3 large onions, finely sliced

3 large potatoes, scrubbed, sliced thinly lengthwise

1 celery stalk, finely diced

4 cloves of garlic, peeled and crushed

8 ripe tomatoes, roughly chopped

½ teaspoon unrefined brown sugar (see page 20)

4 tablespoons finely diced sun-dried tomatoes

¼ teaspoon freshly cracked black pepper

2 handfuls of fresh basil leaves

14 ounces (400g) firm tofu, pressed (see page 18) and finely sliced (optional)

For the garnish

a big handful of toasted pine nuts

½ a handful of fresh parsley, finely chopped

(continued) →

DO IT

Place your eggplant slices into a colander above a sink or bowl and sprinkle with 2 table-spoons of salt. Toss them around until they're well covered and leave for 45 minutes to drain. (If you are in a hurry, don't worry too much about this step.)

Heat the oil in a decent-sized heavy-bottomed frying pan on medium, and fry two-thirds of the onions until they are very crisp and golden. This will take around 10–12 minutes. Stir often and keep your eye on them, lowering the heat a little if they start to brown too much. Remove the onions with a slotted spoon, reserving as much oil as possible. Place them on a thick blanket of paper towels, to absorb the excess oil.

Preheat the oven to 425°F (220°C).

Put the potatoes into a large heavy baking dish and toss them with a good amount of your onion-infused oil and ½ teaspoon of sea salt. You may need a second baking dish. Cover and bake for 15 –20 minutes, until the potatoes have softened a little, but are not fully cooked through. This will depend on the variety of the potatoes. Set the potatoes aside and keep warm. Try not to break any of them up.

Now make a tomato sauce. Spoon 1 tablespoon of the onion oil into a large saucepan on medium-high heat and add the rest of the onions and the diced celery. Cook for 4 min-utes, add the garlic, give it a minute, then follow with the tomatoes, sugar and sun-dried tomatoes. Simmer gently with a lid on for 15 minutes. Season with salt and the black pepper. Tear your basil leaves into the sauce and remove from the heat. Once slightly cooled, blitz the sauce with an immersion blender until smooth, then pop a lid on the pan to keep warm.

Cover the base of a warmed baking dish with a quarter of your tomato sauce. Top with a layer of potatoes, then a layer of eggplants (followed by the tofu, if using), pressing everything gently down. Spoon another quarter of the sauce on top and repeat the layers twice more, finishing with a good covering of the tomato and basil sauce.

Cover with foil or parchment paper, then place in the oven and bake for 1 hour. Scatter the sweet crispy onions on top and bake for another 10 minutes uncovered. Remove from the oven and leave to sit for 5 minutes to cool slightly before serving.

Serve topped with the toasted pine nuts and a sprinkling of fresh parsley.

Leek & Wild Mushroom-Stuffed Potato Skins with Lemon & Chive Yogurt

FOR 4

This is really just a blinged-up baked potato. Hardly any more trouble than the standard, but the simple flavors knock your socks clean off! You can use any mushrooms here, but the wilder and more intense in flavor, the better.

THE BITS

4 large baking potatoes

2–3 tablespoons olive oil

1 leek, finely sliced, green parts included

4 cloves of garlic, peeled and crushed

1 small head of broccoli, florets and stems finely diced

10½ ounces (300g) wild mushrooms of your choice, roughly chopped

½ teaspoon dried rosemary

½ teaspoon dried sage

1 teaspoon dried thyme

(or 2 teaspoons mixed herbs instead of the previous three)

1 teaspoon salt

¼ teaspoon freshly ground black pepper

⅓ cup (75ml) almond milk or soy milk

a big handful of toasted sunflower seeds

2 tablespoons nutritional yeast flakes

2 tablespoons whole grain mustard

For the lemon & chive yogurt

a handful of fresh chives, finely chopped

1¼ cups (300ml) unsweetened soy yogurt

1 tablespoon lemon juice

½ tablespoon lemon zest

a large pinch of sea salt

DO IT

Preheat the oven to 350°F (180°C).

Prick the potatoes all over with a fork and rub them with oil. Bake for 1¼ hours, until golden and soft, turning them over once during that time. Cut them in half and leave to cool.

Heat 1 tablespoon of olive oil in a large frying pan on medium and sauté your leeks for 6 minutes, until softened. Add the garlic, broccoli and mushrooms and cook for another 5 minutes. Pop in the dried herbs, stir and season, then remove from the heat and cover.

The potatoes should now be cool enough to handle. Carefully scoop out the insides and put them into a bowl, leaving the crispy skins intact. These will be our stuffing vessels! Mash the insides with the milk, then stir in the vegetables, seeds, nutritional yeast flakes and mustard, adding a little more salt as needed. Spoon the mash back into the waiting skins, packing them full to bursting, and place them on an oiled baking tray. Pop the potatoes back into the oven for 10–15 minutes, until piping hot.

To make the lemon and chive yogurt, mix all the ingredients together in a bowl.

Serve the stuffed potato skins with a good dollop of lemon and chive yogurt on the side.

Eggplant Involtini with Creamy Spinach Stuffing & Roasted Tomato & Olive Sauce

FOR 4

Involtini means "little wrapped bundles," and in this case the wraps are slices of eggplant. Just a few simple steps and you have a dish that looks as good as it tastes – the contrast of colors on the plate really sets things alight! The bigger the eggplants, the better – big fat involtini are best. Take your time when slicing them, as the more even and straight they are, the nicer the dish. Try laying them on their side and cutting slowly with a long sharp knife. Don't use the last few slices of the eggplant on either side, as they will not be large enough to roll – save them for more eggplant antics at a later date. I like this dish with boiled pasta or new potatoes and watercress. Another nice idea is to add an additional topping of pine nut Parmesan (see page 313) before you bake the involtini.

THE BITS

4 tablespoons olive oil

2 large eggplants, cut into 1cm slices lengthwise

½ teaspoon sea salt

¼ teaspoon freshly ground black pepper

For the roasted tomato & olive sauce

2 tablespoons olive oil

½ cup (125ml) red wine (vegan)

10 ripe tomatoes, quartered

1 onion, finely sliced

1 teaspoon dried oregano

4 cloves of garlic, peeled and crushed

1 tablespoon red wine vinegar

1 teaspoon unrefined brown sugar (see page 20)

a handful of green olives, pitted and finely sliced

a large pinch of sea salt

plenty of freshly ground black pepper

For the creamy spinach stuffing

2 teaspoons olive oil

10 ounces (275g) spinach leaves, washed

2 cloves of garlic, peeled and crushed

a large pinch of sea salt

7 ounces (200g) firm tofu, pressed (see page 18)

3 tablespoons almond meal

a small pinch of freshly ground black pepper

½ tablespoon lemon juice

1 tablespoon nutritional yeast flakes

For the garnish

a handful of fresh parsley, finely chopped

DO IT

Preheat the oven to 375°F (190°C). Put all the tomato sauce ingredients into a large baking dish, combining everything well. Bake for 30 minutes on the top rack of your oven, stirring once, then cover with a lid or foil and bake for another 35 minutes. The tomatoes should have some nice color.

Take two baking trays and pour 1 tablespoon of olive oil onto each, spreading it out so that the trays are well covered. Place the eggplant slices on the baking trays, season with salt and pepper and drizzle the rest of the oil on top. Bake for 15 minutes on one side, then turn the slices over and bake for another 10 minutes, until softened and golden.

To make the creamy spinach filling, heat 2 teaspoons of olive oil in a large pan on medium. Add your spinach, garlic and a large pinch of salt, and panfry for 5 minutes, until the spinach has wilted and most of the liquid has evaporated. Remove from the heat. Place the rest of the filling ingredients in a food processor, add the spinach, and blitz until thick and creamy.

Your tomatoes should now be ready; leave them to cool slightly. Wipe out the food processor and pour in the tomatoes. Pulse a few times – you want a chunky sauce. Taste and season if needed.

Now let's roll! Lay the eggplant slices on your work surface, facing away from you lengthwise with the narrow end closest to you. Spread 2 tablespoons of the spinach filling on each slice and gently roll them away from you. Don't press them down too hard when rolling, otherwise the filling will spill out of the sides. Continue rolling until all your eggplant slices are used up.

Pour the tomato and olive sauce back into the baking dish and place the involtini face down on top of the sauce, well spaced out. Bake uncovered for 15–20 minutes, until everything is bubbling and warmed through.

Serve sprinkled with a little freshly chopped parsley.

Poppy & Herb Rolls

MAKES 18 SMALL ROLLS

Making your own bread takes time, but for me, it's the only way to go. You just can't replicate the flavor and aroma of home-baked bread – it's food for the soul. This is a nice way to serve bread to a gathering of people. The rolls are baked together in a pan and your guests can rip their own rolls off the steaming mass of bready loveliness. You can make these little rolls into a visual treat by making half with all-purpose flour and half with just whole wheat. It's a technique I use over and over and it never fails. Play around with whatever good herbs you have, dried or fresh, and you can use other seeds instead of the poppy seeds.

THE BITS

1 teaspoon dried yeast

1 teaspoon unrefined brown sugar (see page 20)

1½ cups (360ml) warm water

2¼ cups (300g) unbleached all-purpose flour

scant 1¼ cups (145g) whole wheat flour (or spelt/rye flour)

¾ teaspoon sea salt

1½ teaspoons dried mixed herbs

3 teaspoons olive oil

2 tablespoons poppy seeds

For the topping

1 tablespoon olive oil

1 teaspoon poppy seeds

DO IT

In a small bowl, combine the yeast, sugar and 1 tablespoon of warm water. Set aside for 10 minutes and allow to go frothy. Put the flours and salt into a large mixing bowl and combine with a wooden spoon. Add your herbs to the yeast mixture. Make a well in the center of the flour and pour in your yeast mixture and the oil, then gradually pour in the water with one hand, mixing all the time with the other. Very slowly, pour in enough water so that the dough comes away from the bowl, but is still slightly tacky to the touch. You may not need to add all the water.

On an oiled surface, begin to work the dough. Knead it around 100 times or for 10 minutes, getting that gluten elasticity going and your arm muscles toned. Doing this to your favorite tunes helps. Place the dough in a lightly oiled bowl and cover with a kitchen towel, then leave in a warm place for an hour to rise. Slightly warmer than room temperature is best (but no hotter) – near a warm radiator or fire is perfect. The dough should more or less double in volume. If it doesn't, leave for another 15 minutes. (You can even leave the dough overnight in a fridge to achieve the same results.)

Knead the risen dough a few more times, then cut it into 18 even-sized pieces. Roll them around in your cupped hands to form little balls and place them tightly together in an oiled 10-inch (25cm) quiche/pie dish (or any round, shallow baking pan). Cover very loosely with a kitchen towel (careful, they may stick) and allow to rise for another 30 minutes in a warm place.

Preheat the oven to 425°F (220°C). When the dough has risen again, brush very lightly with some olive oil and sprinkle the poppy seeds on top. Bake the rolls for 30 minutes, or until golden brown and hollow-sounding when tapped on their undercarriage. Once the rolls are in, do not open the oven. If you do, it may affect the baking and you will never forgive yourself! Allow to cool for 20 minutes on a wire rack.

Okra, Corn & Black-Eyed Pea Succotash with a Chili Cornbread Crust

FOR 6

This is classic Southern stew, at its best. All the Cajun spices are here, with, of course, the sweetness of roasted corn. I've turned it into something resembling a pie, with a yellow cornbread lid. Succotash is traditionally made with lima beans, but I love black-eyed peas in Southern cooking.

The okra is a nice addition and is best cooked without piercing the main part of the funny, hairy green finger. When you chop okra, the seeds will make whatever dish you are making quite slimy and thick. This can work in your favor if you are looking to thicken a stew or bind a burger, although generally, slime + food = strange looks of revulsion. I like the texture, but you decide – to chop or not to chop.

This dish is really a mammoth meal in itself, but you may like a green salad or some panfried greens served on the side. Oh, and a bottle of fiery chili sauce is a must!

THE BITS

1 large onion

2 celery stalks

1 large carrot

1 red bell pepper

1 yellow bell pepper

9 ounces (250g) okra, trimmed or roughly chopped (see note above)

1 tablespoon olive oil

3 cloves of garlic, peeled and crushed

1 teaspoon dried thyme

1½ teaspoons smoked paprika

½ teaspoon ground cumin

½ teaspoon chili powder

3 large tomatoes, roughly chopped

1 tablespoon tomato paste

½ cup (125g) dried black-eyed peas, soaked and cooked (to give about 1½ cups [275g] cooked beans)

1⅓ cups (400ml) bean cooking liquid or vegetable stock

2 ears of corn, kernels removed (roughly 1⅔ cups [250g] sweet corn)

sea salt and freshly ground black pepper

juice of ½ a lemon

For the chili cornbread crust

¾ cup (100g) unbleached all-purpose flour

1 teaspoon baking powder

1 teaspoon baking soda

1 cup (125g) stoneground (coarse) cornmeal

a large pinch of sea salt

½ teaspoon dried oregano

1 large red chili, deseeded and finely diced, or ½ teaspoon red pepper flakes

½ tablespoon nutritional yeast flakes (optional)

3 ounces (80g) silken tofu, whisked until smooth

½ tablespoon olive oil

1 teaspoon brown rice syrup or unrefined brown sugar (optional; see page 20)

¾ cup (175ml) soy milk

DO IT

To make the cornbread, sift the flour, baking powder and baking soda into a bowl with the cornmeal and salt, and stir in the oregano, chilies and nutritional yeast flakes (if using). Mix in the tofu, oil and brown rice syrup (if using) and gradually add the soy milk, gently stirring together until just combined. The mixture should resemble a thick batter. Cover and pop into the fridge for 20 minutes.

(continued) →

Preheat the oven to 400°F (200°C). Slice the onion and chop the celery, carrot and peppers into 1cm dice. Put the onion, celery and carrot into a large heavy-bottomed pan with the okra and 1 tablespoon of olive oil on medium-high heat and sauté, stirring frequently, for 7 minutes. Add the peppers, garlic, thyme and spices and cook through for 2 more minutes, stirring well. Now add the tomatoes, tomato paste, black-eyed peas (with their cooking liquid or stock) and corn. Warm the stew through for 5 minutes, then season well with salt and pepper. Stir in the lemon juice. Check the consistency – it should be a loose stew, with a good amount of sauce. The veggies will still be a little on the "al dente" side.

Ladle the succotash into a warmed baking dish and flatten it down slightly with the back of a large spoon to make a level surface. Give your cornbread mixture a final stir, adding a drop of water if it's too sticky, and slowly spoon it all over the stew, smoothing gently as you go. Spread it out until it just about meets the edges of the dish. Your dish should be tall enough for the mixture to come 1cm below the rim, as it will rise a little when baked.

Place the succotash into the oven and bake for 25–30 minutes, or until the cornbread has risen and turned golden brown.

Simple Chili Cornbread

MAKES ONE LOAF

A mellow yellow loaf, so simple to make and very nutritious. It is ideal served with smoked Cuban black bean soup (see page 80) or with anything remotely Creole or Mexican. I like it for breakfast, toasted and spread with avocado. This makes quite a dense loaf, which I love, but a lighter loaf can be achieved by adding unbleached all-purpose flour instead of whole wheat. My advice: keep it whole.

THE BITS

scant 1¼ cups (150g) coarse cornmeal

1¼ cups (150g) whole wheat flour

2 teaspoons baking powder

1 tablespoon nutritional yeast flakes (optional)

1 teaspoon red pepper flakes (optional)

1 teaspoon sea salt

1 cup (250ml) soy milk or almond milk

1 tablespoon brown rice syrup (or other sweetener of your choice)

½ cup (90g) sweet corn kernels

DO IT

Preheat the oven to 350°F (180°C).

Grab a large mixing bowl and fill it with the dry ingredients. Whisk together the milk and syrup until combined and beginning to froth. Add the milk and syrup mixture to the bowl of dry ingredients gradually, until you get a soft batter, then stir in the corn and mix gently together.

Pour into an oiled 8½ x 4½-inch (1 pound/450kg) loaf pan and bake for 25–30 minutes. Stick a knife or a wooden skewer into the center of the bread – if it comes out clean, it's ready.

Best left on a wire rack for 20 minutes before serving.

Dearest sweet tooth,

You have arrived in the plant-based Garden of Eden. Not so much the land of milk and honey, more the land of nut butters and dates. Not as poetic sounding, maybe, but equally sweet and rich.

Here you will find delicious treats that not only set the taste buds alight with wonderful flavors, but actually do the body good. You could call this a guilt-free dessert corner, if you approach dessert with your hips, heart and waistline in mind.

Vegan desserts are a BIG surprise (they are still surprising me!). I am regularly astounded by what can be done when the dessert staples are omitted (namely eggs, white flour and cream or milk). Creativity pours out of vegan folk who crave their old favorites and imaginative substitutes are discovered.

Many vegan cakes do contain white flour and quite a lot of sugar; a vegan cake is not necessarily a healthy cake. I do not really buy into this über-sweet approach (although the dark chocolate and beet brownies are quite something!); it's a little like vegetarians who slap loads of cheese on everything. We can do better than that! Much, much, much, better.

Bring on the sweet thangs!

Raw Blueberry & Macadamia Cheesecake

FOR 8 WHOPPING SLICES

If you have yet to enter the magical world of raw desserts, this macadamia cheesecake is a sensational place to start. It's so very rich and surprisingly healthy. If you try one recipe in this book, this is the one. I have yet to meet anybody who can resist it! I often like to use cashews in the filling purely because of the price difference – macadamias are expensive – but for a special occasion, go for it! Depending on the season, any berry can be used for this recipe. Blackberries are a personal favorite – I love their bitter edge with the sweet creaminess of the cheesecake – although blueberries are delicious, too, of course.

THE BITS

For the crust

2¼ cups (300g) raw macadamia nuts

a handful of pumpkin seeds

generous ½ cup (90g) dates, soaked for 1 hour, then pitted

3 tablespoons freshly grated coconut (desiccated is fine)

For the filling

2⅓ cups (360g) raw cashews or macadamias, soaked for at least 3 hours

½ cup (120ml) lemon juice

½ cup (120ml) brown rice syrup (or other sweetener of your choice)

¾ cup (180ml) coconut oil

a large pinch of sea salt

1 teaspoon vanilla extract

½ cup (120ml) water

For the sauce

14 ounces (400g) blueberries

generous ¼ cup (45g) dates, soaked for 1 hour, pitted

DO IT

To make the crust, put the macadamias, pumpkin seeds and dates into a food processor and pulse together until a rough crumble is formed. Add more dates if it's a little dry or more nuts if it's wet. The mixture should be able to be rolled into balls and not be overly sticky.

Scatter a layer of coconut on the base of a springform pan. You can use a normal pie dish – it just makes it harder to extract the cake (you can try lining your pan with a snug layer of plastic wrap). Using your hands, press the macadamia crust onto the coconut, covering the base and forming an even layer.

To make the filling, blitz all the ingredients in the magically cleaned food processor (bless those kitchen elves) until you have a smooth creamlike texture. You may need a few goes to get it all incorporated, scraping down the sides with a spatula. Scrape out your filling mixture into the pie dish, bang it gently a few times on a work surface (to get rid of air bubbles) and smooth the filling down using a spatula.

Place in the freezer and freeze – for best results, eat on the day of freezing, or soon after. Remove the cake from the pie dish using a thin pie server around the edge and gently pushing the base out. Take it easy and slowly. Pop it into the fridge and allow it to defrost – a couple of hours will do.

Place the blueberries and dates into your food processor (now miraculously clean again) and blitz well. Add a little water to thin the sauce out if needed. Pour on top of the cheesecake before serving, and if there is any excess sauce, serve it in a bowl as a berry bonus.

Chestnut Cream
with Gin-Soaked Damson Plums

FOR 4

This super-tasty little dessert can be whipped up in double-quick time. It can be eaten as it is, or thinned down slightly and served with pies and cakes. Chestnuts are lower in fat than all other nuts and are quite starchy, making them perfect for a purée. If you are lucky enough to have a damson tree in your garden, you'll be fully versed in the wonders of these tangy little plums. Any plum will work well here, but I have a particular fondness for damsons.

THE BITS

For the chestnut cream

10½ ounces (300g) chestnuts, peeled, brown skin taken off

2–3 tablespoons brown rice syrup (or other sweetener of your choice)

a small pinch of sea salt

scant ½ cup (100ml) soy milk or almond milk

For the gin-soaked damson plums

4 handfuls of damson plums, cut in half lengthwise and pitted

¼ cup (50ml) of your favorite gin

2 tablespoons unrefined brown sugar (see page 20)

4 long ribbons of orange peel (use a peeler)

For the garnish

3 tablespoons toasted chopped almonds

DO IT

Put the damsons into a large bowl with the gin, sugar and orange peel and gently mix. Make sure all the sugar has dissolved, then place in the fridge for at least 2 hours (overnight is good, and drinking the leftover damson gin is even better).

In a small pan, cook the chestnuts with 2 cups (500ml) of water, until soft – about 20 minutes will do. Drain, then place in a food processor with the syrup, salt and milk and blitz together until smooth and creamy.

Carefully spoon your chestnut cream into small wide glasses – they should be one-third full. Top with your damsons and a sprinkling of toasted chopped almonds.

Charred Pineapple Wedges
with Spiced Caramel & Lime Yogurt

FOR 4-6

This sounds complicated, but is actually a cinch to make. Roasted pineapple is something that transports me directly to the Caribbean. I have added a couple of fancy accompaniments, but the star here is the caramelized fruit. I like to char my pineapple before the main barbecue session gets under way, while the grill is still clean. This dish gets better when doused in the spiced caramel and kept warm in the oven. The pineapple is delightfully sweet, so the lime yogurt makes the perfect tangy companion. For a boozy touch, add a glug of dark rum to the caramel.

THE BITS

1 large ripe pineapple, peeled and all brown eyes removed

For the spiced caramel
1 cup (250ml) water
4 tablespoons unrefined brown sugar (see page 20)

2 star anise
4 cloves
1 cinnamon stick

For the lime yogurt
juice of ½ a lime
zest of 1 lime

½ tablespoon brown rice syrup or other sweetener
1¼ cups (300g) unsweetened soy yogurt

DO IT

In a small pan, bring the water to just about boiling and stir in your sugar and spices. Allow it to simmer vigorously, uncovered, stirring often, until the liquid is reduced by half or a syrup forms. Cover the pan and keep warm on the stove.

Cut your pineapple in half lengthwise, then, with your knife at a 45-degree angle, cut out the tough central stem (you don't have to do this, but the texture bothers some). Cut the pineapple into 1cm thick half-moon-shaped slices.

Bring a barbecue or grill pan to a high heat. Press a pineapple steak onto the grill – it should sizzle and smoke immediately. Place your pineapple pieces in rows and do not move them – this will ensure you get the desired charred-stripe look. Don't overfill the grill; leave enough space between slices to turn them over easily.

Cook for 2 minutes on each side. It's best to have some long-handled tongs available here, as the wedges may stick. Use a metal spatula to quickly scrape them loose with a jabbing motion and then, quick as a flash, turn with the tongs. It's a technique that's easily grasped. You'll be a master flipper in no time.

Place the charred pineapple in a large warmed ovenproof dish. Cover with foil and continue with a fresh batch of wedges. When all the slices are cooked, drizzle some of your spiced caramel over them and place the dish in the oven on low heat (just to keep warm).

Mix the lime juice, zest and brown rice syrup into the yogurt, tasting and adjusting until it is to your liking. Serve the pineapple with extra caramel spooned on top and a nice dollop of lime yogurt.

Charred pineapple wedges with spiced caramel & lime yogurt, page 279

Coconut & Vanilla Rice Pudding with Mango & Basil Compote

FOR 4

This is a heady combination of flavors and richness, finished off with the sweetest and most fragrant of toppings. Ripe mangoes can be hard to come by and must be savored when they do appear. Organic coconut milk and vanilla extract are available, and the extra pennies spent are very much worth it. Cheaper versions of these products taste really lousy once you have tried the good stuff.

THE BITS

1 x 14-ounce (400ml) can of coconut milk

1 cup (200g) uncooked short-grain rice

1⅔ cups (400ml) unsweetened almond milk or soy milk

3 tablespoons brown rice syrup (or other sweetener of your choice)

1 vanilla pod or 2 teaspoons vanilla extract

1 tablespoon coconut oil

finely grated zest of ½ a lime

For the mango & basil compote

1 large, ripe mango

a big handful of basil leaves

1 teaspoon lime juice

½ teaspoon brown rice syrup (or other sweetener), if needed

DO IT

Set aside 3 tablespoons of the coconut milk and put the rest into a pan with the rice, almond milk and syrup. Bring slowly to a boil, keeping your eye on it, as it will boil over quite easily. Get a gentle simmer going, then add the vanilla (split the pod lengthwise and scrape the pulp into the pan). Stir, pop a lid on the pan, and leave on low heat for 20–25 minutes, stirring often. The rice should be slightly more cooked than normal rice: nice and fat and soft.

Stir in your coconut oil, the reserved coconut milk and the lime zest, and leave to rest with the lid on for 10 minutes. The coconut oil will give the rice a nice shine and richness. Thin with warm water if necessary.

While the rice pudding rests, make your compote. Peel your mango. Pit it and slice into thin batons. Set aside half, plus the bits from around the seed (if you haven't munched them already). Take the rest of the mango, pop it into a food processor with the basil and lime and blend until smooth. Check the flavor – if it needs a little sweetness, add ½ teaspoon of syrup. Transfer to a bowl. Add the rest of the sliced mango to the compote. The fragrant basil will infuse with the already fragrant mango.

Serve the lovely coconut rice in warmed shallow bowls or on dessert plates and cover liberally with your gorgeous fruity compote.

Brazil Nut & Chocolate Spelt Cookies

MAKES 16

We all need a standby cookie, something you can whip up almost with your eyes closed. Here is my chunky cookie of choice. The concept of cooking without eggs, white sugar and white flour is daunting to many a baker, but my friend Gillian, a wonderful baker, came up with this recipe, one of the finest vegan cookies I've ever munched on. The best thing that can be done with these cookies is to make them into an ice-cream sandwich with the chocolate and maple ice cream (see page 290). If the cookies are still warm, this is a heavenly proposition. The sandwiches can also be made and frozen for future enjoyment. Sometimes, when feeling daring, I go for 100 percent spelt action here – I find its toasted flavor amazing.

THE BITS

1 cup (120g) unbleached all-purpose flour

scant 1¼ cups (140g) spelt flour (or whole wheat flour)

1 teaspoon baking soda

1½ teaspoons baking powder

¼ teaspoon salt

1 teaspoon ground cinnamon

1 cup (200g) unrefined brown sugar (see page 20)

¾ cup (180ml) vegetable oil

1 teaspoon vanilla extract

2 ounces (60g) vegan dark chocolate, chopped or broken into very small chunks

a handful of raisins, roughly chopped

a handful of Brazil nuts, roughly chopped

2 tablespoons water

DO IT

Preheat the oven to 350°F (180°C).

Sift the flours, baking soda, baking powder, salt and cinnamon into a mixing bowl.

In a separate bowl, blend together the sugar and oil, adding the vanilla. Add to the dry ingredients and stir gently, then add the chocolate chunks, raisins, Brazil nuts and water. Stir a little more until just combined, making sure everything is moist. The mixture should be clumpy. Add more water if it's still powdery and dry.

Spoon out the mixture, using one heaped tablespoon per cookie (roughly ping-pong-ball size), forming them into small balls with your hands. Line three large baking trays with parchment paper and place the balls on the trays, pressing them down into fat cookie shapes with your fingertips. Leave at least a 2-inch (5cm) gap between cookies, as they expand quite a bit in the oven!

Bake for 10–12 minutes, rotating the trays at least once. Cookies are quite sensitive and every oven is different, so keep an eye on them – they will highlight any oven hot spots for you! Take the cookies out when they have just about firmed up; they will continue cooking as they cool.

You should now be looking at a form of chewy cookie-based nirvana. They are supposed to be soft when they leave the oven – let them cool on the trays for a few minutes. When firm, transfer to a wire rack and allow to cool for 10 minutes before diving in.

Carrot, Orange & Pistachio Halwa

FOR 4–6

Halwa seems to be one of those global dishes claimed by so many countries, from Greece to India. It's a brilliantly simple dessert loved by cooks across the world. Normally it's made with semolina, but I have opted for carrots here (you can also use beets). There are no compromises with flavor or texture at all, and you will not believe this dish is vegan, it is so creamy and rich. The orange blossom water is optional, but if you have it, pop some in and enjoy the intense fragrance that it emits when steaming away in your bowl. It adds a touch of citrus perfume to proceedings like no other ingredient. For a special occasion, I add a large pinch of saffron to the simmering milk for that extra touch of luxury.

THE BITS

1¼ pounds (600g) carrots, finely grated

3 cups (700ml) unsweetened almond milk

10 cardamom pods (seeds removed and ground with a pestle and mortar)

4 tablespoons unrefined brown sugar (or jaggery for the full-on Indian feel; see page 20)

a big handful of pistachios, roughly chopped

a handful of dried apricots, roughly chopped

2 tablespoons almond butter

1–2 teaspoons orange blossom water (to taste)

For the garnish
a handful of pistachios or pomegranate seeds (optional)

DO IT

Put the carrots and almond milk into a heavy-bottomed saucepan. Bring to a boil, then lower the heat and set to a slow, steady simmer, stirring regularly. After 45 minutes add the cardamom, cook for another 10 minutes, then stir in the sugar. Once most of the milk has evaporated, add the chopped pistachios, chopped apricots, almond butter and orange blossom water. Stir well and simmer for 5 minutes prior to serving.

I like halwa to be served warm, in small bowls (it's quite rich), sprinkled with pistachios or pomegranate seeds as an added extra. But it can also be eaten cold. You may like to spread it into a square baking tray, pop it into the fridge for a couple of hours (once fully cooled) and serve it cut into slices, Indian sweet-shop style!

Rustic Apple & Whiskey Marmalade Tart

FOR ONE BIG TART

This is the easiest and lightest tart I know, which is why I'm sharing it with you. It's the perfect answer to the old dinner party conundrum of desserts that look great, and are easy to make. You'll want a firm and slightly acidic variety of apple for this tart, so it doesn't turn to mush when baked. Think Granny Smith, winesap, pippin, Rome or Suncrisp.

THE BITS

1 sheet of puff pastry (frozen is easiest)

3 tablespoons rindless marmalade

1–2 tablespoons whiskey (not malt whiskey – never malt in cooking!)

4–5 apples, cored

1 tablespoon unbleached all-purpose flour, plus a little more for dusting

⅓ cup (70g) unrefined brown sugar (see page 20)

a small pinch of sea salt

DO IT

Defrost the pastry in the fridge overnight, or leave it on a plate at room temperature for a couple of hours.

Put the marmalade into a small pan with the whiskey and heat gently until it forms a thick syrup. Do not cook further.

Roll out the pastry on a lightly floured surface to a rectangle about 12 x 14 inches (30 x 35cm). Cut off any straggly bits and place the pastry on a baking tray lined with parchment paper. With a small sharp knife, score a ¾-inch (2cm) border around the pastry and gently press down around the edge with a fork, creating a slightly raised border. Prick the base with a fork. Pop into the fridge for 10–20 minutes.

Preheat the oven to 425°F (220°C). Bake the pastry for 12 minutes, until just risen and golden in color.

Halve your apples lengthwise, leaving the skins on, and chop them into ¼-inch (5mm) slices (so they look like little half-moons). Toss the apples with 1 tablespoon of flour and the sugar and salt.

Press the inside area of the pastry down with a fork to form a level base. Arrange your apples in neat little rows on the pastry. Brush the border with some of the whiskey marmalade glaze, then cover with foil and put back into the oven until the apples are softened – another 15–20 minutes should do it (depending on the apples you are using).

Brush the finished tart with plenty more of your whiskey marmalade glaze and allow to cool for 15 minutes.

Best served with scoops of high-quality vegan vanilla ice cream (it actually exists!).

Dark Chocolate & Beet Brownies

FOR 6–8

This is a super-rich brownie recipe, quite dense and with extra chocolate for good measure. I love adding finely chopped prunes to really bump up the sticky richness, and these brownies also taste great with other dried fruits, such as cherries, blueberries or raisins. Brownies are a funny bake: they don't look done, but they are. You'll need a little brownie experience to get it just right, but generally, they are much stickier than your average cake when probed with a skewer or toothpick. I recommend a gentle press test – if the brownie has formed a decent crust and is slightly springy, you're there. This is best served warm, with vegan vanilla ice cream and a berry compote.

THE BITS

10½ ounces (300g) very dark vegan chocolate (check the package)

⅔ cup (150ml) light vegetable oil

7 ounces (200g) silken tofu

1 cup (200g) unrefined brown sugar (see page 20)

4 ounces (125g) beet, finely grated

2 ounces (60g) dried prunes, soaked until soft, finely chopped

1 cup (100g) walnuts, roughly chopped

1 cup (125g) unbleached all-purpose flour

DO IT

Bring a pot half-full of water to a boil (or just use a kettle), then remove from the heat and cover with a bowl (making sure the bottom of the bowl is out of the water). Put the chocolate and oil into the bowl, stir and let them melt. Once completely melted, set aside and allow to cool to room temperature.

Preheat the oven to 375°F (190°C). Oil an 11 x 7-inch (27 x 17cm) baking dish or line with parchment paper.

With a whisk, beat the tofu and sugar together in a bowl, then grab a spatula and stir in the chocolate and add the grated beet, prunes and walnuts. Slowly mix in the flour, folding it in a few times until just combined.

Pour the mixture into the oiled and lined baking tray, and level out with a spatula.

Pop into the oven on the middle shelf and bake for 25–30 minutes.

Leave to cool in the tray, then cut into squares. Brownies should be nice and moist in the middle, more so than other cakes, since they'll firm up when removed from the oven. The middle of the brownie should have formed a slight crust and the outer edges will be slightly crispy.

Chocolate & Maple Ice Cream

FOR 4–6

I have never owned an ice-cream maker and can never see myself buying one, so I needed a method for making a decent ice cream without the hardware. Frances, our recipe tester, really helped us out here. This vegan ice cream goes beyond any expectations and proves you can achieve excellent results with just a couple of stirs and a nice thick dish. It is not a low-fat ice cream – it's a good-fat ice cream. The kind of fat that makes you shine with well-being and that the body loves (and really needs). Quality maple syrup and coconut oil are not inexpensive, but they are well worth the moderate investment. Drizzling some almond cream (see page 296) on top makes a real sundae of it.

THE BITS

    2 cups (480ml) almond milk
    scant 1½ cups (140g) pecans, soaked for 2 hours
    ½ cup (120ml) maple syrup
    scant 1½ cup (100ml) brown rice syrup
    2 teaspoons vanilla extract (or scrape out 1 vanilla pod)
    1 cup (80g) cacao powder
    3 tablespoons coconut oil

    For the topping
    3 tablespoons crushed toasted almonds
    a handful of sliced seasonal fruits

DO IT

Place all the ingredients in a blender except the coconut oil and blitz together until very smooth. Warm the coconut oil in a small pan until just melted, and drizzle it into the blender while the blades are running. Check that the mixture is sweet enough, and blend for a couple of minutes until light and smooth.

Pour the ice-cream mix into a thick glass baking dish and cover with plastic wrap. Pop it into the freezer. Once it is frozen, take the ice cream out of the freezer and leave it for 20 minutes until it is just starting to soften. Place it in the large bowl of a food processor and whiz until the mixture becomes smooth and light. Don't whiz for too long, though, otherwise it will turn back to liquid. Put the ice cream back into the freezer immediately and leave for 3 to 4 hours.

This ice cream will be very hard straight from the freezer, so take it out at least 20 minutes before serving.

Serve topped with crushed nuts and/or sliced fruit.

Raw Spiced Apple & Date Pie

MAKES 8–10 BIG SLICES

Each summer, Jane and I embark on a monthlong raw food adventure, which we call "Raw Earth Month." This pie is completely raw and brilliantly healthy. It is also easy to put together and only takes some intermediate blender skills and a little spreading to create. No ovens or pastry-making required. It has all the glorious flavors of traditional apple pie, just in a different, more wholesome wrapping. We have also enjoyed this pie with pears instead of apples. Macadamia and pecans make a great crust combination, as do cashews and walnuts, so use whatever is easiest to source.

THE BITS

For the crust

1½ cups (200g) macadamia nuts or cashews

1½ cups (150g) pecans or walnuts

⅓ cup (50g) dates

a large pinch of sea salt

For the filling

5 ounces (150g) dried apples, roughly chopped

2 cups (480ml) apple juice

13 ounces (375g) apples (about 3 or 4)

1 tablespoon lemon juice

8 big fat dates (Medjool are best), soaked until soft

½ teaspoon cinnamon

a large pinch of nutmeg

1 teaspoon vanilla extract

1 tablespoon maple syrup

a small pinch of sea salt

For the topping

scant 1 cup (90g) pecans or walnuts, finely chopped

4 big fat dates, finely chopped

½ teaspoon vanilla extract

a large pinch of ground cinnamon

DO IT

Soak the dried apples in the apple juice for an hour.

To make the crust, pulse all the ingredients in a blender until a rough crumble is formed. You will need to scrape down the sides with a spatula at least a couple of times. The crust is ready when it is sticky between your fingers. Gently press the crust down with your fingers into a shallow pie dish roughly 9 inches (23cm) in diameter, ideally with a loose bottom or springform action. Press down around the edge with a spoon to make it look neat and tidy, then pop into the fridge for 1 hour to firm up.

To make the filling, drain the dried apples, which should now be soft and plump. Core and chop the fresh apples, leaving the peel on, and toss them in the lemon juice to stop them from browning. Put half the fresh apples into a blender with the dates, cinnamon, nutmeg, vanilla extract, maple syrup and salt, and pulse until well combined. Pour in a little of the apple juice from the dried apples if the filling is too thick. Add the rest of the fresh apples and dried apples, then spoon onto the pie crust and smooth out.

To make the topping, mix together the pecans, dates and vanilla in a bowl and spread over the top of the pie to form a crust. Sprinkle with the cinnamon.

Cover and place in the fridge for an hour to chill. Carefully slice and serve at room temperature.

Rosé-Poached Rhubarb with Strawberries & Toasted Almond Buckwheat Crumble

FOR 4–6

A delicious vegan twist on a summer standard. Buckwheat crumble is a new kid on the block, light as a feather and brazenly healthy. Buckwheat's full, nutty flavor is perfect for crumbles. I prefer warming it in a frying pan, where you can keep your eye on it and it's easier to stir. I use rosé wine here, but the recipe works just fine with white or even red wine. The glasses you use for serving should be tall and not too wide, allowing everyone to ogle the careful layering. Any leftover crumble keeps very well in a sealed container and makes a wonderful granola substitute in the morning.

THE BITS

For the rhubarb

1½ pounds (700g) rhubarb, cut into 1-inch (2.5cm) cubes

1 cup (200g) unrefined brown sugar (see page 20)

1 star anise

4 green cardamom pods, crushed with a pestle and mortar

1¼ cups (300ml) rosé wine (vegan)

½ pound (220g) strawberries

For the crumble

2 tablespoons vegetable oil

1¼ cups (200g) cooked buckwheat groats

1½ tablespoons buckwheat or whole wheat flour

⅓ cup (75g) unrefined brown sugar

¼ teaspoon ground cinnamon

3 tablespoons sliced almonds

For the vanilla cream

10½ ounces (300g) silken tofu

2 big handfuls of cashews, soaked for 2 hours

1–2 tablespoons brown rice syrup (or other sweetener of your choice)

1 teaspoon vanilla extract

For the garnish

sprigs of fresh mint (optional)

DO IT

To make the crumble, heat the oil in a large frying pan on medium-high and add the buckwheat. Cook for 15–20 minutes, stirring regularly – the buckwheat will get nicely toasted. The darker the color, the deeper the flavor.

Add the rest of the crumble ingredients to the pan and continue to cook for another 15 minutes. The sugar will stick to the flour, which will stick to the buckwheat, which is then stuck to by almonds, and all is toasted and happy. If it's a little dry, add a tad more oil. If it's a little oily, add a smidgen more flour. Try the buckwheat – it should be crisp, caramelized and light. Pour it out onto a big plate and allow to cool.

To make the rosé-poached rhubarb, put the rhubarb into a small pot with a generous ¾ cup (180g) of sugar, the star anise, cardamom and rosé wine. Bring to a gentle boil, cover, and simmer for 8–10 minutes, until the rhubarb is soft but not mushy. Check the sweet to tart ratio of the rhubarb; you may need a little more sugar.

Remove the rhubarb with a slotted spoon. Cook the liquid down until a syrup forms (reducing the volume by more than half). Spoon out the cardamom pods and star anise. Allow the syrup to cool, then place the rhubarb back in the saucepan.

To make the vanilla cream, blend the tofu in a food processor with the cashews, brown rice syrup and vanilla until smooth and creamy. Taste and adjust the sweetness if needed.

Now for the assembly job. Slice the strawberries thinly. Place some rhubarb chunks in the base of a glass with a large spoonful of rosé rhubarb syrup and cover with some of the vanilla cream. Top with a decent layer of crumble and a scattering of strawberries. I would go for at least two layers if you have enough ingredients.

If it's a warm day, you may like to pop the glasses into the fridge and serve the crumble chilled and topped with fresh mint sprigs.

Chocolate Cake with Almond Cream & Raspberries

MAKES 8 BIG SLICES

This is light and chewy, just how I like my chocolate cake. I use a light olive oil in my chocolate cakes, since I think the bitterness of the cocoa and the acidity of the olives go together well. Use any seasonal berries on this cake. My favorites are raspberries – they just look so striking. Blackberries are also very good.

THE BITS

¾ cup (150g) unrefined brown sugar (see page 20)

scant 1½ cups (220g) unbleached all-purpose flour

⅔ cup (50g) cacao powder

1 heaped teaspoon baking powder

1 teaspoon sea salt

⅓ cup (75ml) light olive oil

1 tablespoon apple cider vinegar

1 cup (250ml) water

For the almond cream

½ cup (80g) raw almonds, soaked in water overnight and skins removed

⅓ cup (75ml) unsweetened almond milk or soy milk

scant ½ cup (100ml) light olive oil

1 teaspoon almond extract

2 tablespoons brown rice syrup (or other sweetener of your choice)

For the topping

2 handfuls of fresh raspberries (or other berries)

2 tablespoons crushed pistachio nuts

DO IT

Preheat the oven to 350°F (180°C). Place the sugar, flour, cacao powder, baking powder and salt in a mixing bowl and mix together with a wooden spoon. Add the olive oil, vinegar and water gradually, and continue to slowly whisk until a batter has formed – don't overwork it.

Pour the mixture into an oiled and lined cake pan (I use a round pan, 9½ inches [24cm] wide and 3½ inches [9cm] deep, with a loose bottom or a springform action) and bake for 25–30 minutes. Leave to cool on a wire rack. A skewer thrust into the center should have very little wet cake clinging to it when removed.

To make the almond cream, put the skinned almonds into a food processor and blend, scraping down the sides, until nice and smooth. Drizzle in the milk and, when this has fully combined to make a very smooth cream, begin to drizzle in the oil. The mix will thicken. Stir in the almond extract and sweetener. Check the flavor, adding more sweetener if required, and the texture – it should be the texture of whipped cream, thick enough to spread all over the top of your cake.

When the cake has just about cooled, spread a thick layer of the almond cream over it. It's fine if the cream drizzles over the edges. It adds to the look. Arrange the berries on top. I like to put them in a circular shape just inside the edge. Why not try a mosaic of mixed berries for a really colorful look? For a final flourish, garnish with crushed pistachio nuts.

Sauces, Dressings, Toppers & Other Extras

Something creamy, something sweet. Something tangy, all full-on unique! Here we slip into the dark art of sauce-making and realize that it's actually quite straightforward when you have a few techniques up your sleeves. I have always been amazed at the secrecy surrounding sauce-making – what's the big deal? The wonderful benefit of vegan sauces is no messing around with large quantities of butter or white flour; as usual, we stay close to the trusty food processor and tofu or nuts, to fantastic effect.

Having a decent high-powered food processor means much smoother sauces and purées. If you don't have one, maybe add it to your birthday wish list!

Looking at this plethora of condiment-based goodness, if vegan food is not the future of tastiness, I have no idea what is! Here we have the opportunity to accessorize our dishes with the most vibrant colors and flavors around, like a colorful scarf in a hailstorm.

This chapter sees us spooning, dolloping and sprinkling our way to shining plates of plant goodness. After all, little embellishments can light up your life.

Mango chutney, page 307

Mango Barbecue Sauce

MAKES A LARGE BOWLFUL

Sticky, fragrant and unctious, like the finest barbecue sauces. The addition of fresh mango really ups the ante on this one. This sauce will cling lovingly to tofu, seitan or tempeh when stir-fried and is a wonder with barbecued food. This tangy taste bud-tantalizer gets thicker and stickier the longer it is cooked.

½ tablespoon vegetable oil

1 small onion, finely diced

2 cloves of garlic, peeled and crushed

1cm fresh ginger, grated

½ teaspoon ground coriander

½ teaspoon smoked paprika

scant ½ cup (100ml) vegetable stock

1 star anise

1 large fragrant mango, peeled
and chopped into chunks

1½ tablespoons tamari

1½ tablespoons tomato paste

1½ tablespoons light molasses
or maple syrup

zest of 1 lime

Put the oil into a small pan on medium heat and sauté the onion for 10–12 minutes, until well caramelized. Add the garlic and ginger, cook for 2 minutes more, then add the coriander, paprika and stock and stir. Add the star anise, mango, tamari, tomato paste and molasses. Bring to a boil and cover, then lower the heat and cook for 10 minutes, stir, cook for 10 minutes, stir, 10 minutes more, stir. It gets nice and sticky. Taste for sweetness and saltiness – there should be a nice balance of the two.

Allow the sauce to cool slightly and remove the star anise. Place in the small bowl of a food processor (or use an immersion blender) and pulse a few times, allowing for some nice chunks of mango. Stir in the lime zest.

Smoky Chipotle & Cauliflower Cheese Sauce

FOR 4

I lived in the highlands of central Mexico for a short while, where the little town market was crammed with piles of chilies of all shades and sizes, and I tried them all! The chipotle, however, stands out. Chipotle is now increasingly popular on the condiment shelves and adds a truly unmistakable dose of Mexican flair to all it graces. That delicious and unique flavor that you get in Mexican food can normally be attributed to these smoked chili delights.

This sauce is almost a meal in itself (just toss some steamed greens in its general direction and you're set!). It's thick enough to dip, or it can be poured over roasted veggies or used in a gratin. I pop any leftovers in the fridge and spread it on bread and grill it until bubbling and golden. Think pasta sauce, too. I like to use potatoes to thicken things up here, but you can use a tablespoon of cornstarch for a lighter sauce.

2¾ cups (650ml) vegetable stock

½ a large cauliflower, cut into small chunks,
stems included

1 large potato, peeled and diced

3 cloves of garlic, peeled and crushed

1 onion, finely diced

2 celery stalks, finely diced

2 large dried chipotle chilies
or ½ teaspoon smoked paprika

½ teaspoon ground turmeric

½ teaspoon mustard powder

2 tablespoons nutritional yeast flakes

½ tablespoon lemon juice

sea salt to taste

1 tablespoon olive oil
(or cashew butter for extra richness)

Put the stock into a pan, bring to a boil, and add your cauliflower, potato, garlic, onion, celery, chipotle (or paprika) and turmeric. Cover with a lid and reduce the heat to medium-low. Simmer for 30 minutes, until the potato is very tender.

(continued) →

Pop the contents of the saucepan into a food processor (or use an immersion blender) and add the mustard and yeast flakes. Blitz to a thick sauce.

Pour the sauce back into the saucepan, add the lemon juice and salt, and heat until it begins to slowly bubble, stirring occasionally. Allow it to cook and thicken for 10 minutes.

Stir in the oil (or cashew butter) and serve warm.

Macadamia Mustard Sauce

MAKES ONE SMALL BOWLFUL

A decadent sauce with a mustard twang. The key here is to blend the macadamias for a while – this makes them extra creamy and smooth. Ideal with the eggplant and tomato nut roast (see page 179).

2 teaspoons high-quality canola oil or olive oil

½ a white onion, finely sliced

2 big handfuls of macadamia nuts,
soaked for 4 hours

2½ teaspoons apple cider vinegar or
white wine vinegar

½ –1 tablespoon mustard powder (to taste)

1½ teaspoons brown rice syrup
(or other sweetener of your choice)

½ teaspoon sea salt

½ cup (125ml) vegetable stock or water

Warm the oil on medium heat. Add the onions and cook for 6–8 minutes, until they are soft and sweet. Place in a food processor with the macadamias, vinegar, mustard, brown rice syrup and salt and blitz until smooth. Now drizzle in the stock, little by little, until you have a thick sauce. Keep blending until very smooth. Pour the sauce back into the pan and warm through, without boiling. It should have the consistency of heavy cream.

Sun-Dried Tomato & Marjoram Sauce

MAKES ONE SMALL BOWLFUL

I love marjoram – it abounds where other herbs wilt. It works perfectly in sauces with a hint of the Mediterranean about them. This sauce is ideal for stirring into pasta and spreading on ciabatta or bruschetta. You can sun-dry your own tomatoes by just leaving them in the oven overnight on the lowest setting, with the door open. This does seem like a complete waste of energy, but it works, and the more the tomatoes shrivel, the tastier they get. I own a dehydrator, which means I can dry the late-summer glut of tomatoes into jars upon jars of sun-dried tomatoes, allowing me to experiment with oil marinades. It takes a little time, but as with most cooking processes, you reap the gorgeous benefits at a later date.

¼ cup (50ml) extra virgin olive oil

4 cloves of garlic, peeled and crushed

½ teaspoon fennel seeds

⅓ cup (40g) sunflower seeds,
soaked in water overnight

2 ripe tomatoes, roughly chopped

1¼ cups (125g) sun-dried tomatoes,
roughly chopped, plus any oil

½ a handful of fresh marjoram leaves,
or 1 teaspoon dried marjoram

freshly cracked black pepper
and sea salt, to taste

Warm the oil in a pan on low heat and add the garlic. Allow it to gently poach for a minute, without coloring, then add the fennel and sunflower seeds along with the tomato and sun-dried tomatoes.

Warm through for 2 minutes more, then add the marjoram, pop a lid on the pan and set aside to infuse. Once cooled, place in a blender, add the seasoning and blend until smooth. The sauce should be a silky, shiny affair and can be served hot or cold.

Creamy Cashew Cheese Sauce

FOR 4-6

A wonderfully versatile dairy- and gluten-free substitute for cheese sauce. So, so creamy, and full of glorious richness. Use liberally on the cauliflower cashew cheese (page 261). I'm a mustard freak! I'd probably opt for a full teaspoon in my sauce, but see how you handle half to start with.

⅔ cup (120g) raw cashews, soaked and drained

2 tablespoons cornstarch

1 tablespoon lemon juice

3 tablespoons nutritional yeast flakes

a large pinch of ground turmeric
(or enough to get a nice shade of "cheesy" yellow)

a large pinch of sea salt

½ teaspoon mustard powder
(or to taste)

1 cup (240ml) unsweetened almond milk
or soy milk

Drain the soaked cashews and pop them into a food processor. Blend until creamy – the texture should resemble smooth peanut butter. You will need to scrape down the sides of the food processor a few times to get things really smooth.

Add the cornstarch and pulse a few times, then add the rest of the ingredients, drizzling the milk in gradually. Blend until a smooth and thick sauce is formed, adding drizzles of water as needed. This sauce can be enjoyed as it is or it can be warmed gently – just avoid boiling it.

Superhero Dressing

FOR 4-6

Great with the superhero sprouted salad (see page 108). Every one of these ingredients is a superhero in its own right, so whisking them all together can only lead to happy salads of death-defying tastiness.

1 inch (2.5cm) fresh ginger, finely grated

1 clove of garlic, peeled and crushed

4 tablespoons olive oil

½ tablespoon toasted sesame oil

1–2 tablespoons apple cider vinegar or
white wine vinegar (to taste)

1 tablespoon white or yellow miso
(gluten-free, if needed)

½ tablespoon brown rice syrup

tamari to taste

Blend all the ingredients, except the tamari, in a food processor, putting the ginger and garlic in first. Thin out with a splash of water if needed. Add tamari to taste (your miso may be quite salty) and balance the acidity – more vinegar may be needed.

Fey's Parsley & Lemon Dressing

FOR 4-6

Our friend Fey is a massive and lovely star. When I sent her some recipes to try out, with her gang of Chicas (mates – Fey lives in Murcia, Spain), she loved them all except for one dressing, so she and came up with this one for us, which is perfect with the Mediterranean tofu tostada with Murcian salad (see page 96).

1 clove of garlic, peeled

a large pinch of sea salt

a handful of flat-leaf parsley, chopped

juice of 1 lemon

(continued) →

1 teaspoon Dijon mustard

½ tablespoon brown rice syrup
(or other sweetener of your choice)

⅔ cup (150ml) extra virgin olive oil

sea salt and freshly ground black
pepper to taste

Crush the garlic in a mortar with the salt and parsley until it becomes a paste. Stir in the lemon juice and mustard, along with the brown rice syrup. Little by little add the olive oil until you get the right consistency and taste, adding salt and pepper as necessary.

Raspberry Dressing

FOR 4–6

It's worth buying raspberry vinegar just for this dressing. It finishes the beet, apple and raspberry salad (see page 111) perfectly.

2 tablespoons raspberry vinegar

1–2 tablespoons apple juice concentrate

4 tablespoons olive oil

1 teaspoon sea salt

Simply mix all the ingredients together in a bowl.

Pomegranate Dressing

FOR 4–6

Great with braised cauliflower and Puy lentil tabbouleh (see page 98). Pomegranate molasses is quite versatile and well worth having handy, especially to jazz up dressings and salads.

4 tablespoons olive oil

2 tablespoons pomegranate molasses or
juice of 1 large lemon

zest of ½ a lemon

(continued) →

1 clove of garlic, peeled and well crushed

a small pinch of dried mint

a small pinch of sea salt

½ teaspoon freshly cracked black pepper

Simply whisk all the ingredients together in a bowl.

Raw Ketchup

MAKES ONE SMALL BOWLFUL

This is much better than bottled ketchup and infinitely more healthy. I feel a tingling sense of smug satisfaction when making substitutes for generic household favorites, especially when they are filled with so many good things. The body loves it, the taste buds love it and sweet potato fries like it a lot, too. Store-bought ketchup is a vehicle for sugar, which is why little kiddos love it so. This homemade ketchup uses natural sugars and beautiful nuts to add richness. It's the kind of recipe that makes perfect sense all around. Blend well for best results.

a big handful of cashews or macadamias,
soaked for 2 hours or overnight

2 handfuls of sun-dried tomatoes,
roughly chopped

2 tablespoons apple cider vinegar
or white wine vinegar

1 clove of garlic, peeled and chopped

1 ripe tomato, roughly chopped

1 teaspoon sweet paprika

4 tablespoons olive oil

1–2 teaspoons tamari (to taste)

3 large dates (Medjool are best, soaked
in water until soft), or 4–5 dried apricots

scant ½ cup (100ml) water (use the soaking
water from the dates)

Place all the ingredients apart from the water in a blender. With the machine running, gradually add the water until you have a thick, smooth ketchup. Will keep refrigerated in a jar for a week or two.

Tarragon Aioli

Great with the portobello pecan burgers (see page 222). Sunflower seeds are a good replacement for the macadamias in this aioli. Unmistakably French, tarragon brings a taste of sweet, herbaceous anise.

1 cup (140g) raw macadamias, soaked overnight

¼ cup (60ml) water

a handful of fresh tarragon leaves

½ tablespoon olive oil

2 tablespoons lemon juice

2 cloves of garlic, peeled and crushed

a large pinch of sea salt

Put all the ingredients into a food processor and purée until smooth, adding water to thin it out, if needed.

Mushroom, Leek & Thyme Gravy

FOR 4–6

I normally make this at Sunday lunchtime, when the oven is filled with roasting goodies. It goes perfectly with a nut roast (see page 179), and is equally at home poured over roasted or steamed veggies with some perfectly roasted potatoes on the side. After a Sunday lunch like that, the real deliciousness of a vegan diet becomes clear. Tofu converts are never far behind.

1 tablespoon olive oil

1 leek, finely sliced

2 cloves of garlic, peeled and crushed

14 mushrooms, finely diced (I normally opt for chestnut, but your favorite variety will be fine)

10½ ounces (300g) silken tofu

5 fresh sage leaves, finely sliced, or ½ teaspoon dried sage

1 large sprig of fresh rosemary, or 1 teaspoon dried rosemary

2 sprigs of fresh thyme, leaves only, or ½ teaspoon dried thyme

2 tablespoons nutritional yeast flakes

2 tablespoons cornstarch (or gluten-free thickener of your choice)

2 cups (480ml) warm vegetable stock

⅔ cup (150ml) unsweetened soy milk

sea salt and freshly ground black pepper to taste

Warm the olive oil in a frying pan on medium heat and add the leek. Cook for 5 minutes, then pop in the garlic and mushrooms. Cook and stir for 5 minutes more, then add the silken tofu and the herbs and cook for 2 minutes more, stirring regularly.

Add the nutritional yeast flakes and sprinkle in the cornstarch (making sure it's well broken up, with no lumps). Cook for 1–2 minutes, then gradually pour in your stock, stirring quickly as you go, and add enough soy milk to make a thick gravy. Warm through gently for 20 minutes, uncovered. Check that there is no "floury" taste to the gravy – if there is, cook for 5 minutes more and re-taste.

Pick out the rosemary sprig, then blend the sauce using an immersion blender or in a food processor until a gravy is formed, adding more milk if needed. Check the seasoning and serve with great pride to happy folk.

Teriyaki Sauce

MAKES ONE SMALL JARFUL

Japanese cooking at home is becoming increasingly popular and is ideal for us vegans, as dairy rarely crops up on the Japanese menu. Teriyaki sauce is my favorite Japanese condiment, the perfect balance of sweet and salty that brings the fresh and clean flavors of sushi to life. This sauce keeps perfectly in the fridge for months. I like mine a little sweet –

(continued) →

(continued) →

give it a quick taste as you may prefer a dash more tamari. If you like a sweet teriyaki sauce, just add 1–2 teaspoons of unrefined brown sugar to the mix (see page 20). Mirin is readily available nowadays in supermarkets.

10 tablespoons tamari

15 tablespoons mirin

Put the tamari and mirin into a small pan over medium heat and simmer gently. Remove from the heat when a third of the sauce has evaporated.

Asian-Style Dipping Sauce

MAKES ONE SMALL BOWLFUL

You know this sauce. You've probably dipped thousands of spring rolls and sushi chunks into something like this over the years. A classic dipping sauce – it also makes a good dressing. Great with raw lumpia (see page 162).

3 tablespoons rice vinegar

2 tablespoons tamari

1 teaspoon toasted sesame oil

1 teaspoon brown rice syrup

1 scallion, finely sliced at an angle

3 small dried chilies, or ¼ teaspoon red pepper flakes (optional)

Simply whisk all the ingredients together in a bowl.

Mint Raita

FOR 4

Soothing raita, an essential condiment when faced with the mind-bending flavors and fiery chili heat of Indian cuisine. Great with spinach bhaji burgers (see page 230).

scant 2 cups (450ml) soy yogurt

juice of ½ a lemon

(continued) →

a big handful of fresh mint leaves, very finely chopped

a large pinch of sea salt and freshly ground black pepper

Mix all the ingredients together in a bowl and serve at room temperature.

Beet Raita

FOR 4

Freakin' pink! Brightens up any feast. Eating food this color makes you feel alive! Good with turnip and spinach Kashmiri curry (page 199).

scant 2 cups (450ml) unsweetened soy yogurt

1 beet, peeled and grated

1 teaspoons fennel seeds

½ tablespoon lemon juice

a large pinch of sea salt

Mix all the ingredients together in a bowl and serve at room temperature.

Horseradish & Dill Yogurt

MAKES ONE SMALL BOWLFUL

Horseradish and dill are a fine pair. I like to keep a horseradish root in the freezer, ready to grate, 24/7. Lovely with beet and cumin fritters (see page 153).

1⅓ cups (350ml) thick unsweetened soy yogurt

1 tablespoon lemon juice

3 tablespoons finely grated horseradish or 1½ tablespoons horseradish purée

a handful of fresh dill, finely chopped

a pinch of sea salt

freshly ground black pepper to taste

extra virgin olive oil, for drizzling

Stir all the ingredients except the oil together in a small bowl. Season and drizzle with olive oil.

Mango Chutney

MAKES ONE SMALL JARFUL

Give this a try – it's like making jam only much, much better. The real chutney deal! Great with the spinach bhaji burger (see page 230) or matar dal (see page 217).

1 pound (500g) unripe green mangoes (or mangoes that are as unripe as possible), washed

1 tablespoon vegetable oil

1 large red chili, finely diced

2-inch (5cm) cinnamon stick

2 teaspoons coriander seeds

8 green cardamom pods, cracked

5 cloves

2 star anise

1 cup (250ml) water

½ teaspoon garam masala

generous ¾ cup (160g) unrefined brown sugar (see page 20)

½ teaspoon sea salt

2–3 tablespoons apple cider vinegar (if the mangoes are sweet)

Cut the mango flesh into ¾-inch (2cm) cubes. Heat the oil on medium in a heavy-bottomed saucepan. Add the chili, cinnamon, coriander seeds, cardamom, cloves and star anise, cook for 30 seconds, then add the mango chunks. Cover with the water and add the garam masala, sugar and salt. Add the vinegar if needed. Bring to a boil and gently cook, uncovered, for 45 minutes to 1 hour, or until nice and thick. Stir regularly to ensure that the chutney doesn't stick – this is especially important towards the end of cooking.

Spoon the chutney into a clean jar right away. It will keep for several weeks in the refrigerator.

Green Tomato, Ginger & Orange Chutney

MAKES ABOUT 3 POUNDS (FOUR LARGE JARS)

I first made this chutney one baking hot day in Spain, when oranges and local green tomatoes were abundant in the fruit bowl. It was while eyeing piles of tantalizing tomatoes that this refreshing chutney sprang to mind. Something to complement the sweetness and ripeness of Spain's summer produce, and a receptacle for wonderfully fruity green tomatoes, which is the preferred shade for many of the local varieties like Raf, Kumato, Pata Negra and Mucho Miel. If you can't go green, try red (tomato-wise). This chutney is sweet and tangy, a one-pot wonder to be reckoned with.

5½ pounds (2.5kg) green tomatoes, deseeded and quartered

2 large oranges (zest of one and both cut into segments, with no white pith)

1 large onion, finely chopped

4 cloves of garlic, peeled and crushed

⅓ cup (50g) golden raisins

1 tablespoon yellow mustard seeds

1 tablespoon cumin seeds

½ tablespoon coriander seeds (smaller ones are best)

1 teaspoon ground turmeric

8 cloves

2 inches (5cm) fresh ginger, grated

1⅔ cups (400ml) white wine vinegar

½ cup (100g) unrefined brown sugar (see page 20)

½ cup (75ml) apple juice concentrate, or apple juice

3 red chilies, deseeded and finely sliced

¼ cup (50ml) olive oil

Place everything in a large heavy-bottomed pot and heat until the sugar is completely dissolved. Bring to a boil, then simmer, stirring regularly, for 1 hour, or until it thickens to a sticky chutney. Remember it will thicken even more as it cools.

(continued) →

Spoon the chutney into clean glass jars and seal well. Store in a cool dark place for a few weeks, ideally, before you tuck into it. Once opened, keep in the fridge, where it will last for weeks.

Red Onion Marmalade

MAKES ONE LARGE JARFUL

A bit of onion marmalade brings things to life. There's vastly less sugar here than in most store-bought varieties. Lovely with a smoked tofu sausage sandwich (see page 232).

1 tablespoon vegetable oil

2 bay leaves

5 large red onions, finely sliced

a large pinch of sea salt

a large pinch of freshly ground black pepper

½ teaspoon red pepper flakes

2 tablespoons balsamic vinegar

2 teaspoons unrefined brown sugar
(see page 20)

Put a heavy-bottomed saucepan on medium-low heat and add your oil, bay leaves and sliced onions. Fry for 20 minutes, stirring, then season with salt. Drop the heat, pop a lid on and cook for 1 hour, stirring occasionally, until the onions are very soft and caramelized. Take the lid off, turn the heat back up, then add the pepper, chili, balsamic vinegar and sugar. Stir well and cook until all the vinegar has evaporated. Make sure the onions don't stick to the bottom. They should be very sweet and sticky by now; if not, continue cooking – they will just get sweeter and sweeter! Set aside to cool.

Fig & Apple Compote

MAKES ONE SMALL BOWLFUL

Thick and sticky! Figs are such a treat: fleshy center, smooth skin, crunchy seeds. Paired with a bit of tart and zest, they are really at home in this compote, which is good with the asparagus and cashew cream tart (see page 176).

8 dried figs, stems trimmed,
cut into quarters and
soaked for 4 hours

3 green apples, cored, peeled
and roughly chopped

2 teaspoons lemon zest

½ teaspoon lemon juice

1 star anise

1 cinnamon stick (about 2 inches [5cm])

Put the figs (with 4 tablespoons of their soaking juice) into a small pan and add the rest of the ingredients. Bring to a gentle boil and slowly simmer uncovered for 20–25 minutes, until the apples are soft but still retain their shape. Remove the star anise and cinnamon stick.

Roasted Red Pepper & Black Olive Tapenade

MAKES ONE MEDIUM BOWLFUL

Like hummus and baba ghanoush, tapenade is part of the bedrock of any great picnic or summer spread, the beating heart of any canapé-based event. It adds a fruity intensity and saltiness, whether stirred into pasta or spread thinly over a cracker or crudité. It has the kind of potent flavor that we don't expect from "just" plants, but I think few things can pack a punch like a nicely piquant tapenade.

⅓ cup (90ml) extra virgin olive oil

2 red bell peppers, deseeded and
roughly sliced

½ cup (80g) black olives, pitted

(continued) →

½ a handful of fresh oregano or
1 teaspoon dried oregano

2 tablespoons nonpareil capers,
well drained and rinsed

½ a handful of fresh parsley, chopped

zest of ½ a lemon

1 large clove of garlic, peeled

½ cup (50g) sun-dried tomatoes

1 tablespoon lemon juice

sea salt, if needed

a large pinch of freshly cracked black pepper

In a small frying pan on high heat, warm ½ a tablespoon of olive oil and add the red peppers. Allow to sizzle, sweeten and soften for 10 minutes, then remove and allow to cool. Reserve any leftover oil.

Put the olives, peppers, oregano, capers, parsley, lemon zest, garlic and sun-dried tomatoes into a food processor and pulse together, gradually drizzling in the lemon juice and the rest of the oil. All should be well combined and shiny to the eye. Check for seasoning and add sea salt, black pepper and lemon juice accordingly.

The tapenade will keep in a sterilized jar in the fridge for weeks, but make sure you bring it to room temperature before using.

Spinach Pistou

MAKES ONE MEDIUM BOWLFUL

This is great with oven-baked squash gnocchi (see page 172). Hazelnuts bring their sweet and mellow flavor to this classic pistou. Try this with nettles and wild garlic if you can (instead of spinach and basil).

¾ cup (100g) hazelnuts

3 cups (100g) spinach or watercress leaves

2 big handfuls of fresh basil leaves

3 cloves of garlic, peeled and crushed

juice of 1 lemon

zest of ½ a lemon

a large pinch of sea salt

2 large pinches of freshly ground black pepper

⅓ cup (75ml) extra virgin olive oil

Place the hazelnuts in a small skillet on medium heat. Keep them moving for 5–7 minutes – they will become roasted and smell so very sweet! Put them into a food processor and blitz for 30 seconds. The nuts should begin to break down into lumps and chunks, which is what we want. Add the rest of the pistou ingredients (except the oil) and blitz, drizzling the oil in gradually until you get a nice runny texture, like a thick sauce. You will need to scrape down the sides of the food processor a few times. Add more oil if the pistou needs thinning.

Pistachio & Cilantro Pesto

MAKES ONE SMALL BOWLFUL

I think you will be pleasantly surprised by this nontraditional take on pesto. It's a meal in itself – spread it on toast! Or stir it into noodles or mashed sweet potatoes. Lovely with chargrilled chorizo pinchos, too (see page 238).

3 handfuls of fresh cilantro leaves

1 large clove of garlic, peeled and crushed

1 cup (115g) pistachios, soaked
for 1 hour and drained

½ teaspoon dried mint

juice of 1 lime

2 teaspoons lime zest

scant ½ cup (100ml) extra virgin olive oil

a handful of sun-dried tomatoes,
roughly chopped

a large pinch of sea salt and
freshly ground black pepper

Put the cilantro and garlic into a blender with the pistachios, dried mint and lime juice and zest, and blitz to a purée, drizzling the oil in

(continued) →

(continued) →

Spinach pistou,
page 309

while the mixture is blending. You should be left with a thick, chunky paste. Stir in the chopped sun-dried tomatoes and season to taste.

Creamy Pesto

MAKES ONE LARGE JARFUL

If you live in a warm part of the US or you have a greenhouse (or a windowsill!), growing your own basil is a must. It's a sacred herb, so fragrant, easy to grow from seed and it thrives come summertime. Pick a handful of leaves from a decent-size plant and be amazed at how it springs back after a short time. Even the potted plants that you can buy in supermarkets will last for a while if sensitively raided for leaves and watered on occasion. This pesto is ideally made the day before use and can simply be stirred into pasta and steamed vegetables or even lathered over a baked potato. When times are tight, I turn to peanuts. They are a decent substitute for pine nuts (use a few more quantity-wise) and they don't break the piggy bank. Try it on your pals – they won't be able to tell the difference!

5 ounces (150g) silken tofu

2 big handfuls of fresh basil leaves

½ a handful of fresh chives, finely sliced

⅔ cup (85g) pine nuts (or ⅔ cup [100g] blanched/skinless peanuts)

2 cloves of garlic, peeled and crushed

2 tablespoons nutritional yeast flakes

⅓ cup (75ml) extra virgin olive oil

Pop all your bits into a food processor and blitz until it has a nice chunky pesto texture, adding the oil gradually and regularly scraping down the sides of your processor. Store in a clean jar – it keeps well in the fridge for up to 5 days.

Pumpkin & Olive Butter

MAKES A LARGE BOWLFUL

Being a vegan pushes you into some pretty creative corners, and that's when things like butter recipes arise. This is not butter – it's better. It's bright orange for a start! It also contains no bad fats and is vastly higher in nutritional value. It will keep well in the fridge or freezer and will firm up when cooled. Enjoy it spread over most edible things. If you prefer your butter unsalted, leave out the olives.

1 small sugar/pie pumpkin, peeled, deseeded and diced

2 tablespoons fruity olive oil

1 small onion, finely diced

1 large clove of garlic, peeled and crushed

3 tablespoons almond, cashew or sunflower seed butter

2 tablespoons finely chopped green olives

1 tablespoon white miso (gluten-free, if needed)

1 teaspoon sea salt

Steam the pumpkin over boiling water for 25–30 minutes, until tender. Drain well and leave uncovered until cool. This will dry it out slightly.

Warm the olive oil in a pan on medium heat and gently cook the onions for 5 minutes, then add the garlic and continue to cook until nice and soft. Pop all the bits into a blender and blitz until smooth. Check the seasoning.

Nice served warm or cold on fresh bread, or as a hearty dip.

Coriander & Pumpkin Seed Topper

MAKES ONE SMALL BOWLFUL

A potent topping for soups and salads, this can also be mixed into stews to add a nice

(continued) →

richness. If you are making a soup or stew that hints at a Mediterranean origin, I highly recommend this. It can even lighten up a curry. Mix liberally with a little oil and you have the makings of a top-notch dressing. This topper keeps well in the fridge in a sealed container. It's a lively little number – use sparingly.

3 tablespoons coriander seeds, toasted

½ teaspoon sea salt

1 large clove of garlic, peeled and crushed

5 tablespoons pumpkin seeds, toasted

2 tablespoons fruity olive oil

Grind the coriander seeds and salt with a pestle and mortar or a food processor, followed by the garlic. When a paste is formed, add the pumpkin seeds and grind well, until some of the oil is released from the seeds. Gradually add the olive oil and grind until a glistening chunky paste is formed.

Pine Nut Parmesan

MAKES ENOUGH FOR ONE GOOD TOPPING

This is as close to Parmesan as you can get for the vegan palate. Toasted pine nuts are so precious: fatty and oily, when mashed they morph into something very special. It's a good recipe to make in a large batch – just multiply the amount of ingredients a few times – as it keeps well for a couple of days, getting better with age. Sprinkle liberally and joyfully over anything that strikes your fancy.

4 tablespoons toasted pine nuts

1 tablespoon toasted sesame seeds

a large pinch of finely grated lemon zest

1 tablespoon nutritional yeast flakes (optional)

a pinch of sea salt

Combine all the ingredients in a food processor, or use a pestle and mortar, and pulse or mash a few times until fine and crumbly, just like finely grated Parmesan.

Tofu & Herb Feta

FOR 4

Massively versatile and packed full of protein and nutrients, the only thing tofu lacks is lots of flavor. However, this gives us the perfect opportunity to show our creativity in flavoring the wonder bean block. This recipe is so simple, and it transforms tofu into something delicious – a staple in the repertoire of most vegans, a basic feta to accompany salads and much more. If you don't fancy some of the herbs, just leave them out.

8½ ounces (240g) firm tofu, pressed (see page 18)

1 tablespoon lemon juice

½ teaspoon sea salt

1 clove of garlic, peeled and crushed

2 teaspoons fruity olive oil

1 tablespoon very finely chopped fresh chives

½ tablespoon very finely chopped fresh dill

1 tablespoon very finely chopped fresh parsley

Place a third of the tofu in a blender with all the other ingredients and blitz until smooth. Break the rest of the tofu up into feta-like chunks with your hands, then add them to the smooth mixture with the fresh herbs and stir to combine.

Taste and season, then leave to marinate overnight for the finest flavor.

Suppliers

We try to get most of our ingredients close to home, but when we buy online, where we choose to spend our money is important: who are we giving it to, and how will they use it? I believe this is one of the easiest and most effective methods of bettering the world we live in. Give your hard-earned money to the good ones, whenever possible. Here are some resources:

Bob's Red Mill (bobsredmill.com)

This employee-owned company was started three decades ago by the man himself, Bob, and has been producing top-quality dried food goods ever since. It's one of the best sources for wholesome grains, flours and legumes, as well as gluten-free alternatives. You've probably seen Bob's products in the organic section of your local grocery store, and their online store offers a plethora of tricky-to-find ingredients, such as chana dal beans, spelt flour, flageolet beans and farro.

Frontier Co-op (frontiercoop.com)

Purveyors of high-quality natural and organic foods, including herbs, spices and extracts, along with vegan staples like nutritional yeast. They get an A+ for their efforts in supporting social and environmental responsibility. Many items are offered in both small sizes and in bulk, so consider getting some like-minded people together and ordering every few months – buying wholesale is cheaper.

Abe's Market (abesmarket.com)

An online store with a focus on natural goods and a wide selection of organic foods. Each of their products has a list of its certifications and qualities, so you can check whether something is vegan, non-GMO, made in the USA, biodynamic or free of pesticides, additives, dyes, etc. It's a great way to find out exactly what you're buying.

Navitas Naturals (navitasnaturals.com)

Specializing in organic superfoods, you can find all sorts of funky green powders here, along with numerous nut, seed and cacao products. An added bonus is that all their products are certified organic and non-GMO, with a focus on sustainability and environmental friendliness.

Blue Mountain Organics (bluemountainorganics.com)

Here you'll find almost anything sprouted that you can imagine, along with other certified organic nuts, nut butters, flours, grains, dried fruits and superfoods.

Last but not least, the two most important food providers for any aspiring/casual/once-in-a-while/hard-core vegan:

Your local organic farmer

Befriend your local organic vegetable farmers: there will be some around. The best place to look is the farmers' market. Support them and revel in the fruits (and veggies) of their toil. Local organic fruits and vegetables are the cornerstone of any healthy, vibrant, ethical diet, and farmers are some of the most important people in our society! Even better, become your own local organic vegetable farmer by growing your own gorgeous fruits and veggies. Seasonal veggies will keep your body and mind singing throughout the year. As Hippocrates said, "Let thy food be thy medicine and medicine be thy food."

Your local health food store

A place of sanctuary and nourishment for vegans, this is probably the hub of all things ethical/organic/vegan in your area. A font of information and support (hopefully!) if you're a new vegan, and a go-to source for many of the ingredients you will find mentioned in this book, from cheap whole foods to funny-sounding Asian condiments.

I also highly recommend regular foraging of hedgerows, coastlines, fields and forests – our free and natural supermarkets.

Index

Big Love!

Some people have a novel in them, but it appears I had a cookbook! The birthing process of this wedge of veganity has been riddled with chaos and many surprises along the way. The opportunity came out of the big blue like a flash of bright green vegetal lightning. The story goes something like this: at a boozy New Year 2011 at my cousin's house, her husband, Mick (who is directly responsible for and a driving force behind my baffling career in media circles), films me cooking and generally waffling on about lentils and the like, and next thing I know I'm in London cooking a blasphemous version of *kitchuri* for some lovely TV folk (cheers, Jo). Then I'm suddenly on a show called *Meat v Veg* (which was a load of fun), leading to me meeting the big man Rob Allison (a top, top geezer and chef), who mentioned me to some top-notch publishers and BAM! I'm writing a massive vegan cookbook and fulfilling a lifetime ambition! How cool!

Getting this book together has been a real trip, like the largest and most vibrant homework assignment ever. It has developed into a proper labor of love and I must firstly and foremostly thank and offer my undying gratitude and love for the complete support, patience, inspiration and constant giggles of my partner in life and travels, Miss Jane Legge. Without you, honeypie, I'd still be on that Filipino beach munching coconuts and reading Jung (in fact, let's get back there soon!). Jane built the Beach House, where we now live together with the coolest animal in the world, Buster, the feral Russian Blue (aka Punk Boy, Little Man, Roonie, Raja, Punkawallah, Bustusmaximus, Buzzywoooo, Buzzman, Funky Monkey . . .).

I've been on the road in India while writing this and have dealt with a constant lack of internet, electricity or even a kitchen in which to create these recipes that reflect my life and mirror the richness of experience I have found by traveling the road less trodden. The recipes encapsulate my past and my present; old favorites and things I just ate for lunch have all made it into these pages. The process was entirely new to me and a big shout must go to Jonathan (my literary agent and a lovely bloke) for his sage advice at every juncture; to Lindsey, for embracing the idea of this cookbook and making it happen (while having a baby!); and to Tamsin (editor supreme), a hugely bright and positive energy who has managed to cajole and tweak *Peace & Parsnips* out of my untamed enthusiasm. I'd also like to send a big thanks to Matthew and all the awesome team at The Experient in New York, including Jennifer, Batya and Elizabeth. You have made my US experience such a pleasure and loads of fun.

Thanks must go to Paul Gayler and Denis Cotter, who have always inspired me and pushed me forward in creating brighter and tastier food with veggies. To all the vegan cooks around the world: you are a creative, shining force! Thanks also to all the good, the bad and the largely ugly chefs with whom I have worked over the years. If you abused me, thank you; if you showed me how to make a simple roux, thank you also; both have made me the hairy, hippy cook that I am today.

Two awesome cooks in particular, Frances and Sophie, worked tirelessly to make this food shine. Frances (recipe tester extraordinaire) offered a considered non-vegan perspective on things as well as managing to locate smoked tofu in Wiltshire. Sophie (home economist and so much more) organized the ingredients and was a cooling presence in the maelstrom of the photo shoots (in the midst of a summer heatwave). Both have kept me on the straight and narrow and added their amazing talent and organizational prowess to these pages. Big thanks to Al (photographer), who is such a talented geezer and a visionary in the field of food photography. And to Sarah, who put her heart and soul into the book and fielded all my demands for something that looked like the inside of a cosmic kaleidoscope and made it coherent and practical, but nonetheless stunning. There are so many of the Penguin UK gang to thank, I hope you know who you are. I was in the best hands and you all made things seem so effortless when I'm sure they weren't!

My family, who have always been a complete source of love and encouragement, giving me the freedom to roam the world freely and feeding me whenever I wandered back in from the wilds. The Legges, who accepted me into the Blue House and beyond with such open hearts, buying me special soy milk when I visit and supporting my bean-bubbling exploits since day one.

The people who have tested the recipes: Fey over in the red valleys of Murcia, and her Chica gang; Dan in Balham for taking an interest in my constant meanderings; Narendra for going through the curry section and not freaking out too much when I "veganized" his nan's favorite recipes; all my friends around the globe – I love you all and hope to see you soon.

Also a "big love" shout goes to all the food bloggers who supported the Beach House Kitchen blog (beachhousekitchen.com), from Hawaii to Tasmania, rural Stafford to Iran: you're all diamonds. Pete Harris, for the tofu and yoga books and kindness; all the magic people at Trigonos Retreat and Education Centre (my summer day job), who give me the opportunity to experiment with their gorgeous home-grown produce and feed such wonderful eclectic folk.

To John, Paul, George and Ringo for obvious reasons.

Alan Watts, Terence McKenna, Lao Tzu, Buddha, Neil Young, P. B. Shelley, Theodore Roethke, India . . .

. . . Gandhi, Martin Luther King Jr., Aung San Suu Kyi, the Dalai Lama, and all those who chose peace before violence and who strive for a harmonious existence for all beings sharing this beautiful earth.

Namaste and peace.

Lee X

PS – To all the people I haven't thanked, thank you!

About the Author

Passionate about vegan food without being preachy, **LEE WATSON** brings a singular sensibility to the vegan cookbook shelf. After he worked in restaurants for more than 20 years, from classical French fine-dining establishments to healthy fast food and raw vegan outlets, a chance encounter with a life-changing taco bought on the streets of Mexico started Lee on his own personal food odyssey. Ever since, he has been ceaselessly touring the world for fresh inspiration.

In Murcia, Spain, Lee helped to build and run a beach restaurant; he has also cooked on TV as one half of the presenting team on Fox's multi-episode program *Meat v Veg*, which has been broadcast in Australia, Brazil, India, Hong Kong and elsewhere around the world. He lives "the good life" with his partner, Jane, in western Wales, where he works as a vegan chef at an idyllic retreat center in Snowdonia National Park. Besides growing his own organic fruit and vegetables, Lee writes poetry and plays guitar, practices all forms of yoga, hikes and runs in the mountains, swims in the sea, surfs and enjoys nature.